MW01701181

memoirs of a superfluous man

THE WORKS OF ALBERT JAY NOCK

The Myth of a Guilty Nation
Jefferson
A Journey into Rabelais's France
A Journal of These Days
Our Enemy, the State
Free Speech and Plain Language
Henry George; An Essay
Memoirs of a Superfluous Man
On Doing the Right Thing, and Other Essays
The Book of Journeyman; Essays from the New Freeman
The Works of Francis Rabelais, 2 vols.
The Theory of Education in the United States
**A Journal of Forgotten Days*
**Letters from Albert Jay Nock*
**Snoring as a Fine Art and Twelve Other Essays*
**Selected Letters of Albert Jay Nock*
**The State of the Union*

Mr. Nock wrote introductions to:
Forty Years of It, by Brand Whitlock
How Diplomats Make War, by Francis Neilson
The Selected Works of Artemus Ward, edited by Albert J. Nock
Man Versus the State, by Herbert Spencer
Meditations in Wall Street, by Henry Stanley Haskins

Mr. Nock contributed to:
The Freeman Book (Selections from the Eight Volumes of the Freeman, 1920-24, compiled by B.W. Huebsch)

*Published posthumously

memoirs of a superfluous man

Albert
Jay
Nock

HALLBERG PUBLISHING CORPORATION
Nonfiction Book Publishers – ISBN 0-87319
Tampa, Florida 33623

The pen-and-ink drawing of AJN on the front cover
by Laura Retter Thornton (1970)

ISBN Number 0-87319-038-6
Library of Congress Catalog Card Number 93-061321

Cover design and front matter by Xpress Graphix.
Printed in the U.S.A. First printing of this edition January 1994.

For information concerning Rights & Permissions or other questions
contact our editorial office:
HALLBERG PUBLISHING CORPORATION
Phone: 1-800-633-7627

CONTENTS

FOREWORD

EDMUND A. OPITZ

page I

INTRODUCTION

ROBERT M. THORNTON

page V

PREFACE

ALBERT JAY NOCK

page XV

CHAPTER ONE

To be ignorant of one's ignorance is the malady of the ignorant.

— AMOS BRONSON ALCOTT

page 1

CHAPTER TWO

[Social life in the Grand Sicèle] is the school of what is called honour, the universal master who shall be everywhere our guide. Three things we observe there, and find constantly mentioned: that our virtues should be touched with a certain nobleness, our morals with a certain freedom, our manners with a certain politeness. The virtues exhibited in this society are always less what one owes to others than what one owes to oneself; they are not so much a response to an appeal from our fellow-citizens as a mark of distinction between us and them.

—MONTESQUIEU

page 19

C H A P T E R   T H R E E

The art of aristocrats, the art of enriching life.

—MARY M. COLUM

page 36

C H A P T E R   F O U R

I have fought my fight, I have lifed my life,
I have drunk my share of wine;
From Trier to Köln there was never a knight
Had a merrier life than mine.

—CHARLES KINGSLEY

page 54

C H A P T E R   F I V E

Haec studia adolescentiam alunt, senectutem oblectant, secundas res ornant, adversis solatium et perfugium praebent, delectant domi, non impediunt foris, pernoctant nobiscum, peregrinantur, rusticantur.

—CICERO

page 75

C H A P T E R   S I X

"Niebuhr was right," said Goethe, "when he saw a barbarous age coming. It is already here, we are in it, for in what does barbarism consist, if not in the failure to appreciate what is excellent?"

—ECKERMANN, 1831

Great things may be accomplished in our days; great discoveries, for example, great enterprises; but these do not give greatness to our epoch. Greatness makes itself appear notably by its point of departure, by its flexibility, by its thought.

—SAINTE-BEUVE

page 97

C H A P T E R   S E V E N

Le monde est inepte à se guarir. Il est is impatient de ce que le presse qu'il ne vise qu' à s'en desfaire sans regarder à quel prix . . . le bien ne succede pas necessairement au mal; un autre mal luy peult succeder, et pire.

—MONTAIGNE

page 117

CHAPTER EIGHT

Peggio assai che l'averla perduta
Egli è il dir: la mia gente è caduta
In obbrobrio alle genti ed a me.

—BERCHET

page 141

CHAPTER NINE

Those who can not remember the past are condemned to repeat it.

—GEORGE SANTAYANA

Man, biologically considered, . . . is the most formidable of all the beasts of prey, and indeed the only one that preys systematically on his own species.

—WILLIAM JAMES

page 162

CHAPTER TEN

A work of art should express only that which elevates the soul and pleases it in a noble manner. The feeling of the artist should not overstep these limits; it is wrong to venture beyond.

—BETTINA BRENTANO

One must, I think, be struck more and more the longer one lives, to find how much in our present society a man's life of each day depends for its solidity and value upon whether he reads during that day, and far more still on what he reads during it.

—MATTHEW ARNOLD

page 175

CHAPTER ELEVEN

Si sine uxore pati possemus, Quirites, omnes ea molestia careremus; set quoniam ita natura tradidit ut nec cum illis satis commode nec sine illis ullo modo vivi possit, saluti perpetuae potius quam brevi voluptati consulendum est.

—SPEECH OF THE CENSOR METELLUS NUMIDICUS, 102 B.C.

I thought love had been a joyous thing, quoth my uncle Toby. 'Tis the most serious thing, an' please your honour, that is in the world, said the corporal.

—LAURENCE STERNE

page 196

CHAPTER TWELVE

"But what do I know of Aurelia, or any other girl?" he says to me with that abstracted air; "I, whose Aurelias were of another century and another zone."

—GEORGE WILLIAM CURTIS

There is no excellent beauty that hath not some strangeness in the proportion.

—FRANCIS BACON

page 218

CHAPTER THIRTEEN

In the course of things, those which follow are always aptly fitted to those which have gone before; for this series is not like a mere enumeration of disjointed things, which has only a necessary sequence, but it is a rational connexion; and all existing things are arranged together harmoniously, so the things which come into existence exhibit no mere succession, but a certain wonderful relationship.

—MARCUS AURELIUS

page 238

CHAPTER FOURTEEN

Nothing in education is so astonishing as the amount of ignorance it accumulates in the form of inert facts.

—HENRY ADAMS

page 258

CHAPTER FIFTEEN

Omnia exibant in mysterium.

—THOMAS OF AQUIN

Illi sunt veri fideles Tui qui totam vitam suam ad emendationem disponunt.

—IMITATIO CHRISTI

page 283

CHAPTER SIXTEEN

Quod amplius nos delectat, secundum id operemur necesse est.

—ST. AUGUSTINE

The primary and sole foundation of virtue or of the proper conduct of life, is to seek our own profit.

—BARUCH SPINOZA

page 304

FOREWORD

ALBERT JAY NOCK
(1870-1945)

Albert Jay Nock came before the public in one capacity only, as a man of letters. That's the way he wanted it, believing that the rest of him was nobody's business. We do know that he was exposed to the "grand old fortifying classical curriculum" at St. Stephens, where he earned a degree in 1892. He did graduate work in theology, was ordained and served three Episcopal parishes for a decade, entered the world of journalism, and won renown as an editor and belletrist.

It was not in him to become a popular thinker and writer; he wrote for the Remnant and tried to do a solid body of work for the future. "The first rate critic's business," he wrote, "is to anticipate the future, work with it, and look exclusively to it for his dividends." The future Nock worked for is catching up with him!

Nock was a virtuoso in these matters, and we shall not see his like again. But we can follow his development as meticulously set forth by the man himself in *Memoirs of a Superfluous Man.* This book (whose title sums up Turgenev) is not an autobiography in the usual sense of that term. Every suggestion that he write a book about his life was rejected with annoyance — until a friend suggested "a purely literary and philosophical autobiography." Nock fell in with this notion because, as he said, "every person of any intellectual quality develops some sort of philosophy of existence; he acquires certain settled views of life and of human society; and if he could trace out the origin and course of the ideas contributory to that philosophy, he might find it an interesting venture." Thus, *Memoirs,* "the autobiography of a mind in relation to the society in which it found itself."

Nock closes his final chapter, privacy still intact; but the attentive reader's mind has been subtly invaded, and it would be a dull fellow indeed who could deny that the hours spent with this book were not among his most memorable reading experiences. Nock discourses on education, literature, women, politics, economics, religion and death, and he does so in matchless, eighteen carat english prose, spiked with apt quotations and laced illusions. Nearly a lifetime of reflection had been spent on each of the topics here aired, and this book is Nock's final statement and testament. It is the book by which he will be finally judged, the one in which he himself took most satisfaction. It is a book to be enjoyed and then mastered; and as a dyer's hand is stained by the medium he works in so does the magic of *Memoirs* work on a person's whole outlook and philosophy.

Those whom Nock has reached do not form a movement or a clique; such men as the eminent sociologist, Robert Nisbet, out in the South Pacific during World War II where he "practically memorized" the *Memoirs*; or the influential scholar, Russell Kirk, at an army camp reading Nock and corresponding with him. Nock was a frequent guest at the Buckley home during the early '40s, and it is safe to assume that the brilliant William F. Buckley, Jr. and his "National Review" owe something to these contacts. Nock inspires the reader to do his utmost for himself or herself as the only way there is for anyone to do some real service for anyone else. There's only one way to improve society, he used to say; present it with one improved unit — yourself.

Nock laid no claim to originality; he sought to give known, tried and true ideas a new twist, a different slant which breaks through current stereotypes. As a critic he stands in the great succession of men like Rabelais and Artemus Ward, who know that *"for life to be fruitful, life must be felt as a joy; that it is by the bonds of joy, not happiness or pleasure, not of duty or responsiblity, that the called and chosen spirits are kept together in this world."*

Nock's books were not best sellers, but they keep coming back into print. The weekly journal he edited from 1920 to 1924, the "Freeman," had a small circulation, but scholars continue to draw on it and discerning souls regard it as the high watermark of American journalism. Nock wrote for the educable few who simply want to get at the plain truth of things — the Remnant. *"You do not know, and will never know, who the Remnant are, nor where they are, nor how many there are, nor what they are doing or will do. Two things you know, and no more; first, that they exist; and second, that they will find you."*

Nock believed that he had uncovered the plain truth of things in several areas, and he set forth his elucidations in impeccable English, serene in his faith that this fully discharged his duty. The assumption back of this faith is that truth has an internal energy of its own enabling it, if we don't stand in its way, to cut its own channels and gain acceptance in minds ready for it. Trying to make truth palatable for minds not ready for it is no service to the people involved, for it clogs whatever thought processes they have.

Truth tampered with is truth lost. The hard truth is what Nock is talking about; truth with the bark on it, truth unsophisticated by even good intentions, undiluted by ulterior considerations. Are there minds ready for this kind of truth? Nock believed that every society has such minds else it would fall apart. Every society is held together by a select few — men and women who have the force of intellect to discern the rules upon which social life is contingent, and the force of character to exemplify those rules in their own living.

The Remnant grows, and they are finding him. Since Nock's death most of his titles have come back into print, only to be sold out. Two collections of letters were published posthumously, and another *Journal.* Two books have been written about Nock, one about his "Freeman," plus several doctoral theses — not bad for a superfluous man!

And there is a Nockian Society with members throughout the world. The letterhead reads "No officers, No dues, No meetings." He would have liked that!

Much of Nock's work defies time, which means that he will be discovered anew by each generation. Many will make his acquaintance in the new edition of this book, whose appearance is a happy portent that Nock's best writing will never for long be out of print.

EDMUND A. OPITZ
180 MAIN STREET, CHATHAM, MASSACHUSETTS 02633

INTRODUCTION

REFLECTIONS ON A SUPERFLUOUS MAN

When I first read *Memoirs of a Superfluous Man,* I was about twenty-six years old. I had been a reader for as long as I could remember but had read few serious books. I dipped into some but simply did not comprehend much of what the authors had to say. I read Will Durant's *The Story of Philosophy* when I was in my late teens and the only part that made much sense to me was the section on Voltaire. About the same time I tried to read C.E.M. Joad's *Guide to Philosophy* but was hopelessly lost after only a few pages. Then came Albert Jay Nock and, for the life of me, I cannot remember who called him to my attention. Perhaps it was Bert Smith, owner of a marvelous second-hand book store in Cincinnati, *Acres of Books*. I purchased a copy of *Memoirs* from him and he remarked that he envied me reading it for the first time. Well, you might say I was impressed with *Memoirs* because when I finished the last page, I immediately turned back to the beginning and reread the entire book!

Albert Jay Nock's *Memoirs* was my key to open doors to the wonderful world of ideas. Of course, most of the people and books he mentioned were unknown to me and much of what he wrote was over my head because I had read so few serious books. But Nock lit my mind as no other writer has ever done. I have read hundreds of serious books in the past forty years, most of them because I had read *Memoirs.*

Reading Nock's *Memoirs* and his other books gave me a large dose of intellectual stimulation and brought to my attention many fine writers who, in turn, introduced me to others. Fellow-book-worms will understand this without further explanation. But for "reluctant" readers, may I add that reading Nock had some very important, "practical," consequences in my life. It is not necessary to describe in detail how all of this came about. Suffice it to say that had I not read Nock, it is unlikely that I would have met my present wife or four persons who are among my closest friends. I believe it was C.S. Lewis who remarked that one "should be very careful about looking into a book because it can be dangerous."

Albert Jay Nock was seventy-three when he published his *Memoirs* and he died two years later in August 1945. In 1943 most people in the United States were mainly interested in defeating the Axis nations — Germany, Japan and Italy. The tide had turned in favor of the Allies in 1942 but there were years of fighting ahead. It was hardly a propituous time to write a philosophical book when all efforts were bent toward achieving victory over the Axis no matter what the cost to civilization in the long run. But Nock writes his *Memoirs* with hardly a mention of World War II or any other current event. Instead, he reflected on twenty-five hundred years of history and took the long view. Nock was never infected with what I call presentism, the belief that yesterday and tomorrow are unimportant; the only time that counts is *now*.

Despite the fact that the United States and other Allied Nations wee fighting against totalitarian countries, individual freedom had few champions fifty years ago. Collectivism, at that time, had been embraced wholeheartedly by only a few nations but many others found its ideas appealing, especially central planning, whereby the government exercises control over the economic life of the nation with, of course, the unfortunate consequences on the lives of individual citizens.

Besides Nock's *Memoirs* there appeared a few other books in 1943 speaking for freedom and against collectivism in any form: Rose Wilder Lane's *The Discovery of Freedom,* Isabel Paterson's *The God of the Machine* and Ayn Rand's *The Fountainhead.* Friedrich von Hayek's *The Road to Serfdom* and Ludwig von Mises's *Omnipotent Government* came out in 1944 and in the same year Frank Chodorov began publishing his broadsheet, *analysis*. There were others, I am sure — H. L. Mencken was always a friend of liberty — but not many. Being a friend of liberty in those days was a lonely job and certainly not a way to achieve fame and fortune.

It is unlikely that anyone would agree with all of Nock's ideas; he would have been suspicious of anyone who made such a claim. He wanted no band of followers, treating his every word as holy writ; that, to him, would have been "a terrible thing to think upon." Nock simply "hung out" his ideas with no attempt to force them upon passersby but only to have them on view should anyone be interested in examining them and deciding what to accept, what to reject, and what to put on hold pending further consideration. Nock had a disinterested love of the truth. His aim was always "to see things as they are" and not fall victim to self-delusion or wishful thinking. The important thing, he wrote, is not *who* is right, but *what* is right. So we need give our allegiance, not to Nock or any individual, but to the Truth.

Nock's books were not big sellers when he was alive; they never will be, so regular publishers are not much interested in them. A relatively small band of admirers helps to keep some titles in print, including the present one. Nock wrote for an enlightened minority, a remnant, and what he has to say will never be palatable to large numbers of people. Such men as Nock never achieve celebrity status as do politicians, popular journalists, television newsmen, and best-selling authors; they pass through life relatively unnoticed, and seemingly have no influence on their fellow-men. But men like Nock have more real influence in the long run than many well known figures because they touch individuals in ways that subtly alter the reader's life and reshape his vision of the world.

Nock avoided publicity as doggedly as most men seek it. The maxim of Epicurus, "Live unknown," was one he adhered to faithfully — compulsively, some might say. Van Wyck Brooks tells us that in *The Freeman* days "no one knew even where he lived, and a pleasantry in the office was that one could reach him by placing a letter under a certain rock in Central Park."

In his *Memoirs* Nock affirmed that "whatever a man may do or say, the most significant thing about him is what he thinks; and significant also is how he came to think it, why he continued to think it, or if he did not continue, what the influences were which caused him to change his mind." One may understand Nock by the simple expedient of reading his books for he was as outspoken in the expression of his beliefs as he was reticent about his private life. What Nock says of Thoreau is, then, true of himself. "One may know him intimately and profitably through his works — there is no other way — but what one may know or not know *about* him is of no importance." So one may *penetrate* Albert Jay Nock only by carefully reading his books. Gustave Thibon expresses this idea so well: "Mere physical proximity without moral intimacy, is the surest way to miss the secret beauty of a soul, to brush by without seeing it . . . It is not close at hand that greatness is seen, but from within; vicinity without intimacy sets up the densest and most impassable of barriers."

Albert Jay Nock was a *clarifying* thinker. He never presented his ideas as being brand new, fresh off the press, but, on the contrary, as being in most cases farily well-established, if, indeed, not ancient. It was his forte to give the known a new twist, to offer a new slant on things which usually conflicted with the stereotyped thinking of his contemporaries. AJN was, too, a radical thinker, if by radical we mean getting to the root of a matter and not being satisfied with superficial explanations. His desire, in every instance, was to find "the reason of the thing" to "get wisdom, get understanding."

As a social critic, Albert Jay Nock stands head and shoulders above most. Much of what passes for social criticism must be taken in small doses, or one will come away depressed and generally in a mood to chuck it all. The reader may agree to everything the critics say, one hundred percent, but he is nevertheless left in a despondent mood. Not so with the greatest critics who are aware "that for life to be fruitful, life must be felt as a joy; that it is by the bond of *joy,* not of happiness or pleasure, not of duty or responsibility, that the called and chosen spirits are kept together in this world."

The great critics help "the truth along *without encumbering it with themselves.*" Hence they are not subject to the shortcomings of so many writers who have something of importance to say, but usually spoil it by the injection of their own personalities. The

> . . . most searching criticism is made by indirection, by the turn of some phrase that at first strikes one as quite insig-

> nificant, or at least quite irrelevant to any critical purpose; yet when this phrase once enters the mind, it becomes pervasive, and one finds presently that it has coloured all one's cast of thought — and this is an effect which only criticism of the very highest order can produce.

The true critic's remarks are made, so to speak, *en passant*. His primary purpose, in other words, is not to offer criticism, this being only a sort of by-product. Nock, like all great critics, was a fine artist and as such he was able to create a mood without mentioning it. His chief concern was creation for he held with Goethe that the critic should be primarily concerned with the processes that build up, and not with those that tear down. "The final purpose of the arts is to give joy." Just so, and it matters not how little joy may be current in the society for,

> the true critic has his resources of joy within himself, and the motion of his joy is self-sprung. Their may be ever so little hope of the human race, but that is the moralist's affair, not the critic's. The true critic takes no account of optimism or pessimism: they are both quite outside his purview; his affair is one only of joyful appraisal, assessments, and representation.

And again as to the primary purpose of art:

> When Hesiod defined the function of poetry as that of giving "a release from sorrows and a truce from cares," he intimated the final purpose of all great art as that of elevating and sustaining the human spirit through the communication of joy, of felicity; that is to say, of the most simple, powerful, and highly refined emotion that the human spirit is capable of experiencing. This, no doubt, does not exhaust its beneficence; no doubt it works for good in other ways as well; but this is its great and final purpose. It is not to give entertainment or diversion or pleasure, not even to give happiness, but to give joy.

Of all other men in American letters perhaps Nock might be most aptly compared with Henry David Thoreau. Nock, like Thoreau, was a discriminating man who was concerned with the quality of life lived and he learned early with Thoreau that a man is rich in proportion to the number of things he can afford to do without.

What Richard Groff writes of Thoreau applies equally to Nock:

> In this emphasis on inner transformation rather than on outward activity, Thoreau echoes the words of Lao Tse, who taught, "The way to do is to be." Insofar as it is the *kind of persons we are* which is at the heart of our problems, then obviously we must begin by changing ourselves. This attitude is at sharp variance with that of those reformers and agitators with plans for reorganizing the old institutions of society or instituting new ones in order to improve the condition of man.

Nock would have nothing to do with the collectivism of his day. As was said of Kierkegaard, AJN "stationed himself to defend the individual against any philosophical, political, or religious teaching that tended to slack off this consciousness of the individual's essential responsibility and integrity." Neither was Nock tempted by the activism of his fellow "intellectuals" who for more than fifty years have been guilty of treason because they have willingly deserted the cause of truth and, in Russell Kirk's words, gone "a-whoring after strange gods, whose blandishments both the traditions of their culture and the discipline of their profession should enable them to resist." The disinterested love of truth has been replaced by a lust for power and prestige; no longer guardians of the truth, they have gone to the service of the states which "would use the scholar and debase him." Nock was one of the few intellectuals to retain his integrity and avoid what Julien Benda called *The Treason of the Clerks*. By clerks Benda meant "all those whose activity essentially is *not* the pursuit of practical aims, all those who seek their joy in the practice of an art or a science or metaphysical speculation, in short in the possession of nonmaterial advantages, and hence in a certain manner say: 'My kingdom is not of this world.'"

The job Nock loved best, though it brought him neither fame nor fortune, was being a spokesman for the remnant. If we belong in the remnant, he wrote, we will

> proceed on our way, first with the more obscure and extremely difficult work of clearing and illuminating our own minds, and second, with what occasional help we may offer to others whose faith, like our own, is set more on the regenerative power of thought than on the uncertain achievements of premature action. Such persons have the power to see things as they are, to survey them and one's own relations to them with objective disinterestedness, and to apply one's consciousness to them simply and directly letting it take its own way over them unchartered by preposession, unchanneled by prejudice, and above all uncontrolled by routine and formula. Those who have this power are everywhere; everywhere they are not so much resisting as quietly eluding and disregarding all social pressure which tends to mechanize their processes of observation and thought. [The remnant is] an order of persons — for order is the proper word, rather than class or group, since they are found quite unassociated in any formal way, living singly or nearly so, and more or less as aliens, in all classes of our society . . .

It is not unlikely that future historians may see Albert Jay Nock as a prophet in the great tradition of Isaiah and Jeremiah; though his habits and vocabulary were not those of the ordinary clergyman, he calls one to the life of the "spirit" — the "inner life" — and away from an existence concerned primarily with things. Susan Stebbing writes of what I refer to, her term being "spiritual excellences" which are

> intellectual and moral capacities lacking which the life of human beings would be nasty and brutish; length of days could not redeem it. The excellence I call *spiritual* includes

> love for human beings, delight in creative activities of all kinds, respect for truth, satisfaction for learning to know what is true about this world (including ourselves), loyalty to other human beings, generosity of thought and sympathy with those who suffer, hatred of cruelty and other evils, devotion to duty and steadfastness in seeking one's ideals, delight in the beauty of nature and art — in short, the love and pursuit of what is worthwhile for its own sake. In this pursuit the individual does in fact have at times to suffer pain and to surrender what it would be good for him to have were it not for the incompatible needs of others, needs which he recognizes as claims upon himself. This is another spiritual excellence. These excellences are to be found in *this* world; no heaven is needed to experience them.

Nock was more concerned with being and becoming than with doing and getting. His was an aristocratic spirit which "is not a matter of birth, or occupation, or education. It is an attitude of mind carried into daily action, that is to say, a religion. [The aristocratic spirit] is the disinterested, passionate love of excellence . . ."

In one of his letters, AJN remarks that "Rabelais was one of the world's great libertarians — he has been a stay and a support to my spirit for thirty years, and I could not possibly have got through without him." His Introduction to *The Works of Rabelais* might also serve to explain why his own books, especially *Memoirs* are worth reading.

> It must be laid down once and for all, that the chief purpose of reading a classic like Rabelais is to prop and stay the spirit, especially in its moments of weakness and enervation, against the stress of life, to elevate it above the reach of commonplace annoyances and degradations, and to purge it of despondency and cynicism. He is to be read as Homer, Sophocles, the English Bible, are to be read . . . The current aspect of our planet, and the performances upon it, are not always encouraging, and one therefore turns with unspeakable gratitude to those who themselves have been

> able to contemplate them with equanimity, and are able to help others to do so. In their writing one sees how the main preoccupations, ambitions, and interests of mankind appear when regarded "in the view of eternity," and one is insensibly led to make that view one's own. Thus Rabelais is one of the half-dozen writers whose spirit in a conspicuous way pervades and refreshes one's being, tempers, steadies, and sweetens it, so that one lays the book aside, conscious of a new will to live up to the best of one's capacity, and a clearer apprehension of what that best may be.

I hope very much that readers will be pleased to make the acquaintance of Albert Jay Nock, a man so well described by that colossal Dutchman, Hendrik Willem Van Loon, as being "endowed with profound knowledge, blessed with immense possibilities for the enjoyment of life, and possessed of a rare genius for the handling of words."

ROBERT M. THORNTON
FORT MITCHELL, KENTUCKY

THE NOCKIAN SOCIETY

The Nockian Society was founded thirty years ago at Valerio's Italian Restaurant in Cincinnati, Ohio. Three admirers of Albert Jay Nock — a doctor, a clergyman, and a businessman — met for lunch, having been brought together in the first place by a common interest in A.J.N. — an affinity for Nock's ideas as well as Nock's nonpushy approach to the idea business. That you may catch the flavor of the Society, here are the words that appear on its letterhead:

PATRONS:	POLICY:
Francis Rabelais	No Officers
Artemus Ward	No Dues
H. L. Mencken	No Meetings

The purpose of The Nockian Society is not to save the world or engage in political action, but to keep Nock's memory green. While we all presumably admire Nock, we do not wish to idolize the man or endorse every idea embraced by him.

Anyone interested in The Nockian Society is invited to send inquiries to: THE NOCKIAN SOCIETY, 42 Leathers Road, Fort Mitchell, Kentucky 41017.

PREFACE

It has several times been suggested to me, always to my great annoyance, that I should write an autobiography. Personal publicity of every kind is utterly distasteful to me, and I have made greater efforts to escape it than most people make to get it. Moreover, biographical writing, especially of the popular type, presupposes a subject who has achieved, or at least tried to achieve, something ponderable, substantial; and I have done neither. I have led a singularly uneventful life, largely solitary, have had little to do with the great of the earth, and no part whatever in their affairs or for that matter, in any other affairs. Hence my autobiography would be like the famous chapter on owls in Bishop Pontoppidan's history of Iceland. The good bishop wrote simply that there are no owls in Iceland, and that one sentence was the whole of his chapter.

One evening, however, an old friend, Mr. William Harlowe Briggs, brought up the matter again, saying he had a new idea. He proposed that I should write a purely literary and philosophical autobiography with only enough collateral odds and ends thrown in to hold the narrative together. As he put it to me, the idea seemed to have something in it. His notion was the perfectly sound one that every person of any intellectual quality develops some sort of philosophy of existence; he acquires certain settled views of life and of human society; and if he would trace out the origin and course of the ideas contributory to that philosophy, he might find it an interesting venture. It is certainly true that whatever a man may do or say, the most significant thing about him is what he thinks; and significant also is how he came to think it, why he continued to think it, or, if he did not continue, what the influences were which caused him to change his mind. In short, what Mr. Briggs proposed was a history of ideas, the autobiography of a mind in relation to the society in which it found itself.

After thinking over this suggestion for a day or two, I decided to do what I could with it. I do not think the result, as here presented, would interest many people or benefit anybody; I did not expect or intend it to do either. I contemplated nothing but a *tour de force,* a literary venture in a field which, if not quite new, was at any rate new to me, and is one which modern autobiographical writing tends to avoid. I now see that I have succeeded with it much better than I supposed I should, and therefore I have turned my manuscript over to Mr. Briggs to do with as he likes. I have no further interest in it, except as I indulge the hope that he will think his idea has been satisfactorily worked out.

ALBERT JAY NOCK

CHAPTER ONE

To be ignorant of one's ignorance is the malady of the ignorant.

—AMOS BRONSON ALCOTT.

FROM first to last, my schooling was so irregular, so out with the whole technique of modern pedagogy, that I suppose I might fairly be said to have had no schooling at all. In its early stages it was as informal as it was irregular. How I learned my letters must always remain unknown; in Lord Dundreary's phrase, it is "one of the things no feller can find out." My parents did not know; nobody knew. Some one must have taught me them, and very early, for I practiced spelling out words when I was getting on for three years of age; but twenty-five years later, although I asked all around the families on both sides, I found no survivor able to say who taught me, or when, or how. As far back as I can push my own memory, it stops at the point of recalling a set of dirty and defaced alphabet-blocks lying about our cellar in company with a dog-eared copy of the New England Primer. There is a bare chance that these may have helped me on with my earliest adventures in the realm of the liberal arts, but I doubt it; indeed, I am almost sure they did not. In the first place, I do not remember ever playing with the blocks, or making any use of them, or even paying any particular attention to them; nor do I remember ever noticing the Primer until such time as I could read it, which certainly would be no later than when I was three. Our house was a rented one; the cellar was really rather more of a basement than a cellar; it was light, dry and clean, a palatial playroom from a child's point of view; so my notion is that the blocks and the Primer were probably among the oddments discarded and forgotten by some former tenant's offspring.

While it is most unlikely that these bits of salvage did much to put me on the way to literacy, the Primer may possibly have had something to do with forming one of the channels through which the course of my thinking was permanently set. Here again the possibility is very frail, and I set no store by it, but it does exist. If today for the first time I met the Primer's statement—

In Adam's fall
We sinnéd all.

—my first question would not be, Did Adam really fall?, nor would it be, Did we all really sin?. It would not even be the previous question, Did Adam ever really exist?. It would be the question previous to all these three questions, namely: How can any one possibly know anything about it? Moreover, not only is this the case now, at the close of a rather uncommonly experienced and reflective old age, but even though I stretch my memory to the utmost I do not recall a time in all my life when I would have met a similar or analogous statement in any other way. I can quite believe that at three years of age, *praemonitis quae praemonenda,* I would have instinctively put the same question as at thirty or threescore. Therefore my impression is that the channel of my reaction to the Primer's doctrine of original sin was somehow ready-cut, that my reaction followed a habit of mind already fixed and settled, and that in so far as the Primer's couplet had any function in the premises, it was merely that of a trigger, a spring of action.

A French friend, the gifted daughter of an immensely gifted father, is much amused whenever she sees this agnostic and skeptical instinct at work, and tells me it is my French blood cropping out; which indeed may easily be so. My mother's people came here as refugees from France at some time between 1686 and 1688. Their descendants were a long-lived lot; four generations of them were on earth in my time. Up to the last generation they were also rather prolific for French folk; the tendency seems to have run out then; they reverted to type so sharply as pretty well to extinguish the line. My mother was one of ten, and I am her only child; I had a sister who died in infancy before I was born. Out of the four generations I knew, every one of them, man, woman or child, was an anachronism, a straight throw-back. Scratch the skin of their mind, and the unadulterated blood of a seventeenth-century Rochellois Protestant would flow. Nothing interests me more now than to look back on the excellent lucidity, integrity, detachment and humour which they brought to bear on all the works and ways of the society around them, including their own works and ways—especially their own; their power of disinterested and humorous self-criticism was superb. They seem to have held place in a true apostolic succession, for as I see them now I see an Amyot, Montaigne, Rabelais, du Fail, des Périers, contemplating the spectacle of Renaissance society, appraising its little infatuations with serene preciseness, and finding them immensely diverting. My observation of these people gave me a far freer entrance than I could otherwise have had into the minds of Voltaire and the Encyclopædists, of Molière, Beaumarchais, yes, of Scarron also; and into minds as diverse as those of Fontenelle, la Bruyère, St.-Simon, in the seventeenth century; or as those of Comte, Scherer, Ste.-Beuve, Halévy, Ernest Renan, the Goncourts and other unheeded prophets of the *fin-de-siècle* who were so nearly my contemporaries; many of them actually my contemporaries, with a generation's difference in our ages.

The general temperament of my mother's family came out in various little ways expressive of a suave irony, characteristically French. Nowhere outside of *Don Quixote* have I come upon so many folk-sayings and proverbial turns of speech as were current among them. Most of these,—all of them, in fact, that I can remember,—I never heard elsewhere, though they can hardly have been original with us. At the end of some boring social function or similar round of duty, they would say, "Well, that burying's got by,"—a simile drawn from the sight of a rural funeral-procession passing a house. Justifying some little extravagance, they would ask, "What's a shilling on a show-day?" They spoke of some enterprise likely to be too much for the person taking it on, as "a store job"; I am unable to make out this allusion. A specious bargain offered "too much pork for a shilling," and an obviously fraudful one would be "cheap at half the money." Carrying too many parcels at once to save a trip, they called "carrying a lazy man's load," and if some one complained of a tough steak, he would be told that "it's tougher where there's none." Once when I came down unusually late for breakfast, my mother said drily, "I think your early rising won't hurt you if your long fasting doesn't." There was a rural flavour about most sayings like these, which makes me doubt that they were at all original with us, for my people were always townfolk as far as I know.

With such a heredity, and having been inured throughout childhood to the spiritual atmosphere of a gentle and pervasive scepticism, it would perhaps not be unnatural that as a general thing I should be found instinctively leaning a little towards the agnostic side. Nor would it be less so, probably, that in encountering controversial matters, such as the theological constructions of the New England Primer, I should always instinctively strike down through all secondary and debatable questions and come to rest upon the one question that is primary and undebatable.

This atmosphere of scepticism fostered another instinctive trait or habit of mind which is characteristically French; the habit of meeting any sudden and unexpected proposal, however interesting, however simple, even trivial, with an instant negative. Our maxim, *Learn to say No*, would have no point whatever in a French copybook, for every French child is born knowing how to say No, and in the circumstances I mentioned he can be counted on to say it with unfailing regularity throughout his life. Like the congenital infirmity of Goatsnose, this habit was mine from "the remotest infancy of my childhood"; and although it amuses me as much as it does my friends, I have long since written it off as unbreakable. I am unable to recall a time when, if some one had proposed something on the spur of the moment,—anything, no matter what, from the hand of the princess to a hand at tennis or billiards—an abrupt No would not instantly have popped out. *Son lo spirito che nega* in this sense truly, like my ancestors; I come by it honestly. This habit might seem like sheer perversity, but it is nothing of the kind. French of the French is the instinct against committing oneself without reflection, and the negative is merely a time-gaining device for holding open the opportunity for reflection, however much or little reflection may actually be required or employed. Even where assent is a foregone conclusion the opportunity must be held open. If the princess's hand were meanwhile forfeited forever, it would be quite too bad and utterly lamentable, but there it is.

II

Although, as I said, there is not the faintest chance of knowing how I learned my letters, there is no doubt about how I learned to piece them together into words. I taught myself to do that. My playroom was in the fore part of our basement-cellar or cellar-basement, and at the other end, against the wall, was ranged a battery of three zinc-lined laundry-tubs with hinged covers, also zinc-lined; a rather pretentious affair for those days. Above the tubs was a window with a cracked lower sash, over which was pasted, upside down, a piece cut out of the New York *Herald*. As I lay prone on the tub-cover with my heels in the air and my chin propped up from my elbows, this piece of print was level with my eyes at a comfortable reading-distance. At irregular intervals, mostly when it rained, I occasionally posited myself in this fashion and spelled out the printed words, reading like a Hebrew, backwards. I did this with no notion whatever of self-improvement, but merely as finding myself some sort of occupation when I had nothing more interesting to do; somewhat as one idly falls back on working out a puzzle; which even so was rather odd, for all my life I have been desperately bored by the mere thought of any kind of puzzle. In this way, however, I learned to read; and like Thoreau, except for the time devoted to this exercise, I am unable to count a moment spent over a newspaper that was not wasted. One effect of this experience remains with me. I can still read print from right to left quite handily, and also print which is upside down.

My first setback was the discovery that English is not a phonetic language. The name of a certain Colonel Harry appeared on my scrap of newspaper in some connexion which I no longer remember. I do not know who Colonel Harry was, or anything about him; probably I never knew; perhaps the nub of his story disappeared when my fragment of paper was cut out. All I remember is that when I pronounced his title phonetically, some one,—I think it was our fine old coloured cook,—corrected me. Gradually I was introduced to anomalies like *cough, tough, hough, bough, through*, and it was not long before my curiosity about them began to give way to a vague indefinite pride in a language too great to trouble itself about anomalies. So far from deserting me, that pride has become progressively overweening and touchy with advancing age. Reason and logic are all against the orthographical antics of our language, and all in favour of the wholesale confiscations which a military despotism will no doubt levy on our speech when all else that belongs to us has been confiscated. As a man of reason and logic, I am all for reform; but as the unworthy inheritor of a great tradition, I am unalterably against it. I am forever with Falkland, true martyr of the Civil War,—one of the very greatest among the great spirits of whom England has ever been so notoriously unworthy,—as he stood facing Hampden and Pym. "Mr. Speaker," he said, "when it is not *necessary* to change, it is necessary *not* to change."

Here, I am told, the English side of my ancestry comes out; and again that may very well be so. My father's parents came from a town in Staffordshire, on the Worcestershire border, where their people appear to have lived so long that the memory of man runneth not to the contrary. My grandfather sprang from a race of ironworkers; I know nothing about them, save that one of them, named Henry, was a gunmaker who had something of a reputation in his day. An odd incident that happened when I was in my late twenties convinced me that he must have been a first-rate artisan. Coming on from the West Coast, I stopped-over in Missouri to visit an old friend, an inveterate Nimrod with whom I had shot black duck in the mouth of the Housatonic in the days when we were at school together, doing post-graduate work—and can one imagine a self-respecting black duck or old-squaw making its way up Stratford harbour now? My friend presently proposed quail-shooting. The only gun he could borrow for me was something that looked like the second or third generation after the flint-lock. It was a long, light, single-shot muzzle-loader, perhaps a trifle over sixteen-gauge, with a beautiful barrel of thin brown steel. I have never handled a gun that shot harder or truer, or one that came up half as prettily; it virtually aimed itself. The end of a day's shooting found me head over heels in love with it and trying my best to buy it, but the owner was obdurate; he treated me as the father of the prize Circassian beauty would treat a common slave-trader. While cleaning the gun with devoted care that evening, I noticed the maker's name in small block-letters on the lock-plate, *H. Nock.* I made up my mind on the spot that if this artist were not one of the family, he should have been; and many years afterward, quite by accident, I learned that he was.

My grandfather came to America to superintend a steel-making concern. My impression is that he was the first in this country to make steel of the highest quality, but I will not answer for the fact. I have been told, though I doubt it, that he was the first to make any kind of steel here. I should say that this could hardly be; but whatever the truth about such matters, I can vouch for his having been a most capable workman. He had a process of his own, which he kept secret; I do not believe he ever wrote out the formula for it, but if he did, it has long since disappeared. He gave my father a razor which he had fashioned out of an old file or something of the kind; an exquisite, dainty little object that one might at first sight take to be a miniature or toy razor, not meant for use, yet for serviceability I have never seen one like it. He also made a sword with an edge like a scalpel's, and so flexible that one could touch the hilt with its point. I do not know what became of this or any other of his artifacts.

He was a man of sterling character, habitually silent, thoughtful, dignified, regarded by strangers as perhaps a little on the dour side. He was in all ways a conspicuous example of the "ancient and inbred piety, integrity, good nature and good humour of the people of England"; which, by the way, remains the truest characterisation ever made of that people, albeit not made by one of themselves, but by an Irishman. My grandfather's forebears were *echt*-English English out of the original Saxon stock that landed at Ebbsfleet; they were English of the sort that as late as my own time still looked down their noses at the descendants of the French bastard of 1066 and his desperadoes, and spoke of them as "foreign devils." His eight children, all but one born here, stood rather in awe of him, though he was always kindly in his stiff English way, never unjust or overbearing, and never intolerant. His tolerance, like all else of his, was English; it had its root in authority and tradition, and was exercised within the limits which these determined. It was therefore, strictly speaking, unintelligent; thus standing in sharp contrast with the tolerance practiced by my mother's family. This was purely French; it was founded on reason and proceeded by logic, tempered and refined by an unfailing sense of what is amiable, graceful and becoming. My mother has told me how often, when one of them passed a hasty judgement on somebody for something, her father would say, "Be careful, children; remember, you don't know the circumstances." It would hardly have occurred to my English grandfather to put the matter that way.

The upright and gentle old English couple spoke such broad Staffordshire that I could seldom make much out of what they were saying. They were deeply religious, exercising an extremely simple and practical faith, and asking no questions. Their type of religion was that on which, for once in his life, Carlyle spoke out with the insight and lucidity of a Taylor, Hales, Chillingworth, or one of the Cambridge Platonists. "Man's religion," he said, "consists not in the many things he is in doubt of and tries to believe, but in the few things he is sure of and require no effort to believe." No Cudworth or Whichcote could do better than that. My grandfather was one of many who became disgusted with the repulsive Erastianism of a State Church, and became a Dissenter, of the Methodist persuasion; in fact, the Methodists formally commissioned him as a lay preacher, and even after he came to this country he would sometimes preach to Methodist congregations when no one was at hand to do it. His preaching seemed acceptable, though I hardly see how American hearers could have understood his speech.

Gogol's story, *Old-Fashioned Farmers*, brings to my mind a good many features of the old couple's peaceful life in their latter days; their devotion, their playful teasings and twittings, their intense busyness with small activities, their hospitality and friendliness for those who found entrance to the household. They lived long and well. When my grandfather was ninety-three he was stepping about New York on a firmer foot than mine is now, and at a pace as brisk as mine; at ninety-six he complained that for some reason his eyesight was not what it used to be. He died at some months past ninety-nine. His children also lived to a great age, except the two youngest who died virtually by accident; if the science of medicine had stood then where it does now, they might have lived as long as the others. Both sides of my family ran to longevity, as far back as they have been traced. My mother died at eighty-seven; her father, at eighty-six; and except for deaths that were virtually accidental, all their contemporaries in the family lived about as long, and some longer. Two of my own contemporaries in a distant connexion are going on for ninety, one for a hundred, and one for seventy-six. Latterly, again like my mother's family and even more abruptly, my father's family pinched out. Of my grandfather's children, four were childless; one had three children, all now dead; one had two; and two had one each.

My father told me of a strange incident in his mother's life which made such an impression on him that he remembered it clearly, although he was no more than five or six years old when it happened. While he was playing in the garden with two of his sisters a very large grey bird appeared, circled slowly two or three times overhead, and settled on one of the window-sills in my grandmother's bedroom. My grandmother came to the door at once, apparently in great distress, and said, "Come in the house, children; your grandfather is dead." Some weeks later (those being the days of sailing-ships) she got a letter telling her that her father had indeed died in his home in Staffordshire at precisely that hour. His illness was short, and his death wholly unlooked-for; he was supposed to be in the best of health. If my grandmother ever gave any account of her sensations at the moment, my father did not know of it; no doubt she did, but he was unlikely to have heard anything about it, since such matters were not much discussed in the hearing of children. The odd thing is that my grandmother would be the last person whom one would associate with any metapsychical or superpsychical or extrapsychical (or whatever the right word may be) experience. She was preëminently placid and wholesome of mind, abounding in the unimaginative good sense so typically English of the Midlands, and one would say quite insensitive to impressions originating at all outside the commonplace.

III

I have spoken of my father's people with this rambling particularity because hardly anything referable to them is likely hereafter to fall within the scope of these memorabilia. The truth is, I inherited almost nothing on the paternal side, and what little I got is almost wholly by way of external characteristics; blue eyes, blonde complexion running to the rubicund, what one of my sinful friends calls the veritable boozehister's complexion, fit to ornament a retired admiral of the Royal Navy. A thin skin, scanty blonde hair, small pudgy hands and feet, a villainous tendency to gout, rheumatism, arthritis; these, I believe, make up the lot. The only internal characteristic that I can identify positively as coming from this side is my unreasoning jealousy in behalf of the appalling vagaries of my native tongue. Nothing else arouses this peculiar emotion; such feelings as I have for other things is wholly a reasoned affair, leading me into no emotional excesses; that is to say, it is fundamentally more French than English. The Englishman holds himself privileged to criticise his people and their most cherished institutions as freely as he likes, but he will not extend that privilege to others; and their assumption of it, even when such assumption is most notoriously justifiable, at once touches off a display of irrational resentment. With the Frenchman (as far as my observation goes) the case is somewhat different. He may be quite as devoted to his Marianne as the Englishman is to his Britannia, and quite as well aware that the object of his devotion has a repulsive birthmark on her shoulder. He will not cover up the birthmark, however, and pretend it is not there; nor will he pretend that on occasion it is not so clearly visible to the stranger as it is to him; nor will he assure the stranger that the thing is not at all a birthmark but a superbly contrived beauty-spot, and that nothing but envy, hatred, malice and all uncharitableness prevents the world from accepting and admiring it as such. Wandering around the Poitou at the time of the last Presidential election in France, I asked a worthy Poitevin who the next President was likely to be. He shrugged his shoulders with an expression of the utmost indifference, and replied, "I don't know,—some old cow." If he had asked the question, and I had given that answer, he might well have thought my manners were none too good, but ten to one he would have smiled at the sally, and said, "*C'est tout a fait ça.*" Hardly so the Englishman.

It amuses me to see how true to type I run in the one particular; I am as unintelligently and absurdly jealous of the injustices, inhumanities, iniquities, of our language as any good Briton is of those inhering in his flagitious imperialism. Like him, I refuse to see them as unjust, inhumane, iniquitous. I insist that they are just, beneficent, and in accordance with the will of God. If foreigners have trouble with them, I agree that it is most unfortunate, but really we can't think of regularising the exquisitely asymmetrical symmetries of our noble tongue merely to accommodate foreigners. Let the foreigner sweat them out for himself; it serves him right for his presumption in having been born to the use of a language so far inferior. My French blood rises up at this, calling it the bland hypocritical arrogance of *l'Albion perfide, la Grande Voleuse.* Then, English-like, I am moved to insist in all honesty that it is nothing of the kind. It is merely the humble and pious recognition of certain verities which were established before the foundations of the world were laid. Since our adorable Creator, in His wisdom and in His loving-kindness, endowed the Briton with the natural right to rule, it was fitting that He should have endowed him with command of a majestic and imperial language. Since He ordained the immeasurable superiority of British character, customs, laws and institutions, the Untouchables of the world must respect the idiom in which that superiority is not only proclaimed but exhibited. It is painful to find this attitude put down as arrogant and hypocritical when we Britons are actually the most simple-hearted of mankind; but what is one to do?

I must confess that when the English half of my being rears

up in this preposterous fashion, the French half laughs most indecorously at the capers I cut. It gently pulls my sleeve, and bids me once more study prayerfully the immortal figure of Homenas praising the Decretals. Fortunately this seldom happens; the French half controls me completely, I think, in every department of spiritual activity save only where this matter of linguistics comes in; and here I am as densely, as impenetrably, English as Palmerston himself.

In respect of vocabulary, like Mr. Jefferson, I am "a friend to a judicious neology," but in respect of style and usage I count myself a hidebound old British Tory, and glory in my shame. Mr. Mencken's great work on the American language is monumental, and I would go almost all the way with it in granting a place in the English dictionary to its verbal neologies of American origin; but its culpable laxity towards matters of style and usage makes the British lion within me growl with rage. The sensitiveness, the delicacy of perception which at once takes the right measure of an occasion and puts a style in right relation to its subject; the instinct for clarity, harmony and balance, the infallible sense for the exact adaptation, often the exact sacrifice, that is needed to maintain them; this is what determines the validity of usage. It passed King James's translators effortlessly on from an Attic simplicity in the story of Joseph to an almost matchless example of the grand style in the book of Daniel, and thence to a sort of bastard Corinthian style faithfully reflecting the crabbed Greek of the Pauline epistles. In at least one instance, where euphony was the primary consideration, it made them sacrifice grammar to euphony. When force was the primary consideration, Mr. Jefferson once sacrificed both grammar and sense to it in saying, "We have nothing scarcely to propose to our legislature." Brand Whitlock years ago remarked to me how greatly Andrew Jackson's execrable grammar strengthened his sentence when he roared, "I know them French; they'll never pay unless we make 'em." I wish Mr. Mencken had compared the kind of prose he sometimes sanctions with the kind he writes himself. *Mutatis mutandis,* his management of style and usage is so unerring that as far as these go I might easily imagine that William Law or Bishop Butler had written his *Treatise On Right and Wrong.*

IV

Unless one counts in the Primer, which never really interested me, the first book to attract my notice was Webster's Dictionary. Probably it caught my eye as being the biggest book in my father's library, and also as being easily accessible in its place at the end of one of the lower shelves. Whatever the attraction was, I dragged the volume out one day, and in the pages of pictures at the end I struck a rich and unexpected vein of interest. Presently I discovered that the pictures were duplicates of those in the text, so I quite made a business of looking them up to see what was said about them. I remember being greatly taken with the pictures of prehistoric creatures, and when somewhere or other I heard somebody recite a scrap of nonsense-verse about certain exploits of—

> The Icthyosaurus
> On the banks of the Taurus,
> And the Pterodactyl
> By the gurgling rill,

—I was delighted to find myself among old friends. The amount of miscellaneous information gained in this way, however, seems not to have done me much good *qua* information, since most of it did not stay long with me; but collaterally, in the matter of reading, and especially of spelling, the case was different. I became an uncommonly rapid reader; and as for spelling, the seed sown by the dictionary must have fallen on good ground, for in my later life I have seldom been seriously put to it for the spelling of an English word; probably not more than a dozen times in all; and this notwithstanding I never studied a spelling-book or did any stated exercises in spelling. I use the figure of good ground advisedly, since there seems to be a sort of congenital instinct for correct spelling in a non-phonetic language, and many of the ablest minds are born without it. Two of my ablest acquaintances can but barely spell their own names twice alike; Henry George was a wretched poor speller; and Count Tolstoy's manuscripts show that the great and good old man must have kept his copyist's teeth on edge. Something of the same sort seems to be true of one's speed in reading; and therefore I feel that my proficiency in these two accomplishments is of little credit to me.

The dictionary became quite literally my bosom friend, for I lugged it about, clasped to my breast with both hands, from one place to another where I should not be underfoot, and there I would lay it open on the floor and read it lying prone as I had lain on the tub-cover when perusing my scrap of newspaper. I must have been very young then, for I could but barely manage the book's weight; I do not know exactly what my age was. Once my devotion put me in the way of a bad accident. My people had never let on to notice my doings with the dictionary, but they may have thought it was under too much wear and tear, for one day I found its place vacant. I said nothing, but kept a sharp eye everywhere, and presently discovered it out of reach on a shelf in a closet. Aided by a chair with a teeter-tottery pile of books built up on it, I somehow actually managed to get the thing out and down again without breaking my neck. Perhaps what Mrs. Malaprop called "an unscrupulous Providence" had decided that a whilom student of the Primer might become a good Calvinist some day, and took a chance on giving me an uncovenanted lift. Nothing was said about my escapade, no questions asked; apparently it was accepted as testimony to the mighty truth that you can't keep a good man down; and so my studies went peacefully on. One trace of them still remains; considered as sheer casual reading-matter, I still find the English dictionary the most interesting book in our language.

V

The net profit of my first few years of life appears to have been a fairly explicit understanding of the fact that ignorance exists. It has paid me Golconda's dividends regularly ever since, and the share-value of my small original investment has gone sky-high. This understanding came about so easily and naturally that for many years I took it as a commonplace, assuming that everyone had it. My subsequent contacts with the world at large, however, showed me that everyone does not have it, indeed that those who have it are extremely few. They seemed particularly and pitifully few when one contemplated the colossal pretensions which, in its modesty, the human race puts forth about itself. I found myself projected into a society which was riotously pretentious, forever congratulating itself at the top of its voice on its achievements and abilities, its virtues and excellences, its resources and prospects, and calling on all the world to admire them; and yet a society by and large "too ignorant to know that there is such a thing as ignorance"! I was immensely amused by this anomaly, yet I surveyed it with a mild wonderment; it was something of a puzzle. In time I found that others had made this discovery before me; also that other contemporary societies were in this respect more or less like the one I was in, essentially like it, the main difference being in the degrees of blatancy wherewith the resemblance was proclaimed; also that past societies of men long dead and gone were like it; also that the reasons why all this should be so had apparently never been any clearer to others than they were to me.

Thus in my early manhood I learned to respect ignorance, to regard ignorance as an object of legitimate interest and reflection; and as I say, a sort of unconsidered preparation for this attitude of mind appears to have run back almost to my infancy. Moreover, when I got around to read Plato, I found that he reinforced and copper-fastened the notion which experience had already rather forcibly suggested, that direct attempts to overcome and enlighten ignorance are a doubtful venture; the notion that it is impossible, as one of my friends puts it, to tell anybody anything which in a very real sense he does not already know. It seemed extraordinary that this should be so. Nevertheless, there it was; and apparently no one could give,—certainly no one, not even Plato, did give,—any more intelligent and satisfying reason why it should be so than I could give; and I could give none at all.

Here again, running back to my childhood there may have been going on a kind of vague and indefinite preparation for this discovery. I speak with caution, for I recall only one incident pointing that way, and withal a trivial one; yet point that way it certainly did. When I was about seven, up in New Hampshire where my mother and I were visiting some relatives, a priggish little boy from next-door, reeking with infantile piosity, said to me one Sunday afternoon, "I did not see you in church this morning, I did not." I replied politely, "Didn't you?" As a matter of fact, I had not been there; but I saw no reason for discussing my absence, and I saw one imperative reason for not discussing it. I disliked the sanctimonious little whelp intensely, on general principles—there was that, of course; and it was clearly none of his business where I had been or not been—there was that also. Yet I remember distinctly that these considerations did not move me to the reply I made. I knew the boy and his upbringing well enough to know that if I entered into explanations with him, his invincible ignorance would estop him from understanding a word I said. In like circumstances I would, and always do, make a like reply today, and for the same reason.

As time went on, I became convinced that Calvin's idea of invincible ignorance had a validity which the Genevese French lawyer did not suspect. I was also interested to see that this view had strong indirect corroboration from the practice of those whom for some odd reason—odd, because no one ever seems to learn anything from them—we misname as "the great teachers of mankind." Apparently they accepted ignorance as a fixed quantity; apparently also their direct attempts at enlightening ignorance were extremely few and futile. But why should ignorance have persisted as a fixed quantity throughout human history, as apparently it has done; and why should the direct effort at enlightening ignorance remain as inveterately impracticable and inadvisable today as it was in the days of Socrates, Jesus, Confucius, Im-hotep, or as it must have been found to be by the wiseacres of the Neolithic period, if any such there were?

These were the questions which interested me, though I was never eagerly curious about them, or much stirred by finding no answer at hand. Now and then some circumstance would bring them to the top of my mind long enough for me to note the circumstance's bearing on them, but no longer. I never broached them for discussion in my student days. The theory of progressive evolution was top dog everywhere at that time, and its energumens would have met my questions with the "one plain argument" with which Lord Peter met the doubts of his brothers, in the *Tale of a Tub*. This flat negation of history and common experience would have done no more than to illustrate the quality from which the questions take their rise, and would therefore have been pointless. Not until I was well along in years did I come on a theory of man's place in nature which provided my questions with a competent and satisfactory answer.

CHAPTER TWO

[Social life in the Grand Siècle] is the school of what is called honour, *the universal master who shall be everywhere our guide. Three things we observe there, and find constantly mentioned: that our virtues should be touched with a certain nobleness, our morals with a certain freedom, our manners with a certain politeness. The virtues exhibited in this society are always less what one owes to others than what one owes to oneself; they are not so much a response to an appeal from our fellow-citizens as a mark of distinction between us and them.*

—MONTESQUIEU.

DURING the period I have been canvassing we lived in Brooklyn, the City of Churches. Our neighbourhood had somewhat the appearance of a moderately well-to-do suburban locality just before a congested population has crept up on it. Chelsea, Greenwich, Harlem, probably looked more or less like it in the early days of New York. The high-life of Brooklyn lived on the Heights, which is still the most desirable residence-site in the city, though the winter winds which sweep up from the bay are colder than death. Between us and the high-life lay a sprawling amorphous population of which we knew little. Residence-blocks had but barely reached us, though they were fast on their way. Apartment-houses were yet to come; I think there were hardly any of them anywhere in Brooklyn. The houses in our locality were roomy in a Victorian style, hence ugly enough; their grounds were spacious, all extremely well-kept, and almost all the properties were owned by those who lived on them.

Our district served the function of a modern suburban town, for the heads of our families mostly had their occupations in what is now called Manhattan, and were actually commuters, going to-and-fro daily by way of the horse-car lines down Gates or Fulton Avenue to the East River ferries. They spent about the same length of time in transit as their successors who now swarm in from Summit or New Rochelle; but the pace being slower, their daily journey was less tiring, and (since comfort largely resides in a state of mind) more comfortable. It was also less tedious, for Ruskin's observation that "travel becomes uninteresting in exact proportion to its rapidity" applies as well to commuters' travel as to any other.

The *rus in urbe* type of existence prevailed among us quite considerably. One neighbour kept a flock of guinea-fowl which ran so wild over his rearward premises that when he wanted one for dinner he would shoot it. Our own place, one of the few rented ones there, must have had at least a hundred-foot frontage, I think more. The house was well back from the street, and the garden running the full length of a long block behind it was remarkable for having large fruit-trees in it and a line of oversized blackberry-bushes down one side. I was more circumspect about blackberries after the day when I came within an ace of pawing in on a hideous huge spider which was sitting in the centre of its web amidst the thick bushes. This monster was of a bright yellow colour with black stripes. I have seen others of the same kind since then, but never one much more than half its size.

Another neighbour, a patriarchal old Englishman with a white beard, kept a great stand of bees. I remember his incessant drumming on a tin pan to marshal them when they were swarming, and myself as idly wondering who first discovered that this was the thing to do, and why the bees should fall in with it. It struck me that if the bees were as intelligent as bees are cracked up to be, instead of mobilising themselves for old man Reynolds's benefit, they would sting him soundly and then fly off about their business. I always think of this when I see a file of soldiers, wondering why the sound of a drum does not incite them to shoot their officers, throw away their rifles, go home, and go to work. Why, instead of producing this effect which seems natural and reasonable, does it produce one which seems exactly the opposite? In the course of time I found that Virgil had remarked the fact about bees, and that in his parable called *The Drum* Count Tolstoy had remarked the fact about the human animal. Neither, however, had accounted for the fact. Virgil had not tried to account for it, and Count Tolstoy's attempt was scattering and unsatisfactory.

Something perhaps worth mentioning, if only for its oddity, is that none of us children ever had any toys except such as we made for ourselves; odder too, possibly, that none of us wanted any. I might have had toys if I had asked for them, but I did not care enough about them to ask, and no one offered me any, even at Christmas when we all had nice things of one kind or another given us. Such cronies as I had seemed to be in the same state of indifference. I vaguely remember seeing a dilapidated rocking-horse in our cellar, but I think it was something I fell heir to, like the alphabet-blocks and the Primer. At any rate, I did nothing with it and cared nothing for it. When I was six or seven I collected some pieces of board and knocked together a very good nest for myself in the upper branches of a tree near the house, whence I surveyed the landscape after the manner of Alexander Selkirk. I also made a practicable swing, but soon got out of the way of using it, being attracted into fields of larger adventure.

One side of our premises was bordered by a big stretch of vacant land which, with the garden, gave us a playground practically illimitable. For some reason, huge piles of broken rock had been dumped on these vacant lots, which vastly increased their interest. We did tricks in Alpine-climbing over these, picking out ways which involved the most hazardous feats of balancing. One day I discovered some ten-cent pieces scattered at the foot of one pile, and this set us off on a gold-rush at once, exploring all the depths and crevasses of the porous heap in a search for further loot, but we did not find any.

In all, I led a very active, busy and wholesome outdoor life, the year round. In summer, we were hard at work in all the primitive occupations which youngsters devise for themselves out of such resources as they happen to find in their way, though curiously little imagination had play in our enterprises. We did not build any castles in Spain or pretend to be Indians, pirates, explorers, or the like. I do not know why this immemorial privilege of childhood was lost to us, but our more prosaic doings filled our days so full that we did not miss it. Apparently our world of practical affairs was so large, abundant and satisfactory that we had more than enough to do with taking it as it was. Our nearest approach to the make-believe was in organising snowball-battles. We would build a snow fort, then divide ourselves into attacking and defending forces, using shields made out of barrel-heads, with leather straps through which to pass the left fore-arm, Roman style. We had a tacit convention against "soakers"—ammunition dipped in water and left to freeze hard—and also against snowballs weighted with a stone core. All such practices were blacklisted according to the doctrine that "fair's fair" even in war. We were too young to know that this doctrine was fast going out of fashion among our elders, but in our innocence it seemed quite the right thing; so clearly the right thing that I do not recall ever having heard it discussed or even mentioned.

Sometimes we got intimations of a larger world surrounding ours. Once I wandered a long way eastward to where a railway ran, and there I saw two locomotives, gorgeous with red paint and glittering brass, bearing the strange names of Wouter van Twiller and Pieter Minuit. This led to my learning that a very fine people called Hollanders or Dutchmen lived across the ocean, and once long ago a colony of them had settled here. Indeed, some of their descendants were still here, and were much respected. I thought their governors must have been most tremendous fellows to have such scrumptious engines named for them, and I was especially keen on seeing some of those descendants. There were none handy to us at the time, however, so my curiosity had to go unsatisfied for many years. This experience not only gave me a justly high opinion of the Dutch, but it also set up a great love for the old graceful type of locomotive, which has never left me; and, by consequence, I now look on the nondescript electric locomotive and the slithering, sneaking, dishonest-looking type of "streamlined" Diesel locomotive with the utmost abhorrence and disgust.

Although there were no Dutch in our neighbourhood, our social atmosphere had a distinct bracing tang of cosmopolitanism which I very early learned to breathe with interest and enjoyment. The only female playmate I ever had came into my life at the age of four, and soon went out again; a tiny frail blonde French girl—she impressed me as frail, but judging by others I have seen since then, I now think she was *fausse-maigre.* She knew not a word of English, nor I a word of French, yet we conversed fluently enough, and like the gifted souls at Pentecost, we somehow managed to come at some sort of understanding, in a general way. I think I never knew what her name was, but for purposes of identification I spoke of her as "little Oui-oui," which answered well enough. She did not take to me particularly, nor I to her, but we carefully observed the diplomatic amenities in all our relations, and the chances of a sentimental attachment, if ever there were any, died a-bornin'.

We had several English families among us, all out of the best that the upper-middle class could show, and with most of the objectionable insular angularities peculiarly British worn down by attrition. One family named Brown came from the Indian civil service. The French critic who said, rightly enough, that in matters of colonial administration *les Anglais sont justes, mais pas bons,* would gladly have made an exception for this amiable family. Mrs. Brown taught my mother to make curry *secundum artem,* the real thing, which was one of the cardinal joys of my life at home. Memories of it today make me explode in wrath like a retired colonel from Poona or Allahabad when I see the messes which miserable defaulting devils stew up and put before me under the name of curry.

A few Germans lived among us, one named Kreuter, a little brisk old man, a great friend of my father, and a master hand at making sauerkraut. When he had got a batch of sauerkraut in prime condition, he would bring over a couple of quarts for my father to sample and pass expert judgement on. The discussions were so long and the aroma so pervasive that my mother finally laid down the law that my father and Kreuter should hold their sessions outdoors or in the woodshed. She said she always knew when Kreuter was coming, if the wind was right, for she could smell his tin pail long before he hove in sight. She also declared she could see the fumes of his sauerkraut push up the cover of the pail once in a while, like the action of a safety-valve, as he was proceeding along; but this may have been an illusion of some kind.

Between the Kreuters and a grocer named Mahnken whom we patronised, I picked up a bit of German which I used sometimes not really knowing whether I was speaking German or English. Probably it is in consequence of this that occasionally now when I try to think of an English word, the German equivalent will come to me long before the English word produces itself. This of course seldom happens, but it has happened, and once or twice very awkwardly, as it did only a few days ago when I was pointing out a stone-quarry as a landmark for some motorists who asked for directions. I lost the word completely, and after fishing around in my mind for a moment or two while the motorists waited, I made the silliest possible show of myself by turning to the people with me and asking what a *Steingrube* is in English.

The cosmopolitan character of our neighbourhood was rounded out by the presence of a north-of-Ireland Scots Protestant family which in the eternal fitness of things bore the name of Irons. When one laid eyes on old Irons one said to oneself,

Behold England's age-long difficulty in governing Ireland! He was a living, breathing allegory of what Burke called "the dissidence of Dissent, and the protestantism of the Protestant religion"; that is, he was everything that a sentimental, quick-witted people like the southern Irish would regard with frantic loathing. He looked like Sir Edward Carson, and his harsh sepulchral voice was Carson's own; or Ralph Nickleby's, as Dickens describes it. He regarded all non-Calvinist doctrine as a lie and a heathenish superstition, and he was especially strong for burning the Romish and High Anglican hierarchies at the stake. Rabelais's description of Gaster fitted him like a poultice. Nothing could be done with Irons, "for he is imperious, blunt, hard, severe, uneasy and inflexible; you cannot make him believe, represent unto him, or persuade him anything; he does not hear." My parents got an immense deal of amusement out of Irons, though none in an ill-natured way, for there was never a grain of ill-nature in our household. In their view, human character in all its unaccountable manifestations is simply the most diverting thing in the world, and as such they accepted it. Irons was a prize exhibit after his kind; luck had thrown him our way as a kind of spiritual windfall, to be highly appreciated for what he was, an uncommonly interesting and comical object of character-study.

I think I am safe in saying that the touch of cosmopolitanism in our surroundings affected me favourably and permanently. What with the Dutch names on the locomotives, Kreuter's sauerkraut, the little French girl, the English, and the inveterate, almost homicidal intransigence of old Irons, all interpreted through my family's humorous, penetrating and tolerant view of humanity-at-large, I got the impression of an interesting and rather delightful variety of cultures, traditions, modes of thought, and habits of life; and I am sure I must also have got some inkling of what always has seemed to me, and still seems, the most rational and practical attitude towards them. One of the most offensive things about the society in which I later found myself was its monstrous itch for changing people.

It seemed to me a society made up of congenital missionaries, natural-born evangelists and propagandists, bent on re-shaping, re-forming and standardising people according to a pattern of their own devising—and what a pattern it was, good heavens! when one came to examine it. It seemed to me, in short, a society fundamentally and profoundly ill-bred. A very small experience of it was enough to convince me that Cain's heresy was not altogether without reason or without merit; and that conviction quickly ripened into a great horror of every attempt to change anybody; or I should rather say, every *wish* to change anybody, for that is the important thing. The attempt is relatively immaterial, perhaps, for it is usually its own undoing, but the moment one *wishes* to change anybody, one becomes like the socialists, vegetarians, prohibitionists; and this, as Rabelais says, "is a terrible thing to think upon."

In all our little cosmopolitan variety, I had the luck to see examples which were invariably good, not only in the older generation, but in my own as well. The boys of our neighbourhood were a well-brought-up lot, manly and decent. By pure accident one day a burly English lad named Growtege hit me on the back of my head with a stone, hurting me severely. When he helped me home and turned me over to my mother, his manly shouldering of responsibility and the equally manly way he "took on" about his carelessness, were quite remarkable. I remember some trivial bits of mischief done now and then, but I do not recall anything mean, low, shabby or wilfully damaging, on the part of any among us.

A mysterious outsider turned up in our midst at irregular intervals, and terrorised the neighbourhood. Nowadays he would probably be called a problem child, whatever that is, but as a matter of fact he was a born cutthroat and plug-ugly. None of us knew who he was or where he came from, or anything about him. Oddly, he was always neat, clean-looking and well-dressed. He had the strange faculty of appearing suddenly out of nowhere and then as suddenly disappearing, like the prophet Elijah; and if he chanced to meet another boy, he would fall on him without a word and beat him unmercifully. We soon became fed up with him and organised a *posse comitatus* or vigilance-committee to lie in wait and demolish him on his next arrival; which we did so effectively that he never reappeared.

II

I have recounted these minutiæ of my upbringing, or I might better say upgrowing, to correct a false impression which I may have given of myself as a sheltered and bookish creature, something of an infant prodigy. Perhaps too, though I hope not, I have given the impression of a family surreptitiously forcing a precocious and repulsive development. Nothing could be farther from the truth. I was a child of the great outdoors, active, strong, full-blooded, never ill. My literary pursuits were purely an indoor sport in which I was neither encouraged nor discouraged, nor had I any more notion of educating myself than I had of flying. I did not know what education was; I doubt that I ever heard the word mentioned at any time in that early period. All the books in the house were free to me, even those in my father's professional library, and my choices were not influenced or even noticed, as far as I could see. There they were, and that was all.

Only one thing took place which might be debited against this account, though I am sure it should not be. My father was far from being a finished scholar, but he knew some Latin, and rather more Greek than Latin. When I was beginning to talk,—at the age when a child is eager to memorise anything, no matter what, so long as somebody gives it something to memorise,—my father taught me a great string of Greek and Latin paradigms. I am sure he had no ulterior motive in this, but did it mainly because he had no other repetitious jingles to teach me; neither he nor my mother knew any nursery-rhymes.

It may seem odd that a child of that period should grow up without hearing a nursery-rhyme, but so it was; and I can cite another fact about my infancy which is perhaps more unusual. My father and mother both had glorious voices, as had most of my aunts and uncles. The love of music ran strong through both families, many of their friends were musical, music of sorts was always going on about the house; yet I was never sung to sleep, never heard a lullaby or a child's song. All hands played or sang around me, none ever to me. Thus the first strain of music to stick in my memory was not a lullaby or a nursery-song or a hymn-tune; it was a few measures from the final chorus in the second act of *la Traviata*. Offenbach's experience with the eight bars from Zimmer's waltz was like mine, but I have not happened to hear of another like it.

Our small section of Brooklyn resembled the modern commuter's town in maintaining a social life of its own, distinct and separate from those of the Heights and the nondescript district lying between. Measured by the standards which the student of civilised man would apply, our social life was perhaps a rather commonplace affair; a poor thing, but our own, as Touchstone said of his lady-love. Yet as measured by the standards then prevailing in America, it had its merits; and as measured by those prevailing now, it was attractive and agreeable. The curse of hardness had not wholly come upon it, nor wholly cleared a way for the attendant curse of hideousness, of a blighting and dishevelling ennui. My mention of Offenbach a moment ago reminds me that it had one thing which was destined shortly to disappear from American life, a sound sense of gaiety. Its spontaneous manifestations of true gaiety were the first I saw in America, and they were also the last. I have seen plenty of vapid frivolity since then; boisterousness, hysterical nerve-tensions, mechanical escape-devices, all manner of pitiful and vulgar travesties on the real thing; but not since I was ten years old have I encountered the free play of a collective instinct for the best in a civilised *desipere in loco*. Nor is it altogether without reason that this should be so, for as a French writer lately remarked, American society is the only one which has passed directly from barbarism into decadence without once knowing civilisation.

III

As a rule our district kept little track of the high-life's affairs down on the Heights, and such news as occasionally seeped through to us came as from another world. I did not come along in time to be caught in the backwash of the great Beecher-Tilton scandal, but I heard casual mention of it in the family circle years afterward. This cataclysm razed the Heights from end to end, and rocked the whole country; there had never been such a devastating social upheaval. It is forgotten now, as it should not be by students of society at least, for its history is a compendious index to the character and quality of American social life in Mrs. Wharton's "days of innocence." No critic can hope to know precisely what representative American society was like in that period unless he makes himself letter-perfect in a study of this affair.

My family's attitude towards all this commotion could hardly have made a distinct impression on me, for I knew nothing about Beecher or his alleged misdoings, and cared as little. Yet when I read Paxton Hibben's excellent study of Beecher a few years ago, it instantly interpreted that attitude for me as one of calm and humorous detachment. Everyone in those days subscribed tacitly to a pretty fairly uniform code of morals, but there was a snuffiness about the ostentatious pieties and moralities of those concerned in the Beecher-Tilton imbroglio which made it impossible to take their contentions or representations seriously. What people! one said at once. What a life! What a society! In its dulness, its fatuity, its simian inability to see when it was making itself ridiculous, was there ever anything on earth like it? My family clearly had little doubt, on the evidence offered, that the scandal rested on a sound basis of fact; that Beecher had been entertaining himself in dalliance with one at least, and perhaps more, of his female parishioners. But to arraign him for that, and then to get up a great pother about it, all on the sheer score of religion and morality (and afterward, yes, actually, on the score of legality, when Tilton haled Beecher into the civil courts on a charge of alienation)—this procedure would seem the acme of a stilted burlesque.

Yet to regard a matter with humour and detachment is by no means the same as regarding it lightly. My parents would have been the last to regard any matter of adultery lightly, the last to dismiss it with Lincoln's droll saying that for those who like that sort of thing it is probably about the sort of thing they like. On the contrary, their view would naturally be, and I am sure was, much more serious than any which the affair brought to light. The eye of common sense would see simply that the courts of law, religion and morals were not courts of competent jurisdiction. Their sanctions were of debatable validity in the premises, and when as egregiously overpressed as they were in the case of Beecher, the effort to apply them became ridiculous. The court of undebatably competent jurisdiction would be the court of taste and manners. Whatever law, religion and morals may say or not say, the best reason and spirit of man resents adultery as in execrably bad taste, and from this decision there is no appeal. Moreover, the three incompetent courts could not take proper cognisance of the fact that Beecher and Tilton were intimate friends. The court of taste and manners could and would; and a properly enlightened social resentment would be accordingly enhanced, for all but the very lowest of bad manners exempts the wives of one's friends. On the other hand, the three courts can and do take into account the principle of raw expediency, which in the affair of Beecher was made almost paramount, to the intense disgust of all who had any sense of what was due to common propriety and decency. The court of taste and manners takes no account of it.

I grew up in the conviction that in a truly civilised society the sanctions of taste and manners would have a compelling force at least equal to those of law, religion and morals. By way of corollary I became convinced that expediency is the worst possible guide of life. Bentham's doctrine of expediency, on which Michel Chevalier a century ago observed that American society was founded, seemed to me thoroughly false, corrupting and despicable; and in my opinion the present state of the society based on it affords the strongest evidence that it is so. I would not say in the broad didactic manner that it was this-or-that piece of experience,—say, the code governing our snowball-fights, or my family's view of the Beecher-Tilton affair,—which first put me on the way to that conviction. Rather I would say it was the general view of human conduct prevailing around me which did this; a view which these experiences and many others essentially like them, fitted in with and illustrated.

Whether by one means or another, I was somehow prepared to see, as when I was still quite young I did see, that in our society the purview of legal, religious and ethical sanctions was monstrously over-extended. They had usurped control over an area of conduct much larger than right reason would assign them. On the other hand, I saw that the area of conduct properly answerable to the sanctions of taste and manners was correspondingly attenuated. One could easily understand how this had come about. Law is the creature of politics, and the general course of politics, as among others Mr. Jefferson, Franklin and John Adams had clearly perceived, is always determined by an extremely low order of self-interest and self-aggrandisement. Changing the legal maxim a little, *est boni politici ampliare jurisdictionem*, as we everywhere see. Again, when Christianity became organised it immediately took on a political character radically affecting its institutional concept of religion and its institutional concept of morals; and the same tendencies observable in secular politics at once set in upon the politics of organised Christianity. Thus the area of conduct in which men were free to recognise the sanctions of taste and manners was still further straitened.

The consequence was that the one set of sanctions atrophied, and the other set broke down; thus leaving human conduct bereft of any sanctions at all, save those of expediency. In other words, each person was left to do that which was right in his own eyes. What with Bentham on one side and the hierarchs of law, religion and morals on the other, American society had got itself crosslifted into a practical doctrine of predatory and extremely odious nihilism. When the sanctions of law, religion and morals broke down through persistent misapplication to matters of conduct quite outside their purview, the sanctions of taste and manners had become too frail and anæmic to be of any practical good. For obvious reasons the resulting state of our society seems beyond hope of improvement. Attempts to galvanise the sanctions of law, religion and morals for further misapplication are ineffectual; and ineffectual also must be the attempt to root the saving criteria of taste and manners in an ethical soil laid waste by the Benthamite doctrine of expediency.

IV

Besides the qualities I have previously mentioned, the social life in our section of Brooklyn preserved some vestigial characteristics which made it especially wholesome and pleasant for children. It was leisurely, kept down to the tempo of the horse-car. It was also cheerful. Nothing needful to our pleasure or contentment cost much. Our people had resources in themselves which enabled them to get on with few mechanical aids to amusement. Living among them, one could see a great deal of force in Spencer's observation that "happy people are the greatest benefactors of society." I think our people were perhaps as nearly happy as people could be in a land where so acute an observer as Stendhal found that "the springs of happiness seem to have dried up" in the general population; and where Edison, at the end of his life, told reporters that "I am not acquainted with any one who is happy." Like Napoleon in exile, they may have been "not happy, precisely, but contented," but their contentment was a very passable imitation of happiness, quite good enough to enable us unthinking children to get a vast deal of enjoyment out of very little.

Once or twice each summer I was taken down to Coney Island's "long, bare, unfrequented shore," a Sabbath-day's journey at that time. These excursions were usually made in behalf of some visitor's turn for sight-seeing. Even then Manhattan Beach was by no means so desolate as Whitman's line suggests. It had a hotel of credit and renown, where some notable persons spent their summers, and several smaller enterprises had sprung up for the accommodation of day-trippers like ourselves. There was a similar development at Brighton. Gilmore's band played at one of the two beaches, but I do not remember which one; I think it was Brighton. I remember the cornetist Levy's playing to my complete satisfaction, and I was also impressed by the fine stirring effects of a small park of artillery brought in at the ending of the programme with some piece like *1812*. I do not remember what the piece I heard actually was, but it was something in the military way.

What I most enjoyed on these excursions was digging clams to take home. Excellent small quohaugs abounded on those shores, especially at Canarsie; I suppose the last one disappeared from Coney Island all of forty years ago, probably dying of chagrin. The general cheapness of things in our neighbourhood is fairly well indicated by the price of clams. Once a week or so a large round man in his shirt-sleeves, with a yellow paintbrush beard and a tattered straw hat, would drive up from Canarsie and around our district with a wagon-load of quohaugs in bulk. My mother said he had three prices; his cry was "Hard clams, twenty-five cents a hundred; hard clams, quarter a hundred; hard clams, two shillin' a hundred." Four fresh sweet quohaugs for a penny, delivered, seems nowadays like good living; and indeed we did live royally well.

The outings I most enjoyed were when my father would take me over to New York with him for the day. He had an office there, where I was vastly entertained by observing all sorts and conditions of men who dropped in to hob-nob with him. I never knew another man who had a genius for friendship like his; I have sometimes wished I had inherited some of it. He had what Cardinal de Retz called "the terrible gift of intimacy"; a terrible gift indeed, if one misuses it, which my father never did; with all his gregariousness and his immense power of attracting people to himself, he remained always one of the best of men. He had an unerring flair for queer originals, odd fish like old Irons, and got no end of amusement out of them. My mother did not share his partialities, regarding these peculiar cronies as mostly the scum of the earth, though she never interfered with his enjoyment of them, but rather countenanced it and even mildly encouraged him in it.

Aside from these human oddities, the feature of my excursions to New York which most fascinated me was the shipping in the East River. The wharves were lined with sailing-ships; it is hard to believe now that the harbour was full of sails right up to the turn of the century. Now they are no more, and sailors are no more; only mechanicians of sorts. Coentjes Slip was full of canal-boats when I saw it then; they are scarce now, and I presume the canalboatman of early days has given way to some anomalous type. Once our ferryboat passed close to a steamer of the Royal Netherlands line. I could read its name, another Dutch name to be filed away in my memory alongside the names of the locomotives; it was the *Prins Willem III*. It had but just backed out of its slip and was almost motionless, poised to stand downstream on its long glorious voyage of almost a month's time. It would make seven or eight West Indian and Caribbean ports with fascinating names like Jéremie, Miragoane, Jacmel, Aux Cayes, all the way to Surinam; then cut over to Madeira and up to Amsterdam. What an entrancing voyage! What an incomparably delightful way to reach Europe, if one liked the sea and had the time! I made a firm resolve to take that journey some day, and of course on that very ship, no other. But I did not know then how short the life of a steamship is, even as measured by the little life of man. When I was travelling by that line a few years ago, Captain Haasters stopped me on the deck one day, and said, "The purser tells me you can remember the *Prins Frederik Hendrik.*" "Yes, sir," I said, "and I can do better than that. I can remember the *Prins Willem III.*" He shook his head. "Too far back for me," he said, and went on.

Once when my father and I were on a Fulton ferryboat, there happened a most amusing incident which profoundly affected my practical attitude towards men and things throughout my life. It was on a clear winter evening, with a bright moon which threw a sharp streak of light about three feet wide on the after deck of the boat while it was tied up to the bridge. Presently a man appeared, carrying a carpet-bag, such as one almost never saw any more, even then; they probably went out of fashion in the days of reconstruction, when the carpet-bagger gained an evil name, deservedly enough. As this man came down the bridge, he saw the streak of moonlight and took it for an open space, thinking the boat had started. He charged down the bridge at full speed, made a tremendous leap over the streak of moonlight, slipped and fell; the carpet-bag flew out of his hand, flew open, and distributed its contents all over the deck.

As I said, I have never forgotten this incident. In principle, as the diplomatists say, the same ludicrous thing has come under my observation time and time again, in every relation of life. That it has so seldom happened to me is due wholly to the salutary object-lesson furnished by the man with the carpet-bag. Many times in my life I have seen it happen, not only to individuals, but to great masses of people, even sometimes amounting to whole populations. Considering the causes and circumstances of its happening, and the kind of people whom these causes and circumstances victimise, one is lost in wonderment as the Psalmist was when he faced the kittle question, *What is man?*, and could find no answer.

CHAPTER THREE

The art of aristocrats, the art of enriching life.

—MARY M. COLUM.

THE tenor of my intellectual life ran smoothly, being wholly self-directed up to my eighth year. My father's library was large but unpretentious; it existed only for the sake of what lay between the book-covers. There was nothing in it to gratify a collector's spirit; indeed, the collector's spirit had no foothold anywhere in our family. One can understand book-collecting as a business, but only on the seller's side, not the buyer's, except as one would buy in order to sell; one can understand it, that is, as brokerage. I never knew a person who collected books, bric-à-brac, postage-stamps, anything, for the sheer sake of having them, who impressed me as being good for much else. True, I have not met many such, so I may be recording only a set of coincidences. Perhaps also my distaste for accumulating any kind of possessions has affected my judgement, though I am by no means persuaded that it has.

I read some books, looked into others, and looked at a great many, thus putting myself on the way to realising, as I did much later, the amount of education one gets by looking at the backs of books. One's mind is broadened and loosened by simple observation of the immense variety of subjects that have engaged men's attention. Then too it sometimes happens that the casual impressions made by certain subjects do something towards preparing the mind to receive more serious impressions later. As an illustration of this, I remember rummaging out a thin little elementary Hebrew grammar (I have no idea how such a thing happened to be there) and leafing it over by the light of a flickering momentary curiosity, then laying it aside for good and all. Years afterward, however, when an interest in Hebrew poetry caused me to do a little work on the language, I was astonished to see how much I remembered noticing on those few pages, and how clearly I remembered it.

Good literature was much easier come by in my early days than it is now, and it was also much cheaper. One reason for this was that the United States had no international copyright-law until some time in the early 'nineties; American publishers could reproduce the works of foreign authors at no more than the cost of printing and binding. Concerns like the Seaside Library and Lovell's Library drove a roaring trade in pirated books at ten cents a copy, paper-bound, or twenty cents for "double numbers." Their lists were incredibly long. I got my first taste of French literature from a translation of Eugène Sue's novel, *The Wandering Jew*, which the Seaside Library put out at twenty cents. The time I put on it was well spent, for in his architectonics Sue was unquestionably as great a storyteller as Dumas, though not so great in his management of detail. Curiously, I read nothing of Dumas until much later. I was fifteen when *Monte-Cristo* came my way *via* one of these cheap editions; and after that, nothing until I was past thirty. My first detective-story was Gaboriau's gorgeous old shocker, *File no. 113*; it came to me by way of some pirated reprint, I think in the Seaside Library which also carried me through the infinite variety of Jules Verne.

We were all *receleurs* in those days. Not being a Benthamite, I am unable to defend literary piracy on high moral grounds, but I must admit that the massive testimony of our book-catalogues from, say, 1860 to 1890 comes nearer to making a complete case for the whole doctrine of expediency than anything else I know of. If Bentham's "greatest good to the greatest number" sums up the whole canon of right and wrong, no more convincing evidence could be adduced. The foreign authors and publishers suffered, but as Bentham might have said, "what are they among so many?" Their loss was the gain of innumerable thousands. Probably American authorship also suffered by competition in a rigged market, though I do not remember that protectionist spellbinders ever brought this aspect of law-made privilege up to public notice.

Another reason why good literature was more easily accessible then than now is that the proportion of literacy in our population was much lower, and publishers were not under such heavy economic pressure to block up the access to good literature with trash. In Massachusetts, where literacy would be presumably highest, there were nearly a hundred thousand persons unable to read or write. Things were no better in Connecticut, where one-tenth of the child-population got no schooling at all; and it would be fair to suppose that in the more newly-settled regions of the country the level of literacy would be very considerably lower. One might assume that as the level of literacy rose, the level of general intelligence would rise with it, and consequently that the economic demand for good literature would also rise. This, roughly, was Mr. Jefferson's idea, and indeed it has always been at the root of our system of free public instruction for everyone. It has, however, somehow failed to work out according to expectation. The level of literacy has been pushed up very nearly to the practicable limit, but the level of general intelligence seems not to have risen appreciably, and the economic demand for good literature is apparently no greater in relation to a population of a hundred and thirty million than it was to one that was going on for sixty million; in fact, one would say it is much less. The reason for this is plain enough; there is nothing recondite about it. In his view of literacy, Mr. Jefferson was only half right. He was obviously right in premising that no illiterate person can read; but he was guilty of a thundering *non distributio medii* in his tacit conclusion that any literate person can read. On the contrary, as I discovered as long ago as my undergraduate days, very few literate persons are able to read, very few indeed. This can be proven by observation and experiment of the simplest kind. I do not mean that the great majority are unable to read intelligently; I mean that they are unable to read at all—unable, that is, to carry away from a piece of printed matter anything like a correct idea of its content. They are more or less adept at passing printed matter through their minds, after a fashion, especially such matter as is addressed to mere sensation, (and knowledge of this fact is nine-tenths of a propagandist's equipment), but this is not reading. Reading implies a use of the reflective faculty, and very few have that faculty developed much beyond the anthropoid stage, let alone possessing it at a stage of development which makes reading practicable.

As I said, the fact that few literate persons can read is easily determinable by experiment. What first put me on track of it was a remark by one of my old professors. He said that there were people so incompetent, so given to reading with their eyes and their emotions instead of with their brains, that they would accuse the Psalmist of atheism because he had written, "The fool hath said in his heart, There is no God." The remark stuck by me, and I remember wondering at the time whether the trouble might be that such people hardly had the brains to read with. It seemed possible. At nearly the same time I came across the observation of Bishop Butler, who was for a few years a contemporary of Mr. Jefferson—he died in 1752, and Mr. Jefferson was born in 1743—the observation that most people were handier at passing things through their minds than they were at thinking about them; and therefore, considering the kind of thing they read, very little of their time was more idly spent than the time spent in reading. Again I wondered whether this could mainly be accounted for on the grounds of sheer inability to do otherwise. The curiosity excited by these two *obiter dicta* has caused me to keep a weather eye out on the reading-habits of my fellow-beings ever since, and they have testified with monotonous regularity to the fact that while the ability to read must presuppose literacy, literacy is no guarantee whatever of the ability to read, nor even would it suggest that ability to an ordinarily observant mind. One might suppose that so simple and easily demonstrable a fact as this would long ago have attracted attention and caused comment; but it seems not to have done so.

The ex-president of one of our colleges tells me that for a dozen years he carried on experiments in the value of literacy, using freshmen as his guinea-pigs; that is to say, he experimented on persons who were not only literate, but who had gone so far as to pass their entrance-examinations. Selecting a paragraph of very simple but non-sensational prose, he asked his students, taking them one by one, to read it carefully; then to read it carefully again; then to read it aloud to him; then to write down the gist of it in their own words. Hardly any one could do it; hardly any one was able to bring anything like an adequate power of reflective thought to bear upon the substance of a simple paragraph. In other words, they could not read.

II

Few diversions have interested and amused me more than watching the operation of Gresham's law as it bore progressively on the permeation of a whole people by Mr. Jefferson's faulty logic. Our primary assumption was that literacy is a good-in-itself, an absolute good; therefore everybody should be taught to read and write. Any question about this was inadmissible; any doubt that everybody could be so taught was disallowed. When I came on the scene, our system of popular instruction was driving straight ahead with all its might towards its goal of universal literacy, naïvely unaware that any such formidable obstacle as Gresham's law lay in its way. True, this obstacle was not yet in plain view, but surely one would think that the collective foresight of a whole country would have suspected that it must be there. Plenty of bad literature was knocking about in my boyhood, but not enough of it to drive out the good; that is to say, nothing like the full force of Gresham's law had as yet been brought to bear on literary production. Publishers could make a decent profit out of producing books designed, not for persons who were merely literate, but for a relatively small and steady market composed of persons who could read. But within my lifetime the country became largely literate, thus opening an immense market made up of persons who were unable to read but, as Bishop Butler said, were able to pass literary produce through their minds. As this market widened, the satisfaction of it became increasingly profitable, and therefore the best energies of publishers, dragooned under the iron hand of Gresham's law, were bent that way. Moreover, this market was unsteady; being based on nothing but irrational fancy, it had its ups and downs, its hot and cold fits of susceptibility or indifference towards this-or-that type of produce, this-or-that lure of sensational appeal. Forecasting such a market became mostly guesswork, and the character of publishing changed considerably in consequence; from a business it became essentially a gamble bolstered by shrewdness in a meretricious mode of salesmanship. Thus the operation of Gresham's law progressively edged publishers farther and farther out of the category of merchants, properly so called, and farther towards the category of gamblers and touts.

I have seen the fortunes of periodical publications follow the fortunes of books, showing even more clearly what the irresistible force of Gresham's law can do. When literacy was at a low level they could maintain themselves at a high level of quality and command a fairly profitable market. As the level of literacy rose, their level of quality sank and their market thinned. In the middle 'seventies, when our population was getting on for sixty million, Harper's Magazine had a larger circulation by one-third than it has now over a population more than twice as large. Its average circulation from year to year for the first fifteen years of its existence, 1850-1865, was all of ten per cent more than its average for the fifteen years last past.

In the matter of quality, Harper's deserves all praise for standing out against deterioration as long as a ray of hope was left; yet comparing the issues for any year, say between 1875 and 1885, with those for any year between 1930 and 1940, a person of any literary experience can return but the one verdict.

I speak of Harper's with deep affection because I knew it so well and owe it so much. We subscribed for it and also for Scribner's Monthly, which in 1881 was merged into the Century. My father had volumes of these running back as far as 1873, Harper's in austere black leather binding, and the others in dark red cloth ornamented in gold. Publishers of periodicals profited by our parochial copyright-law, like book-publishers. Harper's, for instance, carried long serials in the magazine, then ran them off in book form from the same plates to sell at fifty cents in paper, $1.50 in cloth. At these prices the publishers could afford to pay the authors something, and I think Harper's did pay some authors, though I am not sure about this being a regular practice; Thackeray, I know, was paid $2000 in 1858 for *The Virginians*. The Franklin Square Library, which the Harper brothers built up almost entirely out of British reprints, was several cuts above the Seaside and Lovell's in workmanship. There is nothing like such commercial bookmaking being done today. Its contents also averaged higher, reproducing most of the first-class and second-class British fiction of the period. In the early days these magazines illustrated their pages lavishly with jack-knife pine board woodcuts which seem rather ridiculous now, but which have a certain antiquarian interest as giving an idea of the actual appearance of men and things at the time. Later the magazines did better; in the hands of Pennell, Frost, Abbey, illustrating showed itself as a great art.

Continental literature scarcely existed for us. On a mere perusal of our book-lists one could understand Matthew Arnold's observation that in the things of the spirit America could hardly lay claim to be more than a province of England. Yet it was Scribner's which fixed forever my veneration for Tourgueniev as incomparably the greatest of artists in fiction;

it published a translation by Professor Boyesen of the two stories of the nobleman Tchertapkhanov, and the story called *A Living Mummy*, both from the *Annals of a Sportsman*. Harper's gave me a translation of the beautiful little prose idyl of *Germelshausen*, from the German of Gerstäcker. Again, Scribner's published a couple of delightful Flemish folk-tales, and a charming German legend of the water-princess Ilse. It also introduced me to Jules Verne through an abridged version of *The Mysterious Island*, run as a serial; which led to my reading every work of this truly fascinating man that I could get my hands on, and through the Seaside Library I got my hands on all of them, I believe, but two. Moreover, one of these periodicals,—I no longer remember which one,—brought me the affecting story of Mother Michel's cat, so dear to the heart of French children. I have always been meaning to look this story up and find out what its source was. It may have been lifted from the *Journal des Enfants*, the first child's periodical to appear in France, if not (as I think it was) the first to appear anywhere. None was ever better done or more successful. It was an enterprise of the able and fastidious Lautour-Mézerai, which brought him in $20,000 a year, even after paying men of letters like Paul Lacroix and Charles Nodier to write for it, and keeping up a solid backlog of best-sellers such as the elder Dumas, Léon Gozlan, Emile Souvestre and Eugène Sue. The joys and sorrows of Mother Michel's cat made a story that was plenty good enough for the authorship of any of these, even as seen through the hazy medium of a translation.

In comparing Harper's Magazine of that period with the Harper's of today, one notices that the reader got about four times as much reading-matter to the issue as he gets now. Harper's was lavish with serials; it ran them two and three abreast; and they were something which one could really call serials. Harper's ran Thackeray's *Virginians* through 1858, and in 1865 it ran *Armadale* and *Our Mutual Friend* side by side. The earliest volume to which I had access, the one for 1873, carried serials by Anne Thackeray, Wilkie Collins and Charles

Reade. Through subsequent volumes I got acquainted with George Eliot, Trollope, Miss Mulock, Professor James de Mille, (his fine old sob-starter, *The Living Link*, full of mystery and horror, ran through 1874), R. D. Blackmore, Thomas Hardy, and William Black, who sometimes put his heroes and heroines through most distressing situations. His *Macleod of Dare*, which ran as a serial, brought out a protest in verse from one of Harper's readers. I can recall the first few lines of it:

O Mr. Black! Dear William Black!
Why will you be so blue?
For hypochondria's deepest dye
Seems surely dyed in you.

Oh, why with living corpses fill
The darkling dreadful main,
Or fish them out again at will,
Only to go insane?

—I forget the rest. Black wrote good novels, however; his *Madcap Violet*, *Kilmeny*, *A Princess of Thule*, were good enough for anybody, and still are. In fact, the second-raters of the period were considerably bigger men than modern opinion credits them with being. One turned to them with especial relief after first-raters like Reade and Dickens were bitten by the bug of the Uplift and took to preaching. After *Hard Times*, for example, or *Put Yourself In His Place*, a turn at *Shandon Bells* or *A Castle In Spain* would taste uncommonly good. Only a few years ago, somewhere, somehow, I happened on an old novel by C. Welsh Mason, called *Rape of the Gamp*, which I had read as a boy; Harper's serialised it in 1875. When I re-read it I found that my childish impressions were correct; a cultivated reader of today would find more merit in it than he might expect. These disparaged second-raters seem to me to have understood the true function of the ποίησις as Aristotle and Hesiod expound it, much better than the first-raters who took to pulpiteering, and to have served it with far greater fidelity.

But it was not only fiction that Harper's serialised. It serialised anything that was too good to be lost and too long to be run in one piece. Emilio Castelar's work on the republican movement in Europe, still in many respects the best treatment of the subject, ran through ten or more issues; so did another elaborate historical serial called *The First Century of the Republic*. I recall one on house-furnishings; one on exploration in Central Africa; one called *South Coast Saunterings in England*; one on travel in Mexico; and one in particular called *Recollections of an Old Stager*. This was made up of informal backstairs gossip about actors who had strutted and fretted through their little hour on our political scene in the days of Webster, Clay and Calhoun.

One is struck by the scope of the older periodical, the range of topics it presents. It gives a vivid idea of the number of things in the world which are interesting to the best reason and spirit of man, and also gives a lively sense of how interesting they are. Again, one is impressed by the amount of material in it which is addressed to reflective thought, and is therefore as good and as fresh today as when it was first read, fifty or sixty years ago. The modern periodical is relatively devoid of such material; whereas in my youth, besides what magazines like Harper's and the Century contained, we had three national monthly reviews, one of them very distinguished, which dealt in nothing else. Henry Adams said that the succession of Presidents from Washington to Grant was almost enough in itself to upset the whole Darwinian theory; and if he had lived to see the succession extended to the present time he would perhaps say it was quite enough. So one may say that the course of the North American Review from its illustrious editorship under Sparks, Everett, Dana, Lowell, Adams, down to the present time, is quite enough to upset the notion that universal literacy is an absolute good. The North American Review stands today as intellectual America's most impressive monument to the genius of Sir Thomas Gresham.

In forming an editorial policy, the brothers Harper apparently decided that out of fifty million Americans, more or fewer, there were probably about 100,000 who could read, and that out of these there was a respectable number who enjoyed the exercise of reflective thought. They appear to have taken this hundred thousand as their prospective clientèle, and to have baited their trap with an appropriately diversified lure. The temporary abeyance of Gresham's law enabled them to take this course and follow it profitably up to the last decade of the century. They could not do this now; no one could do it at any time these forty years.

The result was nuts for the inquiring disposition of a small shaver like myself. My parents took in St. Nicholas for me; I read it and liked it, but I had no such interest in it as I had in Harper's and the Century. When I was through with an issue or a volume, I was through with it, while with the others I was never through, nor would I be through now if I could provide myself with a full file of Harper's and the Century down to 1890. St. Nicholas left me where it found me; the others followed my growth. I have often thought that the most unfortunate thing about children's literature is that it is written for children; when one ceases to be a child one has hardly anything left to go on with as a permanent asset. I read St. Nicholas for five or six years, and the only thing in it that I could read now was Lucretia Hale's stories of the Peterkin family, and these, like *Alice*, the *Bab Ballads* and the *Snark*, were not written for children; children were rather their occasion than their cause. Possibly I could re-read Frank Stockton's *A Jolly Fellowship* which ran as a serial in St. Nicholas, but I am not sure. I think I might, though I remember little about it, because I know that a year or so after I read it I did go back to it and read it again.

One of the luckiest strokes in an uncommonly lucky life was my liberty to wander freely over the field opened to me by Harper's and the Century, especially by Harper's. They gave me my start towards a sound sense of what culture is, and of how desirable it is. Long afterwards, when I found culture defined as knowledge of the best that has been thought and said in the world, I could appraise these publications at their true value. Their aim was to clear and strengthen this sense in those who to some degree presumably had it, and to arouse it in the casual person like myself, whom good fortune had somehow made eligible. The snippets which they distributed were a *Vorspeise* clipped off the best available for this general purpose; not always the best there was, perhaps, but the best that for one reason or another could be made serviceable.

Five years ago I spent a delightful summer in the truly delightful country of Portugal, where I saw a state of things which once more set me wondering about the actual net value of universal literacy in any society. Portugal was densely illiterate; apparently no one knew what the volume of illiteracy was, for I got all sorts of estimates on it, running anywhere from fifty to eighty per cent of the population. I missed the customary roadsigns and roadside advertisements; in fact, advertisements of any kind were strangely infrequent; and I was told that they would not pay because too few people could read them. I noticed the absence of anything like what we call "popular literature," the production whereof has become so gigantic an industry with us. Lisbon had a newspaper which seemed fairly prosperous. Knowing no Portuguese, I floundered through one issue with what help I could muster from Latin, French and Italian, and gathered a provisional notion that it was pretty good, though it appeared to be written for a degree of intelligence somewhat above the ordinary, rather than for popular consumption. Its methods of distribution also indicated this, as well as I could make them out. I already knew that Portugal, as a French authority says, had *une petite élite extrémement brillante et cultivée*, and the evidence was overwhelming that this was the only possible clientèle towards which publishers might look.

One consequence of this interested me particularly. Lisbon's population comes to something like half a million, and it is a considerable retail trading-centre for the country at large. I was there at rather a bad moment for trade; goods were moving slowly just then, and the commercial exhibits were not especially impressive, except in two lines where they were indeed impressive—jewellery and books. Judging in relation to the volume of population and the volume of literacy, I have never seen so many, so well-stocked, and so handsome bookstores in any city. Judging in the same way, I calculated that in order to match Lisbon, New York would have to show very nearly as many bookstores as it used to show beer-saloons in the days before Prohibition.

To me the implications of this were obvious and striking. I saw, however, that, (to use our current jargon), the more socially-minded and forward-looking Portuguese disregarded them, and that the country was out to follow the fashion of modern republics since 1789 by pressing for an indiscriminate spread of literacy. I could find no evidence that the wisdom of this course had been challenged or even considered; apparently Mr. Jefferson's estimate of universal literacy's value was taken as axiomatic. I thought that instead of going in for this policy hand-over-head and sight-unseen, the Portuguese might have been wiser first to examine it thoroughly by the light which the experience of other societies could throw on it; the experience of our own society especially, since we have been most heavily committed to that policy and have done most with it. I did not suggest this to my Portuguese friends, however; my opinion was not asked, nor would I have given it if it had been asked. I had no wish to wet-blanket the amiable and kindly Portuguese, nor did I have any exalted notion that I could or should enlighten them, least of all that it was my good-neighbourly duty to try; and a person who feels no such stirrings within him is a superfluous man in any *Kulturkampf*.

It is one of my oddest experiences that I have never been able to find any one who would tell me what the net social value of a compulsory universal literacy actually comes to when the balance of advantage and disadvantage is drawn, or wherein that value consists. The few Socratic questions which on occasion I have put to persons presumably able to tell me have always gone by the board. These persons seemed to think, like Protagoras on the teaching of virtue, that the thing was so self-evident and simple that I should know all about it without being told; but in the hardness of my head or heart I still do not find it so. Universal literacy helps business by extending the reach of advertising and increasing its force; and also in other ways. Beyond that I see nothing on the credit side. On the debit side, it enables scoundrels to beset, dishevel and debauch such intelligence as is in the power of the vast majority of mankind to exercise. There can be no doubt of this, for the evidence of it is daily spread wide before us on all sides. More than this, it makes many articulate who should not be so, and otherwise would not be so. It enables mediocrity and sub-mediocrity to run rampant, to the detriment of both intelligence and taste. In a word, it puts into a people's hands an instrument which very few can use, but which everyone supposes himself fully able to use; and the mischief thus wrought is very great. My observations leave me no chance of doubt about the side on which the balance of social advantage lies, but I do not by any means insist that it does lie there.

III

When I was eight years old I began to study Latin and Greek under—what shall I say? Should I say under my father's teaching, instruction, direction, supervision, tutorship? No, I have precisely the right word in mind, but unfortunately the dictionaries say it is not a good word; that is, they say so by implication, for they do not mention it at all. My able and distinguished friend Mr. Charles A. Beard long ago remarked to me how sorry he was that the word *l'arn*, so well and truly seasoned by hard service in New England, should have gone completely out of currency as a transitive verb. "You can't *teach* a person anything," he said, "and certainly you can't *learn* him anything, but maybe you can *l'arn* him something." There is a nice distinction here, and one so highly valuable as to seem especially well worth preserving for the sake of those whose concern with pedagogy is professional; and yet I suppose it is a dynasty of doctrinaire schoolmarms of both sexes which has done most to wipe it out.

I do not recall that my father ever taught me anything, but in the course of two years, no question, he l'arned me a huge deal of Greek and Latin. It was all done informally and briefly; he never tried to do more than keep my chin above water. We had no schedule, no fixed daily tasks, no regular hours. When he had time, he would ask me what I had been up to, try me out on the knotty bits to make sure I had got them properly straightened up, throw in a word or two here and there which usually anticipated something lying ahead, and that was all there was to it. In the first instance, my interest in these studies, or rather my curiosity about them, was sprung by noticing that the dictionary gave so many of our words as coming from these sources. Naturally, however, it was not long before I became interested in the languages on their own account and rather keen to know what the people who spoke them were like and what they did with themselves. For these reasons, I suppose, pottering about with the languages never seemed like work to me, and I can take no credit whatever to myself for any proficiency which may have come of it; no more than for my proficiency, or lack of proficiency, at billiards, baseball, tennis, teaching, writing, editing, or any one of the many pursuits to which I have set a 'prentice hand in the course of my life. Certainly no one ever pointed my nose towards Rome and Athens; in fact, I had puzzled out the Greek alphabet correctly and memorised it before my father took hold, or, (I think), even before he noticed what I was about. I took up the job on my own, kept at it as I pleased, and was fully prepared to drop it if it failed to pan out. Apparently it is in the constitution of man that nothing done under these conditions seems like work. It may also be that these are the primary conditions requisite for l'arning a person something, and that l'arning him consists merely in taking advantage of them intelligently; but I do not know that this is so; it is only my opinion.

Being alone in my undertakings, I had the inestimable advantage of being unaffected by the law of diminishing returns. I got all I could take in of everything that was coming my way. Not until much later, when I had seen something of mass-education and observed its results, did I perceive how great this advantage is. With Mark Hopkins on one end of a log and a student on the other, the student gets the best out of Hopkins and gets as much of it as he can absorb; the law of diminishing returns does not touch him. Add twenty students, and neither he nor the twenty gets the same thing; add two hundred, and it is luck if anybody gets anything remotely like the same thing. All Souls College, Oxford, planned better than it knew when it limited the number of its undergraduates to four; four is exactly the right number for any college which is really intent on getting results. Socrates chatting with a single protagonist meant one thing, and well did he know it. Socrates lecturing to a class of fifty would mean something woefully different, so he organised no class and did no lecturing. Jerusalem was a university town, and in a university every day is field-day for the law of diminishing returns. Jesus stayed away from Jerusalem, and talked with fishermen here and there, who seem to have pretty well got what He was driving at; some better than others, apparently, but all on the whole pretty well. And so we have it that unorganised Christianity was one thing, while organised Christianity has consistently been another.

IV

It was while we were living in Brooklyn that politics first came under my conscious notice. I wrote an account of this in an essay published a dozen years ago, so I can do no better than to repeat the substance of it here. A short distance over the line which separated our semi-rural section from the more densely-populated central district of Brooklyn stood a ramshackle one-storey turtle-shaped wooden building known as the Wigwam. In some way I had heard it was a "political headquarters," but I did not know what that meant, and was not interested enough to ask. It was an evil-looking affair, dirty and disreputable, and the people who frequented it looked to me even more disreputable than the premises. We children were never actually forbidden to investigate it, as far as I know, but I recollect my mother saying once in an off-hand way that it was a good place to keep away from. I believe none of us was ever inside it, or wished to be.

One summer a campaign came on. I think it may have been a Presidential year, but I am not sure; something at any rate important enough to stir up a great commotion in Brooklyn's political circles. In the evenings the Wigwam became a kind of Malebolge, spewing up long columns of drunken loafers who marched and counter-marched, some carrying banners and transparencies, and others carrying tin torches that sent out clouds of kerosene-smoke. What first attracted my attention to these obscene performances was the sound of a steam-calliope at the head of a troop of marchers. I took this to mean that a circus-parade was going on, and when I went down there and found that there was no circus, I was disappointed and did not care what was taking place.

Thus my first impression of politics was unfavourable; and my disfavour was heightened by subsequently noticing that the people around me always spoke of politics and politicians in a tone of contempt. This was understandable. If all I had casually seen,—the Wigwam and its denizens, the processions of disgusting hoodlums who sweat and stank in the parboiling humidity of our Indian-summer nights,—if all this was of the essence of politics, if it was part and parcel of carrying on the country's government, then obviously a decent person could find no place in politics, not even the place of an ordinary voter, for the forces of ignorance, brutality and indecency would outnumber him ten to one. Nevertheless there was an anomaly here. We were all supposed to respect our government and its laws, yet by all accounts those who were charged with the conduct of government and the making of its laws were most dreadful swine; indeed, the very conditions of their tenure precluded their being anything else. For a moment I wondered why this should be so; but my wonderment almost immediately petered out, and I did not brood over the rationâle of politics again for a great many years.

One incident of election night, however, stuck in my memory. Some devoted patriot, very far gone in whisky, wandered up in our direction and fell by the wayside in a vacant lot where he lay all night, mostly in a comatose state. At intervals of half an hour or so he roused himself up, apparently conscious that he was not doing his duty by the occasion, and tried to sing the chorus of "Marching Through Georgia," but he could never get quite through the first three measures without relapsing into somnolence. It was very amusing; he always began so bravely and earnestly, and always faded out so lamentably.

Having devoted a great part of my latter years to a close observation of public affairs in many lands, I have often had occasion to remember that man. His sense of patriotism and patriotic duty still seems as intelligent and competent as that of any one I have met since then, and his mode of expressing it still seems as effective as any I could suggest.

CHAPTER FOUR

I have fought my fight, I have lived my life,
I have drunk my share of wine;
From Trier to Köln there was never a knight
Had a merrier life than mine.

—CHARLES KINGSLEY.

BETWEEN the ages of ten and sixteen my social environment changed twice so sharply as almost to suggest von Humboldt's observation that no one could pass from Siberia into Senegal without losing consciousness. When I was just past ten my father accepted an unusually attractive professional opportunity offered him from a town on the upper shores of Lake Huron, so we pulled up from Brooklyn, bag and baggage, which was a herculean chore in those days when long-distance trucking was unknown. We and our belongings went by rail to Detroit, and thence by steamboat to our journey's end. Our new home was forty-five miles from a railway, and our only means of communication with the outside world was by steamboat in summer, and in winter by a mail-stagecoach, or oftener a sledge, which covered those forty-five miles daily over what was no better than a logging-road.

No one ever took this hideous ride except on an errand of life or death. From the day navigation closed to the day it opened we were shut in tight, a community of some seven or eight thousand persons utterly isolated, thrown flat on their own social resources throughout a winter that was nothing to trifle with. When you saw how much of those winters there was and how much in earnest they were, you got up a deal of wholesome respect for them. Every year regularly the bay would show a blanket of ice ten miles long, ten miles wide, and five feet thick. Shopkeepers stocked up in the autumn, but usually missed their guess, so when a housekeeper wanted a spool of thread or a pound of crackers in the late spring, she would be told that "we are just out of that, but we'll have some in as soon as navigation opens." My mother used to say she heard that refrain so often that if she heard it once more before the boats ran she would be out of her mind. The whistle of the first steamboat was the event of the year, literally. No matter at what time of day her whistle blew, everyone would let go all holds and rush for the wharf; and if she came in at night, she would find the whole population awake and on hand. If the county court were in session, it would adjourn; and if the churches were in session, as happened once at least to my knowledge, the congregations, choirs, janitors, probably the parsons also, though I did not wait to notice, all promptly quit the way of salvation and joined dogs with the ungodly in a joyous stampede.

One night when the first boat was more or less expected, for we could never be sure of her until we heard her whistle, four or five of my father's pet cronies were smoking and lying and having a general good time with him downstairs, while my mother, who was upstairs with me, saw the prospect of their keeping the household astir until all hours, and said she wished they would clear out and go home. I said I thought it might be managed; so I hunted up an empty quart bottle with a thick lip, went to the back of the upper hall to give the illusion of distance, and blew three long deep blasts on the bottle. Before the sound ceased the men had gone through the front door like a football-rush, struggling into their overcoats as they went. The boat did not come in until the next afternoon, and though the incident caused considerable talk and speculation in the town, the whistlings were never satisfactorily accounted for. Some, remembering that the air was fresh that night, said they might have been the sounds of wind rumbling in a chimney; while another school of thought, somewhat more cynical, held to a theory based on the well-known properties of Ben Kaichen's whisky; but nothing was ever actually determined.

The economic climate was as sharp a change from Brooklyn's as the physical climate. Living in Brooklyn, one was at arm's-length from the nearest thing to a metropolis that America could show; one rubbed elbows with a great variety of interests and occupations. Here there was only one primary interest and occupation—lumber. Brigades of lumberjacks went into camp each winter, felling and stripping trees and rolling the logs to the river. In summer the logs were floated down to the town, sorted, made up into rafts and towed to the various sawmills to be cut. The lumber was then piled on great docks, inspected, and loaded on barges which were towed, two or three in a string, behind a steambarge to Buffalo, Cleveland, or some other Lake port where their market lay. Except for a fairish industry in frozen fish, this was the whole economic life of the town. When we returned to the East after eight years the pine timber was near exhaustion, and pessimists were saying that the place would soon become a ghost-town, as so many single-industry towns had done and are still doing; but this did not happen. A railway came in, followed by other industries, and though I have never since been there to see how the town is getting on, I have heard it is doing well, though hardly anything that an old resident would recognise is left. I have even heard that no steamboats touch there now, which seems utterly incredible and impossible. The railway drove them off, as it drove them off the Mississippi.

Curiously, the social and cultural climate was not so great a change from Brooklyn's as one might suppose. Our town was a first-generation affair, like Jamestown and Plymouth in their early days; it had no history, no tradition. The inhabitants had come in full-grown, mature, and were still in full vigour, not old enough to give way, still less die off. The children they had brought with them were as yet young, and those who had been spawned here were quite young. This matter of settlement by adults gave rise to a rather interesting peculiarity. We were exceptional among American towns in having no Main Street. The business section lay in a rectangle marked by the conjunction of Second and River Streets. Our Main Street, what there was of it, lay along the shore, quite off to one side, and was devoted to the more pretentious residences of the well-to-do. Actually, however, it was not Main Street at all, though the spelling did become corrupted into the conventional form. It was Maine Street, short for State-of-Maine Street, so-called originally because so many of those who had built their fine houses there were lumbermen from Maine.

In this remote, isolated, unsightly region, a wilderness of stumps and sand-barrens, and in a settlement so new which seemed to have no more stability than a mining-camp, one would have expected to find only the ill-favoured and repellent social life of an American frontier town. By some odd freak of chance this was not the case. The millowners and those directly concerned with the production of lumber were a hardheaded, hardfisted lot, with no interest in the amenities of existence, but displaying an amused and rather generous tolerance towards any effort to promote them. They were a good lot, too, as far as their lights led them; self-reliant, hard-working, honest, hating restraint, fiercely independent, yet friendly, kindly, and in many unexpected ways, liberal. In a word, they were standard specimens of the kind that one of my friends speaks of in a nostalgic strain as the old-fashioned, free-thinking, free-speaking, free-swearing American. They interested me immensely; I had never seen anything like them, and I studied their ways with delight. Their virtues,—and they were great virtues,—gave our society its prevailing tone of wholesome vigour which I look back upon as something uniquely formative in my experience.

But our society had an overtone as well. Many of our immigrants were not directly concerned with lumber, but had come to town in the wake of the industry as professional men or tradesmen; and among these an astonishing number were intelligent, thoughtful, and fairly well read. Their conversation was excellent, they had good taste, good manners, and a good attitude towards life's amenities. I have seldom seen so small a town with anything comparable to our array of musical talent; there were so many who not only had superb voices, but who also knew how to sing and were musically literate to a remarkable degree. We had a lyric tenor, a lumber-inspector, who could have made his everlasting fortune in a Continental centre, practically as he stood; also two baritones, both in the insurance business, and a magnificent bass, a lawyer, who could have turned the trick almost as easily. The pretty wife of one of our tradesmen,—a charming couple, I think from Boston,—got extraordinary effects out of whistling; her lower register had something very near the real wood-wind timbre. Visiting connoisseurs of vaudeville who had listened to the best that professional whistlers could do, said they had never heard her equal. The odd thing about our fortuitous aggregation of talent was that it had no root in any established tradition. None of it came of any Continental stock where music was a fixed and necessary part of life. These people were all of the Anglo-Saxon breed, some New Englanders, some "York State Yankees," some from the Western Reserve; and their only traditional music was the ensemble of the bucksaw, the anvil and the flail.

Our choral society, about forty in number, kept hard at it all winter, giving excellent concerts. Their programmes conceded nothing to popular taste, for there was hardly any popular taste to be considered. Our leading citizens, the millowners and their entourage, all turned out handsomely in support of the society, not because they knew much about its work or enjoyed it particularly, but because it reflected uncommon credit on the town and was something to be proud of. They took more actual pleasure out of the shows that our rather meagre dramatic talent vamped up from time to time. These were unpretentious, for we were as weak on the dramatic side as we were strong on the musical side. But, like our concerts, they were undertaken purely for the fun of the thing. The playlets and farces were clever, all hands did the best they could, the audiences were in a mood to be pleased, and things went off as well as one would wish.

When all came to all, I am inclined to think that my parents were socially better off here than they were in Brooklyn. One missed the occasional larger opportunities of a semi-demi-metropolis, but on the other hand, our isolation and our long stretches of enforced leisure kept the congenial elements in our society together in a closer, more sustained, and more intimate association. One thing that gave a perennial freshness to our family life was that my father could indulge to his heart's content his gregarious fancy for cultivating rare and fruity characters. There was no end of such; the town was simply crawling with them, all of the very first order, and positively guaranteed no two alike. Each of them was an inexhaustible mine of diversion for one of my father's peculiar taste. Their incessant pranks, the practical jokes they thought up to play on one another, were a marvel of devilish ingenuity. They were in all stations of life, some rich, some well-to-do, some less so; we had no poor; the grisly social phenomenon which Mr. Dooley called the prolotoorio, ("A prolotoorio, Jawn, is the same thing as a hobo"), had not yet appeared among us. All these congenital nonconformists uproariously clave to my father at first sight, and kept seeing to it that he never had a dull day while he was in their midst; and save for those caused by failing health, I truly think he never had one. If he went out no farther than around the block, he would come back roaring with laughter over some absurd *rencontre*. My mother did not take so much stock in these rugged individualists. She told me once in a burst of confidence that they were the finest assortment of human sculch she had ever laid eyes on. But her sense of humour being what it was, she had to admit, when I pinned her down to it, that they were also probably as diverting as anything in the whole anthropoid creation that was ever allowed to run at large.

Life here gave me a close view of qualities which I was of course too young to appraise at their full value, but when I came to review them in later life I saw that my impression of them had been clear and germinal. Independence, self-respect, self-reliance, dignity, diligence,—often narrow and primitive in their manifestations, if you like, ill-rounded, not at all *durchgearbeitet*, but there they were, the virtues that once spoke out in the Declaration of Independence. It was noticeable, too, that these virtues flourished as well as they did in a state of freedom. Our life was singularly free; we were so little conscious of arbitrary restraint that we hardly knew government existed. Aside from the county sheriff and one deputy, the town had no police, nor seemed to need any; I heard of no crime being committed there in my time. On the whole, our society might have served pretty well as a standing advertisement for Mr. Jefferson's notion that the virtues which he regarded as distinctively American thrive best in the absence of government. I am quite sure that John Adams, George Mason, John Taylor, Mercer of Maryland, Jackson of Georgia, Jones of North Carolina, would have found something admirable and congenial in the Americanism of our citizenry at large; more congenial and far more admirable than anything they could find in the shoddy article now on sale everywhere under that name. I use the words "now on sale" deliberately and advisedly.

II

During my first four years of life in these new surroundings, only two matters out of many which came my way are entitled to a place in this narrative. One was my scraping up a couple of valuable acquaintances; valuable because it was through them that I got up not only a great lot of first-class conversational German, but also considerable insight into German life and character; and all with virtually no effort. Certain inhabitants of our town seemed strangely above their station; above it in education, breeding, culture, views of life. No one knew why or how they came to be where they were, and no one asked. The town kept to the admirable unwritten rule of frontier etiquette which regarded a person's antecedents as quite beyond question. "All I care to know," said Mark Twain, himself a product of the frontier who lived always in its spirit, "is that a man is a human being; that is enough for me—he can't be any worse." Such was the invariable attitude of our society.

Among these misplaced people were a *ci-devant* German-Polish count and his wife. He did some sort of routine work, I forget what; something in the insurance way, I think. He was a taciturn unsmiling person, while she was a lively bright little soul, happy when she had some one to chatter with. For some reason, the epitaph that Callimachus wrote for the sweet-spirited Samian girl who died so young, *τὴν πολύμυθον, ἐπισταμένην καλὰ παίζειν, ἡδίστην συνέριθον, ἀεὶ λάλον,* always puts me in mind of her. Finding that I knew a word or two of German, this childless and more or less companionless woman made friends with me and kept me with her whenever she could, telling me about the charms of her native country and the attractions of life there. She gave me an impression of Warschau as being truly a *civitas Dei*, one of the world's wonders, and I forthwith resolved to see it, which I have never done, and now of course never shall.

Another misplaced person was of a military type somewhat gone to seed, and well on the far side of middle age; tall, large, extremely handsome, and speaking the true pure German of the Hanoverian aristocracy. Whether or not a titular aristocrat, he had every mark betokening generations of good breeding. He seemed singularly content in the humblest of occupations, —he was the janitor of a church,—apparently seeking nothing beyond a very poor living and a maximum of leisure. He had a room somewhere in which he cooked his food and slept, but he had also converted the church's rear basement into a large neat *Gesellschaftszimmer*, where he spent most of his time, and where I too spent many hours in his witty, humorous, philosophical company. I recall him now as one whom experience had shown, as it showed Montaigne, that human beings are very much what they are, that the collective character of their society is very much what it is, and that nothing of any conceivable consequence can be done about either, save to entertain oneself with the kaleidoscopic spectacle of their incredibly absurd exorbitances and divagations. The man suddenly disappeared one day, and we never heard of him again. Probably some turn in his affairs took him back to the Fatherland; I hope so. He got letters and newspapers regularly from Germany, so it seems likely that some arrangement for his return had been managed, though it would be impossible to say on what grounds. One could never think of him as a political refugee, for the *Politiker* of whatever stripe would be no more to him than a creature of sheer obscenity, more or less amusing. He was too honest and upright to have been concerned in any scandal, unless perchance somehow victimised. Since he was a man of deep and simple-hearted sentiment, a true German, I have sometimes thought that in his earlier days an untoward sentimental attachment might have made him break with his surroundings. Once indeed, I remember, he spoke casually of having had a sweetheart in Germany, and when I thoughtlessly asked what had become of her, he replied, "*Sie ist längst im Grabe.*"

So much for these two dear and good friends of my boyhood. I shall always love their memory, and always be grateful for their influence in enlarging my views of life and shaping my demands on life.

The second matter pertinent to this record was a matter of bad luck with my studies. At twelve or thereabouts, for my sins I was sentenced to do time over the "standard authors" which a schoolboy at my stage of progress was supposed to read,—Cæsar, Xenophon, Homer, Virgil, Cicero,—and God wot it was the dullest, dreariest, most unrewarding task I ever set my hand to. If the language-difficulties attendant on it had been even a shade more obstructive than they were, I would have thrown Greek and Latin to the winds forever. These were the least of my troubles; my tribulations rose from the substance of what these wretched men wrote about; it was all so far over my head. I was not interested in bridge-building, in Ariovistus or Vercingetorix, or in what the father of the gods and king of men had done for Æolus. Like Pet Marjorie's turkey, I "did not care a single dam" about the gardens of Alcinous, the Manilian law, or the fate of the poet Archias. The only clear impression made on me by the Catilinian orations was that the great orator was a good deal of a stuffed shirt; an impression which abides with me to this day.

The schools in our town were somewhat worse than none, and I did not attend them, but had hitherto gone on with my studies in the same happy-go-lucky fashion as in Brooklyn. My readings in Greek and Latin had consisted of scraps culled from various works; they were mostly short, and all were appropriate to my age. They dealt with matters well within the compass of a child's understanding, affairs of ordinary life, ordinary experience; many of them were light, amusing, humorous. This slipshod curriculum was invaluable to me in one respect. It set me on my way to see the men and women of antiquity as I have always since then seen them, not as story-book heroes and heroines, but as people exactly like us, each with twenty-four hours a day to get through somehow or other, and for the most part getting through them quite as we do; people of the same instincts, passions, desires, ambitions, abilities, as ourselves, and employing them precisely as we employ them. This may seem a commonplace observation, perhaps a stupid commonplace; yet it does point straight to the enormous difference between knowing history and understanding history. One is often astonished to see how many there are who seem to know a vast lot of history, but to understand hardly any of it. Nine-tenths of the value of classical studies lies in their power to establish a clear commonsense, matter-of-fact view of human nature and its activities over a continuous stretch of some twenty centuries. If one gravitates into that view at an early age, as I did, naturally, unconsciously, not knowing that there is any other view to take, so much the better.

But my parents had the notion of some day sending me to college. They had one particular college in mind for me, and to enter it one had to comply with some of the most preposterous requirements that a hidebound traditionalism could devise. They might well have come down from the curriculum which master Tubal Holophernes imposed upon Gargantua. Their intention was sound enough, probably, but their prescriptions were redundant, pointless. Early in the last century Harvard College required its candidates to show on examination that they were able "extempore to read, construe and parse" any Latin prose or poetry presented to them, and also "to write true Latin in prose, and to be skilled in making Latin verse"; and the same with Greek. This was exactly right, exactly as it should be, for the best way to find out whether or not a person can do something is to set him at it; and that should end the matter, then and there. Why should a poor little devil be required, over and above this proof of competence, to have read through a dreadful slather of what must be to any child the most uninteresting, unassimilable and odious literature that could be put before him? If he had got his facility by unwonted ways, out of Aulus Gellius's scrapbook, Pliny's letters, bits from Cornelius Nepos and Eutropius; epigrams of Martial, Ausonius, the Anthology; fables out of the Græca Minora, stories out of the Vulgate,—what odds, so long as he has it? The authors whom tradition has labelled "preparatory" have a great place in literature, but that place is far out of a child's reach. My notion is that Cæsar and Cicero come in with Tacitus, Sallust and others, far along in one's course, as topical reference-reading in a critical study of Roman political history, as Homer and Virgil should in a critical literary study based on Aristotle's *Poetics*. Taken thus, the student will read and re-read them with understanding and pleasure, but taken as a *corpus vile* of "preparatory" material, he will detest them. I have not read a word of Cicero's speeches since my schooldays, (though I have read his philosophical treatises with great attention); nor have I looked into a copy of the *Gallic War* but once, and that was to settle a bet.

III

When I was just turning fourteen I was sent off to boarding-school, a long way from home, down in the prairie country on the banks of the Illinois River, where again I was plumped into a brand-new set of physical and social surroundings. The town had about ten thousand people; it made its living out of agriculture and miscellaneous manufactures, the principal products being organs, ploughs, alcohol and corn whisky. It had been settled by 'forty-eighters, the best stock that Europe ever exported here, and the descendants of those superb people were keeping very closely to the old ways and traditions. All their social activities and amenities were German. They had three flourishing musical societies; a *Männerchor*, a *Liederkranz* of mixed voices, and a less formal *Gesangverein* of younger folk from whom in course of time I learned practically the whole *Kommersbuch* pretty well by heart. Also with the help of some of them I learned to read music as an extra-curricular activity, with no idea of doing anything with it in a practical way, but only with a vague notion of some day becoming musically literate. The theory and history of music has always interested me, and I have kept at them in a desultory fashion all my life. For some reason there was no instrumental music, except for the piano. In a town brimming over with vocal music of a high order, and harbouring excellent pianists, one would at least look for a string quartette of sorts, but I can not recall a single person who had ever scraped a string.

A great deal of social interest centred in the *Turnverein*, which was an exclusive institution. One had to have credentials running back as far as Henry the Fowler to belong to it, so I got my knowledge of its doings mainly by hearsay. It put on two or three really remarkable gymnastic exhibitions each winter, which were invitation-affairs, though a few plebeians with a "pull" were sometimes grudgingly allowed to crash the gate for standing-room, and were promptly hunted out again when the show was over and the festivities beginning. Some of the beauty and chivalry off the very top layer of two neighbouring cities were usually on hand to grace the occasion; and speaking of beauty, this region blossomed with more pretty girls than I would have supposed there were in the world. They were somewhat on the alfalfa-fed order, innocent of cosmetics, and making an excellent appearance, whether singly or in groups. They gave me the beginnings of a critical taste in such matters, for outside of my own family I had not seen any female beauty worth speaking of, except in some older women. Since then I have been in regions which I thought were a shade or two more productive, and the product rather better. Belgium, for example, seemed on long acquaintance to be keeping up to its mediæval record in this respect, as appears in the old monastic hexameters,

> Gandavum laqueis, formosis Bruga puellis,
> Lovanium doctis, gaudet Mechlinia stultis.

Of course one can't know exactly what sort of thing Bruges kept in stock to fluster the monks of the Middle Ages, but at any time these thirty years I would have put Brussels far and away ahead of Bruges or any other town in the kingdom. I understand, however, that connoisseurs unite *nem. con.* in giving the first prize for this pleasing commodity to Poland, but I have never been in Poland or seen more than a very few Polish girls, so I can have no opinion.

I also acquired, quite unconsciously, the beginnings of a creditable taste in beer. The town had a small brewery which brought forth a most superexcellent product, and the proprietor's son being a day-pupil in our school, its hospitalities were open to us. It was an impressive experience to go down to the brewery when the bock-beer season opened, and see a jury of grave old pundits assembled, austere colossi of learning, taciturn, profoundly scrupulous, sampling the new brew with reverent care and finally delivering judgement. With such a start, I quite naturally grew up in the prevailing superstition that all German beer is good, but when I went into Germany I found a great deal that was bad. I also found that our little brewery was an exception to the rule discussed by Herbert Spencer, that the worst place to look for a product is the place where it is produced. In my day Brussels imported beers from Munich and Dortmund that were beyond belief; they were too good to drink; yet in Munich and Dortmund the same brands of beer were not nearly so good. Thirty-five years ago, the dark beer one got at Lüchow's in New York, and especially the Bavarian black beer that Jansen imported, were far better than anything I found under the same name in Würzburg and Kulmbach, where they were made.

Our school ran to a dozen or fifteen boarders and as many day-pupils, all from good substantial families. It was a strange affair in some ways. Its material equipment was poor and primitive; well-to-do parents today would not dream of putting boys in such a place, though it was well-kept in the sense that nothing was let go dirty or slovenly. Our food was abundant and good; quite on the coarse side and thoroughly uninteresting, but we got on with it and saw no reason to complain. But our living-quarters, dormitory, schoolrooms, were bare, bleak, repellent, as anything one would find in a county jail. One could get up as tear-compelling a story as Copperfield's about our discomfort and wretchedness,—breaking a skin of ice in our wash-pitchers mornings, and all that sort of thing,—but it would hardly go down with us, for we were not conscious of being uncomfortable and wretched; on the contrary we were having a very good time out of our situation. We had all known better things, but not so much better that the contrast was heartbreaking. I sometimes think a superheated passion for the Uplift rather overplays the sense of hardship and misery ensuing upon circumstances like ours; at all events, we laboured under no such distress.

With regard to my studies at the school, my extraordinary luck still held good. Poor as the place would seem if judged by modern notions of the American standard of living, whatever that is, it was just the place for me. I wish now that I had thought to ask my parents how they came to hear of it and what had moved them to send me there. The head of the school was wise, capable, kind, hard-working, and had an excellent literary sense. He woke me up to the fact that Greek and Roman poetry really has some merit; he even caused my detestation of Homer and Virgil to fade out; and he introduced me casually to a great deal that is good in English verse. He had three assistants. One of them managed to sluice some arithmetic and algebra into my head, but it all promptly seeped out again, so that I had to do an extra year's preparatory work in order to enter college, which was humiliating. All I did in mathematics, then or ever, was done by sheer effort of unintelligent memory. Today I am unable to add a column of ten figures and get the same result twice, unless by chance, and the simplest sum in long division is as far beyond me as driving a locomotive.

Like my two friends at home, the other assistants gave the curious impression of not belonging where they were, and one could not help wondering how they had found their way there. One was a cripple, moving about on crutches. He bore one of the most distinguished names to be found in the academic circles of Massachusetts, and everything about him betokened the indefinable quality of distinction. His culture, manners, humour, easy affability, delightful conversation, all had the unmistakable mark of superiority. We had boundless respect for him, and great affection; whatever he might want from us was his. In return, he liked us, treating us as friends, and above all invariably as gentlemen. It was his influence in particular, even above that of the head-master, which set the social tone of the school.

The other master was a gentle-spirited young German, an excellent musician, (though he taught no music), who seemed always very sad. He was a capable teacher, but outside of his work and his music there seemed little that he had the heart to care for. He rather took to me, mainly on the score of music in the first instance, but we soon established a friendship on general grounds. His conversation taught me a great deal about music and musicians, and when I left school he gave me a book of musical exercises to remember him by, seeming to set a great deal of store by it, much more than the book was actually worth. It bore a blue bookplate with a woman's name printed in heavy, bold German script, *Welda Reichels*. I have sometimes wondered whether it was connected with some romance that had missed fire.

It appears to me now that the most unusual and salutary thing about our life in that school was its atmosphere of freedom. Within our hours of work the discipline was strict enough to keep things going as they should, but it was not unkind, unreasonable, or on a proper occasion, inflexible. Out of hours we had all the range there was, free to wander in the fields, row on the river, hob-nob with the townspeople, and strike up acquaintances where we chose. The policy worked well enough. We were never cautioned against putting beans up our noses, or subjected to any snivelling talk about being on our honour, or keeping up the credit of the dear old school, or any such odious balderdash. Nevertheless we somehow managed to behave decently, no doubt because we had no overweening inducements to behave otherwise. I do not recall any pranks serious enough to come in for more than a good-natured reprimand. Yet we were not holding any brief for Condorcet's or Rousseau's views on the essential goodness of human nature. There was always plenty to do that was legitimate and more interesting than anything likely to land us in trouble, so why get in trouble? This was all there was to it; this was the sum of our ethical imperative.

Not so long afterwards I began to suspect that this might also be the sum of the ethical imperative affecting the conduct of mankind-at-large. What first drew my attention that way was the very eloquent and splendid passage of poetry in which Juvenal contrasts the social behaviour of other animals with that of man.[1] On a first reading it struck me that for a first-class

[1] Sat. xv, 159-171.

satirist Juvenal must have been a shocking poor observer. When he said that there is greater concord among serpents than among men, that the stronger lions and boars always spare the weaker, he was saying something which I made bold to believe simply wasn't so.

> Indica tigris agit rabida cum tigride pacem
> Perpetuam.

—but, I said to myself, that is just what she doesn't do. She keeps the peace only unless and until some circumstance arises which in her opinion justifies her in breaking it. I thought that if Juvenal had been a better observer he could not have helped seeing that his tigresses and bears behave precisely as men and women do, and for the same reason. There seemed to me to be some principle at work here, some general law of conduct prevailing throughout the animal world. But all this was casual at the time, something that popped into my head and at once popped out again to stay gone for years. I scribbled a ribald note on the margin of a Tauchnitz text, and was amused by it in my subsequent re-readings of Juvenal, but gave the matter no further thought. My mind reverted to it immediately, however, when long afterwards I learned that there is indeed such a law, though its universality had not been established at that time, nor its implications fully apprehended. I found that Aristippus, Epicurus, Aristotle and St. Augustine had brushed elbows with this law without clearly recognising it, and so in modern times had Bishop Butler. Bentham and Mill had occasional glimpses of it. Spencer's view of it and Henry George's was clear but limited; they did not go the full length it should have led them. Not for a long time did I come upon a competent exposition of that law and its effects; and when I did, curiously, I did not get it from an academic philosopher, but from a retired businessman. I shall have something more to say of this hereafter.

IV

My summer vacations I spent at home in the Lake region, and also the eighteen months intervening between my leaving school and entering college. During these periods I went pretty well on furlough from routine study, reverting to my old practice of desultory reading, and not too much of that. One book, Tylor's *Primitive Culture*, which I read at this time, did set a line of permanent interest; it got me into a hospitable frame of mind towards the works of Darwin, Huxley, Herbert Spencer, and other expositors of progressive evolution, when I came upon them some years later.

As for my other pursuits, I edged my way into baseball of the bush-league type, doing so well that I was thought to have a promising professional future ahead of me if I stuck at it; but although I toyed with the idea, I never went farther with it than playing now and then irregularly, at college and elsewhere, for a number of seasons. I fished a bit, and shot a bird or two sometimes, but only for food; never any large game, though it was plentiful enough. Hunting as a sport was not much done, for some reason, so the bears and deer remained quite tame and friendly. Once at sunset of a winter's day, I remember, a bear and two large cubs strolled through the middle of town, crossed the Second Street bridge and went out again, all quite nonchalantly, tourist-fashion, as people who were out merely to see the sights.

Occasionally I worked at various jobs around the sawmills, partly for something to do, but mainly because I found a fascination in the process by which large wet logs were converted into handsome pine lumber; there was something rather pretty about it. I especially liked the niceness of swift calculation of the way each individual log should be trimmed and cut to insure the least wastage. The foreman had only a moment or two to make up his mind about this, while the logs were coming up the "brow" three or four at a time, so it was a skilled job. Then too it is always a pleasure to see a process all the way through, complete, instead of some mere fraction of it. Here one's eyes could follow the history of a piece of lumber from its origin in a standing tree down to its final state as a two-by-four on the deck of a barge outward-bound to market. It is an amusing thought to me nowadays that as far as knowledge goes, not physical strength, I still could do anything there is to be done around a sawmill, except filing the saws. I should not know how to do that, but I doubt it would take me long to learn.

I was in the timber-woods only once or twice; it was all very still and sombre in their depths, and probably poetic, but the only thing that interested me was that one could look up and see the stars in the daytime, as one does from the bottom of a well. The absence of underbrush and the flatness of the land gave me somewhat the feeling of being in church, so I suppose I should have been touched by the religious awe which poets write of, but somehow I was not. Yet our woods had a lore of their own, and even a mythology. A few years ago, when there was quite a run of research into the tales of Paul Bunyan and other legendary creatures of the timberlands, I was astonished to see no mention of the principal figure in our mythology, the hodag. I was astonished, because in my time the horrific deeds and prowesses of this creature were known *ubique et ab omnibus* in our region, wherever lumber was cut.

Like the fourth beast of Daniel, the hodag was "dreadful and terrible and strong exceedingly; and it had great iron teeth: it devoured and brake in pieces, and stamped the residue with the feet of it." It also had a long flat tail of bone with serrated edges, thin as a band-saw and hard as steel. The hodag subsisted on bears, deer, wildcats and such, but its favourite article of diet was landlookers; these being men whom the millowners sent out to explore and report on unexploited areas of timberland. When the hodag got on trail of a landlooker, nothing could be done; it was just too bad. On the ground, escape was impossible; and if the landlooker climbed a tree, the hodag would saw the tree down with its tail, and that was the end of the landlooker. I never saw the hodag, but landlookers have entertained me by the hour with lurid stories of its doings. I suggest that students of American mythology look into this matter and give the hodag its proper place in their pantheon.

In those years I undoubtedly built up and fortified the singular immunity to infirmity and disease which has lasted all my life; but in those years also my congenital indifference to nature in the wild, natural scenery, rocks, rills, woods and templed hills, hardened into permanent distaste. Like the Goncourts, I can see nature only as an enemy; a highly respected enemy, but an enemy. "I am a lover of knowledge," Socrates said, "and the men who dwell in the city are my teachers, and not the trees or the country." The great Guizot never saw the ocean until he was forty-four, and would not have seen it then if he had not had an errand in a part of Normandy where he could not help seeing it. "At that time," he said, "I would not have gone a couple of miles to see the most magnificent bit of natural scenery. I would have gone a thousand to see a man of talent." This sentiment being so precisely mine, I am wholly unable to understand the passion for rusticity and rural life. In England and the United States, urban life is so deplorably ill-organised that one must exist in the country as best one can; but this is a forced put. In Europe, where urban life is better organised, one views a sojourn in the country as more or less something to be got through with. Apparently it was always so. "What is pleasanter than the city?" cries Tibullus, "What kind of place is a farm-house to park your best girl in?"[2] True, some of the Roman poets, even Tibullus himself, now and then dutifully churned out praises of rural life, but they do not carry the tone of complete conviction to my ears. In a denizen of an American city one can understand a slight exaggeration of the joys of life "up at my little place in the country," but in one accustomed to the urban society of Rome, it sounds a trifle effortful and strained. My notion is that for the moment

[2] Dulcius urbe quid est? An villa sit apta puellae?

Horace and Virgil were perhaps not quite serious, perhaps saying somewhat the conventional thing; but even so, one must admit that, like the House of Lords in Gilbert's delightful satire, "they did it very well."

The nearest I came to feeling the divine afflatus was in my sixteenth summer when I was making a long, slow, lazy trip on a steambarge. The millowners used to let me travel on them when I could persuade my father to exercise his "pull," which was seldom. On this particular trip we passed Port Huron at sunset and were all night going through the Detroit and St. Clair rivers and Lake St. Clair, out into Lake Erie. The night was clear and warm, there was no wind, the moon was full, and I was so delighted by the resultant fine effects that I sat up all night to enjoy them. Perhaps something might have been made of me in a poetic way if the charm of the picture had not been so largely due to the works of man; the farms, the houses, voices on the shores, the lights of towns and villages, the passing boats. With these taken away and the landscape left in a state of nature, I am quite sure I should have looked at it for a while, said it was all very fine, very good, then turned in for a night's sound sleep, and afterwards thought no more about it.

CHAPTER FIVE

Haec studia adolescentiam alunt, senectutem oblectant, secundas res ornant, adversis solatium et perfugium praebent, delectant domi, non impediunt foris, pernoctant nobiscum, peregrinantur, rusticantur.

—CICERO.

CONSIDERED as a vestigial survival, the college I attended is worth a good many words, but I doubt that the tongues of men or of angels could convince the modern American mind that such an institution actually existed short of the Jurassic period, if then; and still less that a person now living actually attended it and remembers it and knows that it was real. Hence in speaking of it I feel uncomfortably like a lecturer trying to reconstruct the civilisation of Atlantis or Avalon before an incredulous and derisive audience. To begin with, it was small, never running quite to a hundred students; it wanted no more and would take no more, preposterous as the fact may seem. It was situated on the blank countryside, approachable only by something over three miles of the pre-motorcar type of clay road which lay between us and the railway. There was no settlement near us; a couple of undersized hamlets lay four miles off, and the nearest pretence to a city, which was not a very plausible pretence, was twenty miles away.

It would be hard to imagine a set of young men living more strictly on their own. We devised our own relaxations and extra-curricular activities with no encouragement from the authorities and no discouragement; nothing but a tacit *nihil obstat.* We had no central meeting-place, and our only gymnasium was an ancient bowling-alley, much out of repair. Our food was pretty much the regular thing in institutional provender; good enough, what there was of it, and plenty of it, such as it was. We took care of our own living-quarters, with no supervision; if we chose to tidy up, we might do so; but if we preferred to live in squalor, we might also do that. In this way the slacktwisted among us soon learned that neatness paid, and the tidy ones got into habits that were almost old-maidish. One would hardly expect it to work out that way, perhaps, but I have often noticed that the most slovenly people are those who are most accustomed to having things done for them.

The authorities had nothing to do with us in a social way; our only contact with them was in business hours and for business purposes. They were men of vast learning, great dignity, always punctiliously polite, but with no affectation of cordiality. For our part, we put up no pretence of fondness for them, but our respect, pride, admiration of them, knew no bounds. We would have fought for them like Stonewall Jackson's soldiers, at the drop of a hat. Their character impressed us even more than their learning, great as that was; and their aloofness just suited us, because it was so completely in character. If they had once tried to make themselves informal, chummy, big-brotherly,—in a word, vulgar,—we would have resented it with contempt. No student was ever spoken to, or spoken of, as Jim or Bill, Smith or Jones, but always as Mr. Smith or Mr. Jones. Our preceptors were gentlemen as well as scholars.

There was not a grain of sentimentalism in the institution; on the other hand, the place was permeated by a profound sense of justice. The most important extra-curricular lesson we learned,—and we learned it properly,—was summed up in Chief Justice Jay's dictum that "justice is always the same, whether it be due from one man to a million, or from a million to one man." We learned this, not by precept, but by example, which is the best way to learn such lessons. In all circumstances we were treated justly, never coddled or pampered, but never overborne or sat upon. Each day's work was a full day's work, union hours, but we could never say we were overtasked. In my four years there I never heard of any one getting a word of commendation for a piece of good work, though I saw a great deal of good work, even distinguished work, being done. The motto of the college might well have been taken from St. Luke's words, "When ye shall have done all those things which are commanded you, say, We are unprofitable servants." Yet we rather liked this attitude, as being in a way complimentary. We were made to understand that the burden of education was on us and no one else, least of all on our instructors; they were not there to help us carry it or to praise our efforts, but to see that we shouldered it in proper style and got on with it.

We learned not only that justice is always the same in small matters as in great, but we also learned thoroughly the consequent lesson which seems so unaccountably hard for Anglo-Saxons ever to learn, that justice is always the same in the case of men and things you do not like, as in the case of those you do like. An uncommonly striking illustration of this truth once came my way. At the beginning of my senior year there entered a fine big handsome freshman,—a first-rate student, too,—who would have interested George Borrow, for he turned out to be a sap-engro, a snakemaster. He was fond of snakes, and not only kept a round dozen or so in his room, but also usually had two or three coiled around him under his loose flannel shirt. When you were talking with him you were likely to see a snake's head emerge from his shirt-front and work its tongue at you in a sinister fashion. His peculiarity was disconcerting at first, but we soon got used to it and became interested in the tricks he did with his snakes; it was in this way that I found out something I did not know before, that snakes are very playful. One evening I had to see the president, a rotund old Scots philosopher of the university of Aberdeen, a formidable figure, loaded to the guards with all the logic and metaphysics that ever were heard of. The old man reposed in his favourite attitude while listening to me, half lying in an easy-chair, legs extended, hands folded, head thrown back, eyes closed. Another couple sat in the far end of the room, conversing in low tones. While I was in the midst of what I had to say, the president suddenly drew himself up with a half-turn towards the other couple, and said, "Heh—heh—snakes?—who said snakes?—what's that about snakes?" Explanation took some time, but when finally he got the whole story through his head, and was satisfied that the snakes were harmless and did not stray off the reservation, he turned again to me, and said, "What an extraordinary taste!—I can't imagine such a thing,—most revolting!—abominable!" With that he paused a moment, and then snapped out, "However, I can't see but that he is within his rights, and he shall have them."

I never forgot this, because it represented almost the last possibility in the way of a strain on the spirit of justice. The old man was fastidious to the point of crankiness, mortally detesting physical contact with any living thing. Only under the *peine forte et dure* could he bring himself to shake hands with any one, and when he did, he extended only the tips of two lifeless fingers. He was also irascible; he controlled more temper every fifteen minutes than most men control in a lifetime. If lynch law were ever called for, it would seem to be under just these circumstances. But there it was; "justice is always the same," and no stress of personal taste or distaste can force a way around the fact; and so the incident was closed.

Moreover, it was closed without prejudice. The young sapengro never had the faintest official hint that his bizarre taste had come under notice. Here, as always in like cases, the force of invariable example brought out a third great truth about justice, namely: that justice is seldom enough. It showed how necessary it is that matters should be managed, not only with justice, but with the appearance of justice, and that very often the appearance of justice is as important as the substance of justice.

Our academic course was fixed and unchangeable as the everlasting hills. You took it or you left it. A student in one of our undergraduate colleges today would regard it with horror as a straight hand-me-down from Standonck and Noël Béda in "that lousy college" of Montaigu where Ponocrates indignantly refused to place Gargantua, and where Erasmus nearly perished. Elective courses, majors and minors, "courses in English," vocational courses, and all that sort of thing, were unknown to us; we had never heard of them. Ours was the last institution in America, I think, except probably some managed by the Jesuits, to stick uncompromisingly by "the grand old fortifying classical curriculum." Readings and expositions of Greek and Roman literature; mathematics up to the differential calculus; logic; metaphysics; a little work on the sources and history of the English language; these made up the lot. If you were good for it, you were given a bachelor's degree at the end of four years, and you were then expected to get out promptly and not come back. The incursions of alumni were most distasteful to the authorities, and were firmly disallowed. If, on the other hand, you were not good enough to stand the appointed strain, it was presumably a matter of God's will, and nothing could be done about it.

With my usual good luck, I barely got under the wire of this salutary régime in the nick of time. The college shortly expired; it was "reorganised" off the face of the earth. There was no longer any function in the American educational system for it to fulfil. Even in my time there was none; it was running on momentum; in the view of the victorious revolutionary pedagogy it was a *chimaera bombinans in vacuo*. In its new form it led a futile and exiguous life for a while, and indeed may still be dragging on at something of the kind, for all I know.

Education is usually described, or perhaps one should say defined, as a preparation for life; but like all general statements, this one will stand a little sifting to make sure we know what we mean by it. My fellow-students and I were sent out from college with the equipment I have described. Over and above that, I do not think any of my fellows had any more in the way of special particularised equipment than I had, which was virtually none at all. If preparation for life means accumulating instrumental knowledge as a means of getting a living, our equipment was defective. If it means laying a foundation of formative knowledge on which to build a structure of instrumental knowledge, our equipment was as complete, I believe, as could be devised. Our preceptors painstakingly kept clear the difference between formative knowledge and instrumental knowledge. Their concern was wholly with the one; with the other, not at all. They had the theory that a young man who had gone through their mill could turn his hand to anything in the whole range of intellectual or manual pursuits, and do it to better advantage in the long-run than one who had not. Without claiming too much for this theory, which is now so heavily discounted as archaic, there is yet perhaps something to be said for it. We were not worrying about our economic future, however, or indeed thinking much about it. There were plenty of opportunities still open throughout the country at that time, and we saw no reason to doubt that we could somehow manage to make our way.

If education be a preparation for living, rather than for getting a living; a preparation for getting the most and best out of this gift of existence which has been dealt out to us unasked, undesired, and which at times seems specious,—if this be so, our equipment gave us two advantages which could hardly have been come at by any other means. I have never seen either of them mentioned in any apologia for the ancient régime, though they are so obvious that they must have been noticed by some one. Perhaps they seemed too obvious to be worth mentioning; or more probably, like the names of countries on a map, they are so obvious as to be easily overlooked.

The literatures of Greece and Rome comprise the longest, most complete and most nearly continuous record we have of what the strange creature known as *Homo sapiens* has been busy about in virtually every department of spiritual, intellectual and social activity. That record covers nearly twenty-five hundred years in an unbroken stretch of this animated oddity's operations in poetry, drama, law, agriculture, philosophy, architecture, natural history, philology, rhetoric, astronomy, logic, politics, botany, zoölogy, medicine, geography, theology,—everything, I believe, that lies in the range of human knowledge or speculation. Hence the mind which has attentively canvassed this record is much more than a disciplined mind, it is an *experienced* mind. It has come, as Emerson says, into a feeling of immense longevity, and it instinctively views contemporary man and his doings in the perspective set by this profound and weighty experience. Our studies were properly called formative, because beyond all others their effect was powerfully maturing. Cicero told the unvarnished truth in saying that those who have no knowledge of what has gone before them must forever remain children; and if one wished to characterise the collective mind of this present period, or indeed of any period,—the use it makes of its powers of observation, reflection, logical inference,—one would best do it by the one word *immaturity*.

For example, most of us probably remember the "great radio-scare" which swept over the country a few years ago, when some radio-entertainer gave a dramatic description, based on a story by Mr. H. G. Wells, of a supposititious invasion of America by warriors from the planet Mars. People everywhere from coast to coast, even students in our universities and colleges, took this egregious yarn as a *bona fide* alarm, and responded to it by going into the most extraordinary excesses of fear and panic. My fellow-students would have greeted such a burst of semi-lunatic idiocy with harsh, unfeeling laughter. It would have sent them back at once to Livy's account of similar absurdities;[1] and their inference,—discouraging indeed, but inescapable,—would have been that despite all the nineteenth century's vaunted progress in science, despite all the revolutionary and expensive elaboration of modern educational systems, the masses of mankind remain precisely as childlike in their credulity and gullibility as they were in the year 217 B.C.

This, then, was the first advantage, usually overlooked, which our régime gave us; it was the means of our absorbing a vast deal of vicarious experience which ripened our minds; and as I said, I do not know of any other discipline which could have done just that. The second advantage usually overlooked is that, somewhat on the principle of *lucus a non lucendo*, our equipment was as valuable to us for what it did not equip us with as for what it did. We left college ignorant of practically everything but what came within the lines of study which I have mentioned. We knew nothing of the natural sciences this side of Aristotle, Theophrastus, Pliny; nothing of any history since A.D. 1500, not even the history of our own

[1] For example, among those reported in 218 B.C., during the Second Punic War, we find an exact parallel to the "miracle of the Marne" reported by eye-witnesses in the last war. "Romae aut circa urbem multa ea hieme prodigia facta, aut . . . multa nuntiata, et temere credita sunt: in quis ingenium infantem semestrem in foro olitorio *Triumphum* clamasse: . . . et in agro Amiternino multis locis hominum specie procul candida veste visos, nec cum ullo congressos." Livy, xxi, 62.

Again, in the following year we see a population terrified by tidings that the god Mars had gone on the warpath. "Augebant metum prodigia ex pluribus simul locis nuntiata: . . . et Praeneste ardentes lapides coelo cecidisse: et Arpis parmas in coelo visas, pugnantemque cum luna solem: et Capenae duas interdiu lunas ortas: et aquas Caeretes sanguine mixtas fluxisse, fontemque ipsum Herculis cruentis manasse sparsum maculis: et in Antiati metentibus cruentas in corbem spicas cecidisse: et Faleriis coelum findi velut magno hiatu visum; quaque patuerit, ingens lumen effulsisse: sortes sua sponte attenuatas, unamque excidisse ita scriptam, *Mavors telum suum concutit*: et per idem tempus Romae signum Martis Appia via ad simulacrum luporum sudasse." Livy, xxii, 1.

Livy further observes that from these modest beginnings people went on to take stock in reports of prodigies too trivial to be worth mentioning, such as goats being turned into sheep and cocks into hens. No doubt they did; plenty there are among us today who believe that a horsehair left to soak in rainwater will turn into a worm!

country. Our ignorance of other subjects was quite as complete. Therefore when subsequently a new idea or a new set of circumstances presented itself to us, it had free entrance to an unpreoccupied mind. There was no accumulated lumber of prepossession or formula to be cleared away. Like the child in Hans Christian Andersen's fable of the king's garment, we saw it as it was, not as somebody had told us it was, or as we thought it might be or ought to be; and at the same time we had a great fund of vicarious experience at hand to help us judge it correctly and make correct inferences from it.

Plato made it the mark of an educated man that he should be able, and above all that he should always be willing, to "see things as they are." Our régime did as much to put that mark on us as any educational régime could do, and more, I believe, than any other will ever do. It did its very powerful best to save us from what the great Stoic philosopher deplored as "the madness and the misery of one who uses the appearance of things as the measure of their reality, and makes a mess of it." Thus I believe our régime abundantly vindicated its character as a preparation for living. One might put it that our education served the function of Mr. Titbottom's spectacles, which George William Curtis described in his exquisite little prose idyl called *Prue and I*. When Mr. Titbottom looked through his lenses, the appearance of the object he was looking at instantly vanished, and he saw its stark reality.

Incidentally (or was it so? I should be disposed to say primarily rather than incidentally, but if the reader has scruples I do not insist),—incidentally, then, our education also served us well in a moral way; and here our parallel with Mr. Titbottom continues. Sometimes the reality of things was more agreeable to Mr. Titbottom than their appearance; sometimes less so; sometimes it was hideous and horrible, as when he looked at an eminent financier and saw a ruthless and ravening wild boar. But after having used his spectacles occasionally for a while, he developed an insatiable appetite for reality. Whatever the object he looked at, whatever the cost of possible disillusionment, he could not rest content until he had put on his spectacles and seen it as it was. Even when the lovely Preciosa came in his range of vision,—but the story ends there abruptly, leaving only the suggestion that Mr. Titbottom may have found Preciosa's reality in some respect seriously dissatisfying.

At first Mr. Titbottom was moved by curiosity, but later he seems to have seen that the avoidance of self-deception is as much a matter of integrity as of convenience. Our régime did a great deal to impress us with that view. I can not say precisely how it did this; mainly, perhaps, by some sort of spiritual osmosis, set up by the whole general course of things being bent that way. By one means or another, however, it was so that we did come out with a fairly clear notion that the deliberate acceptance of appearances, the conscious exclusion of reality, is a distinct failure in integrity, a moral failure. If we had come upon Bishop Butler's great saying, "Things and actions are what they are, and the consequences of them will be what they will be; why, then, should we desire to be deceived?"—we would have taken it as merely a reinforcement of moral integrity by the strongest kind of common sense.

Therefore in a moral way as well as intellectually and culturally, our commerce with the minds of the ancients gave us something of a preparation for living. I have lately observed with interest that some cautiously counter-revolutionary critics are suspecting that the educational revolution, like all revolutions, threw out the baby with the bathwater, as the Germans say, and that some of the old régime's values, ethical as well as cultural, might be profitably salvaged. Three or four years ago, indeed, one American undergraduate college astonished the natives by vamping up a sort of *Ersatz*-classical curriculum which calls for the reading and discussion of one hundred of the world's best books; using English versions of such Greek and Latin originals as are on the list. This enterprise was a nine-days wonder in the journalistic world; the newspapers and popular periodicals took it as an unprecedented innovation, and gave it at least half as much space as they would normally allot to a minor happening in Hollywood! Some hardy journalists thought that this experiment might be the precursor of "a return to the classics," but a product of the old régime would be bound to view this prospect with an eye of benevolent scepticism. It would mean not only the unscrambling of a revolution, which is a tall order in itself, but it would also mean unscrambling a post-revolutionary frame of mind, which I believe has not been done since the early days of Israel in Canaan. Even then, even with the intervention of Jehovah thrown in, it seems not to have been done any too successfully, according to the record.

II

My life has afforded me few diversions more engaging than that of watching the progress of our educational revolution. I have viewed it from the outside for a great many years, and also from the inside for the year or two in which I made a notorious failure at going through the motions of teaching undergraduate collegians. The revolution began with a drastic purge, a thorough guillotining of the classical curriculum, wherever found. Such Greek and Latin as escaped the Reign of Terror was left to die of inanition in dens and caves of the earth, such as the school and college I attended. The elective system came in as a substitute, proposing instruction *in omni re scibili* as its final consummation. During a visit to Germany, the president of Harvard, Mr. Eliot, had taken note that the elective system was working well in German universities, and he saw no reason why it should not work as well in an undergraduate college like Harvard, so he introduced it there. The country promptly carried his logic to its full length. If the thing was good for the university, good for the college, why not for the secondary school, why not for the primary school? Why not try a tentative dab at its being good for the kindergarten?—surely in a free democracy the free exercise of self-expression and the development of an untrammelled personality can hardly begin too young.

So the old régime's notion that education is in its nature selective, the peculium of a well-sifted élite,[2] was swept away and replaced by the popular notion that everybody should go to school, college, university, and should have every facility afforded for studying anything that any one might choose. Our institutions grew to enormous size; the country's student-population exceeded anything ever known. Gifts, grants, subsidies, endowments, brought in an incredible flow of money; and our system at once began to take on the aspect of a huge bargain-counter or a modern drug-store. The results, however, were increasingly unsatisfactory, so much so that in forty years the revolution has not been able to consolidate its gains. After its preliminary clean sweep of the old régime, the succeeding period has been one of incessant and unsuccessful tinkering with the mechanics of the new. At the present time it seems that about all the possibilities of further tinkering have been exhausted, and that nobody can think of anything more to do; the experiment with the hundred best books, to which I have alluded, appears to be the last possible dig for the woodchuck, if I may be permitted the expression. Yet, appraised in terms of actual education, the net result at the end of forty years thus spent still seems to give as poor an account of itself as at the beginning.

Knowing that the theory, the fundamental idea, is all there actually is to any revolution, I became interested in finding out what I could about the theory on which this one was proceeding. If a revolution liberates an idea, that idea will emerge and take hold of the public mind for good or ill, thus making the revolution successful, whether or not its immediate object be attained. If it does not liberate an idea, it amounts only

[2] For the benefit of those who believe in democracy, or think they do,—or rather, who think they think they do,—I may observe that this was Mr. Jefferson's notion. The scheme of public education which "the great democrat" drew up for Virginia is more mercilessly selective than any that has ever been proposed for any public system in this country.

to a riot which fizzles out with the gain or loss of its immediate object, and leaves no mark. The French Revolution liberated the idea of the individual's right of self-expression in politics; the Russian Revolution liberated the idea that politics are governed by economics,—the idea which John Adams held to so staunchly, and which marked him as being a century and a half ahead of his time. I knew what the theory of the old régime in education was, and I had no interest whatever in the interminable cobblings and overhaulings of the new régime's machinery, its curricular changes, "honour schools," "reading periods," its heavily publicised "plans," such as the Wisconsin, Yale, Chicago plans, and all that kind of thing. I was interested only in the new régime's fundamental theory, and in marking the differences between that and the theory which it had displaced.

When I had learned what I could, an invitation came my way to give three lectures at one of our universities; so, since this matter was uppermost in my mind at the moment, I chose it as my subject. The lectures were then published commercially.[3] The book had a curious experience. Professional educators for the most part snubbed it; those who did not, with two exceptions, abused it heartily. I was duly chastened by this, feeling as the Psalmist might, that I should not have been caught meddling in great matters which are too high for me. But while I was disconsolately looking over my work, (since I am really the most teachable person alive), and wondering what I had done that was so bad, I began to hear from the Jesuits. These brethren seem to have facilities for passing the word around whenever a member of the order hits on something which interests him, so in a short time and from all parts of the country I got an astonishing grist of most sympathetic and encouraging letters. This caused me to take heart again, saying to myself that the only body of men in America who have the faintest notion of what educa-

[3] *The Theory of Education in the United States*: Harcourt, Brace and Co., New York.

tion really means are the Jesuits; so if Jesuits go out of their way to say that a work on the theory of education has some merit, the chances are that it has. I had already observed the workings of their system and method in some of the European institutions under their control. Once, I remember, long before my book was written, when I was listening to some young American educators who were all agog over this-or-that new wrinkle in curricular gadgetry, I said, perhaps with some impatience, that the *Ratio Studiorum* of Acquaviva had been doing very well by itself for a little matter of three hundred years or so, and if any one had ever suggested any valid essential improvements on it, or could do so now, he was just the man I should like to see. I got no takers. It turned out that these educators had not heard of the *Ratio Studiorum*, and I suspect they were not quite sure whether Acquaviva was the hero of Rossini's opera or the name of a Pullman car.

The theory of the revolution was based on a flagrant popular perversion of the doctrines of equality and democracy. Above all things the mass-mind is most bitterly resentful of superiority. It will not tolerate the thought of an élite; and under a political system of universal suffrage, the mass-mind is enabled to make its antipathies prevail by sheer force of numbers. Under this system, as John Stuart Mill said, the test of a great mind is its power of agreement with the opinions of small minds; hence the intellectual tone of a society thus hamstrung is inevitably set by such opinions. In the prevalent popular view, therefore, —the view insisted upon and as far as possible enforced by the mass-men whom the masses instinctively cleave to and choose as leaders,—in this view the prime postulate of equality is that in the realm of the spirit as well as of the flesh, everybody is able to enjoy anything that anybody can enjoy; and the prime postulate of democracy is that there shall be nothing for anybody to enjoy that is not open for everybody to enjoy. An equalitarian and democratic régime must by consequence assume, tacitly or avowedly, that everybody is educable.

The theory of our régime was directly contrary to this. Our

preceptors did not see that doctrines of equality and democracy had any footing in the premises. They did not pretend to believe that everybody is educable, for they knew, on the contrary, that very few are educable, very few indeed. They saw this as a fact in the order of nature, like the fact that few are six feet tall. Instead of regarding the thought of an élite with the mass-man's dogged, unintelligent, invincibly suspicious resentment, they accepted it as pointing to a fixture in nature's established order. They accepted the fact that there are practicable ranges of intellectual and spiritual experience which nature has opened to some and closed to others. They may or may not have wished that nature had managed otherwise, but saw quite clearly that she had not done so. There the fact was, and all that could be done about it was to take it as it stood. If any irrelevant doctrine of equality or democracy chose to set itself against the fact, so much the worse for the doctrine.

All complaints against the unsatisfactory course of the post-revolutionary régime can be run back to the continuous effort, by some miracle of ingenuity or luck, to translate a bad theory into good practice. The worst result of this was a complete effacement of the line which sets off education from training, and the line which sets off formative knowledge from instrumental knowledge. This obliteration was done deliberately to meet the popular perversions of equality and democracy. The régime perceived that while very few can be educated, everyone who is not actually imbecile or idiotic can be trained in one way or another, as soldiers are trained in military routine, or as monkeys are trained to pick fruit. Very well then, it said in effect, let us agree to call training education, convert our schools, colleges, universities into training-schools as far as need be, but continue to call them educational institutions and to call our general system an educational system. We will insist that the discipline of instrumental studies is as formative as any other, even more so, and to quite as good purpose, in fact much better. We will get up courses in "business administration," bricklaying, retail shoe-merchandising, and what-not, agree to call our graduates educated men, give them all the old-style academic degrees, dress them out in the old-style gowns and hoods,—and there we are, thoroughly democratic, thoroughly equalitarian, in shape to meet all popular demands.

For the looks of the thing, nevertheless, something had to be done to make some sort of show of cultural balance to all this; and here the régime was in difficulties. Its institutions were loaded up with great masses of ineducable persons, and it was necessary to find something for them to do which they could do; and in a cultural way they could do nothing. Presumably, however, they were literate; that is, they could make their way more or less ignorantly and uncertainly down a printed page; and therefore innumerable "courses in English" were devised for them.[4] To me, this was the most amusing *démarche* in the whole revolutionary programme, for as I said somewhere back in these memoirs, we would not have known what courses in English were. Nobody taught English in our day; or rather, everybody taught it all the time. If we expressed ourselves in slipshod English, unidiomatic English, we heard about it on the spot, so we made a point of being careful. One curious hold-over from this discipline still sticks by me. I can do fairly well with a bit of translating from another language if I have time enough to write it out; but doing it extempore, "on my feet," I halt and feel my way around in the English idiom like a beginner.

As far as my observation goes, the new régime's discipline, for all its incredible litter of "courses in English," does not give nearly so good an account of itself as ours did. I was once in a position where for four years I encountered a steady succession of persons who had "majored in English," "specialised in English," or even, *Gott soll hüten*, taken a master's degree

[4] If the reader thinks I am talking at random here, I suggest he look the matter up and get an idea of the number of these courses given annually by our high-schools, colleges and universities. If he does this, he has a surprise awaiting him.

in English. After sampling a good fair taste of their quality, I got into the way of telling them I would take their word for all they knew about English, since obviously the one thing they did not know was what to do with it, and that was the only thing that interested me. Moreover, during the same period I had many letters from persons who taught English professionally. Half of them were written in a disreputable journalistic jargon, and fully one-third of the remainder rubbed elbows with illiteracy. In my day there would have been joy in the presence of the angels over a sinner repenting, if such infamous English had come under the eye of one of our preceptors; and that it could emanate from a master of arts, a professor or instructor, would have been "one of those things that simply will not bear thinking about."

I doubt that any of my fellow-students ever saw the inside of an English grammar; I know I never did. But knowing Latin and Greek grammar as well as we did, we managed to drag on quite creditably through the intricacies of English composition. As for English literature, it was our literature, we had a native command of it, its attractions were in plain sight, so all we ever thought of doing was to strike into it anywhere and enjoy it. Teaching English literature would have seemed to us like teaching a hungry man the way to his mouth when he had a feast before him. Almost the only chance to make myself useful that my country ever offered me came when the president of a huge sprawling mid-Western state university asked me (I am by no means sure how seriously,—still, he did ask me) to go out and be the head of his department of English literature. I was no end delighted by the compliment, but the mere thought of such an undertaking made me shiver. I told him I had not the faintest idea of how to set about it; I should be utterly helpless. All I could do would be to point to the university's library, and say, There it is,—wade in and help yourselves. Like a very gracious man, he laughed and said that was just what he would wish me to do; but it seemed to be clear to both of us that I should be eminently a superfluous man in the realm of modern pedagogy, so we got on no further.

III

In fairness it must be said that the revolution was not altogether without reason. The earlier discipline was as a rule administered poorly and, which is worse, indiscriminately. My fellow-students and I simply had the luck to find ourselves where it was administered admirably and with austere discrimination. Too often a routine of elementary Greek and Latin was forced upon ineducable children; too often those who forced it even on the educable were themselves ineducable. The academic world never took proper account of the fact that an ineducable person can be trained in the mechanics of a language or a literature, and as well trained, as in the mechanics of dentistry or bond-selling. I have seen many a graduate student who had gone to Germany to study under some great classicist, like a colour-blind botanist going to a flower-show with a bad cold in his head; he came back as a doctor of philosophy, knowing a great deal about his subject, I dare say, but not knowing how to appreciate or enjoy it. So between the ineducable pupil on the one hand and the ineducable mechanical gerund-grinder, as Carlyle calls him, on the other, the system, speaking generally, did fail; it failed, as many a good system has failed, through getting into bad hands.

For us, Latin and Greek were purely literary languages; we were not much taken up with their science except as it served a literary purpose. None of us had any ambition to spend his life on the dative case. If we found what looked like a false quantity in Statius, we did not theorise over it; we concluded that the old boy had probably made a mistake, and let it go at that. If we came on unfamiliar terms and neologisms in Lucian, we were not tempted to make any of them the subject of a learned thesis. Fortunately for us, our dealings with these literatures were set in the ways of French, English,

Irish scholarship, rather than German, which was all the go in America when I came on the scene; this predilection being largely due once more, I suppose, to Mr. Eliot's pernicious influence. The ideal towards which we were steadily directed was that of the man of letters, not the man of science, the philologist, the grammarian, the textual critic. Of course we were all the time accumulating science as we went along, but this was not the be-all and end-all of academic existence. Scholars like Gaston Boissier in France, Tyrrell and Purser in Ireland, Mackail in England, Gildersleeve in America,—these had all the science there was, but they were primarily men of letters, and we, in our small way, were encouraged to make the same use of our scientific equipment that they made of theirs; and all our lives, again in our small way, we have done so. The services of German philological scholarship were inestimable, prodigious; the man of letters will always gratefully make use of them; he must do so; but no amount of philology will of itself qualify a person as a man of letters.

I suppose it may be better to read Latin and Greek in translations than not to read them at all. Yet what one gets is so little by comparison with what one misses that one can never be sure; and when one thinks of the very small amount of preliminary labour involved in getting acquainted with the originals, provided one starts early enough, one feels that for the primary purpose of reading, a reliance on translations is unrewarding. It must be so, for the command of a language means the command of everything written in that language, and one grazes on a very short tether with translations. Many of the English classics have been translated into French, yet a Frenchman who reads no English can have only a poor and limited idea of the content of English literature. We have remains of hundreds of authors in Greek and Latin, and only a toothful of them translated. While one might not go so far as to say with the elder Pliny that no book is so bad as to have nothing good in it, one who is unable to make any way in this vast mass of literature misses an incalculable amount of what is vital to one's purpose; that purpose being to get the run of twenty-odd centuries of the human mind's activity, and thus enable oneself to see contemporary men and things ever more clearly as they are. At the present time, for example, Plutarch's treatises *Concerning Exile, On Hearing Rightly, On Getting Good Out of Enemies*, are worth more than gold and precious stones to a reflective mind.[5] As a shelter against a hurricane of propaganda, nothing could be better than his great saying that right hearing is the first approach to right living; for so indeed it is.

Then, too, most of our translations are not good. Matthew Arnold remarked that this kind of work, which he called "the journeyman-work of literature," is as a rule much better done in other countries; and a comparison of translations in the Loeb series, for example, with those put out by the *Association Guillaume Budé*, gives ample evidence that this is so. Moreover, in the life-long effort to "see things as they are" one must have help from the sense of taste and style, the instinct of beauty and poetry; and even the best of translations can hardly excite this help. A reader who has Mr. Long's translation of Marcus Aurelius needs no Greek; if he has his translation of Epictetus he will perhaps do well enough without Greek. On the other hand, Plato's story of Atlantis amounts almost to a liberal education in æsthetics, and no one, not even Mr. Jowett, can reproduce its quality; the whole genius of the language is against him. The total effect of a page of Thucydides, Livy, Tacitus, even a page of the *Imitation*, is simply unreproducible upon one reading it in translation. And if this be true of the prose of these literatures, what must one say of their poetry; not alone the poetry of their prime, but the poetry of their decadence, such as the verse of Theocritus and the rest of the host who appear in the *Anthology* from 300 B.C. on? Who has

[5] I confess I am not *au fait* with translations, so if my friends at St. John's College turn up with one in their teeth and shake their gory locks at me, I shall accept the correction humbly. I believe a translation of the *Moralia* was once made long ago, but I never saw it, and I think my friends will acknowledge that if it exists at all it must be too nearly inaccessible to be worth considering.

not tried his hand at translating elegiacs from the *Anthology*; and who has succeeded in reproducing anything like their total effect upon a reader?

So when all comes to all, I doubt that a study of translations has enough carrying-power to encourage much hope of a "return to the classics." I do not find this altogether lamentable, however, because I am by no means sure that a return to the classics, even if it were practicable, would be desirable. I am not sure that the post-revolutionary frame of mind is so awry, not sure that any more should be done with education, properly so called, than is being done; or that the final end and aim of education,—the ability to see things as they are,—should any longer be taken into account. The question at issue, obviously, is whether the educable person can any longer be regarded as a social asset; or, indeed, whether in time past his value as a social asset has not been overestimated. As I came to understand much later, the final answer must be referable to the previous question, What is man? On one theory of man's place in nature, the final answer would be yes, and on another, no. The immediate answer, however, I should say would be in the negative. In a society essentially neolithic, as ours unquestionably is at the moment,—whatever one may hold its evolutionary possibilities to be,—there can be no place found for an educable person but such as a trainable person could fill quite as well or even better; he becomes a superfluous man; and the more thoroughly his ability to see things as they are is cultivated, the more his superfluity is enhanced. As the process of general barbarisation goes on, as its speed accelerates, as its calamitous consequences recur with ever-increasing frequency and violence, the educable person can only take shelter against his insensate fellow-beings, as Plato says, like a man crouching behind a wall against a whirlwind.

IV

The unfailing luck which attended me throughout my nonage, and indeed through most of my life thereafter, held good in one most important respect to which I have not yet alluded. I am profoundly thankful that during my formative years I never had contact with any institution under State control; not in school, not in college, nor yet in my three years of irregular graduate study. No attempt was ever made by any one to indoctrinate me with State-inspired views,—or any views, for that matter,—of patriotism or nationalism. I was never dragooned into flag-worship or hero-worship, never was caught in any spate of verbiage about duty to one's country, never debauched by any of the routine devices hatched by scoundrels for inducing a synthetic devotion to one's native land and loyalty to its jobholders. Therefore when later the various aspects of contemporary patriotism and nationalism appeared before me, my mind was wholly unprepossessed, and my view of them was unaffected by any emotional distortion. I could see them as through Mr. Titbottom's spectacles; I could see them as they are.

I do not know how it happened that I escaped these contaminations, for the centres of infection were abundant enough; not as now, of course, but there were plenty of them. The magnificent possibilities of the school as an instrument of propaganda had been perceived very early; Alexander Hamilton, who never missed the boat on a chance of this kind, expounded them in 1800; but in my time their development was only nearing completion. It was quite natural, quite inevitable, that the school should take over from the Church in this capacity. In the Middle Ages and afterwards, when the Church was strong and the State was weak, the Church attended to what little secular thimblerigging was needed to keep things moving in the right direction. When the Church became weak and the centralised, nationalist-imperialist State grew strong, the State began to do its own dirty work; and with the schools, press, cinema and radio under its control, this work is now child's play. I can testify that it is what our Methodist friends used to call a searching experience, to look at the bemused and unsuspecting dupes of these flagitious agencies, and say to oneself, There but for the grace of God, go I!

CHAPTER SIX

"Niebuhr was right," said Goethe, "when he saw a barbarous age coming. It is already here, we are in it, for in what does barbarism consist, if not in the failure to appreciate what is excellent?"

—ECKERMANN, 1831.

Great things may be accomplished in our days; great discoveries, for example, great enterprises; but these do not give greatness to our epoch. Greatness makes itself appear notably by its point of departure, by its flexibility, by its thought.

—SAINTE-BEUVE.

AFTER leaving college I did graduate work for the best part of three years in different institutions, shopping around irregularly like the *vagantes*, the wandering scholars of the Middle Ages, from one man to another who had something on foot that interested me and who would let me sit under him. Not being in quest of an advanced degree, (though finally I did qualify for one, more by accident than intention), I could do this. It still seems to me that the *vagantes* had the right idea for getting the best out of graduate study. When a notable man appeared anywhere on their horizon they would go where he was and camp out with him until they had pretty well got what he had to give them, and then they would "move on to the next pub." Abraham Flexner once remarked to me that getting education is like getting measles; you have to go where measles is. If you go where it is, unless you are by nature immune, you will get it,—no need to worry about that,—but if you don't go where it is, you will never get it. An effective distribution of educational germs, moreover, is a matter of individual persons rather than of institutions. Rabelais has Pantagruel making the rounds of the French universities, as in all probability Rabelais himself had done, and the chapter shows that in itself this might mean very little; but when Bridlegoose says that he had studied law at Poitiers under *Brocadium Juris*,[1] or when Panurge speaks of having dipped into the Decretals with "the most decretalipotent Scots doctor," that really meant something.

In one institution where I spent a full year and more, I formed a close friendship with four fellow-students; and this association was the means of my getting my first clear view of the society in which my little academic world was encysted. It also gave me a lively interest in finding out what the actual collective character of that society was, how it got that character, and what reasonable expectations might be put upon a society which bore that character. We five always ended our evenings, after our routine of work was done, in a sort of *cénacle*, a forgathering for a couple of hours of philosophical discussion helped out by Bass's ale. One of our number, C. J., was the most nearly complete person I have ever seen. He had great ability; like Posidonius, according to Strabo, he was τῶν καθ' ἡμᾶς φιλοσόφων πολυμαθέστατος, combining sound scholarship with a vast deal of general knowledge and information. His ability and attainments were balanced by a splendid integrity, kindness, equanimity and unfailing humour. His tastes were simple in the extreme, and the gentle sincerity of his manner made his conversation most attractive. As Bishop Burnet said of Lord Rochester, "he loved to talk and write of speculative matters, and did it with so fine a thread that even those who hated the subjects that his fancy ran upon, yet could not but be charmed with his way of treating them." His interests

[1] Students nicknamed their professors then as now. This was a students' nickname for Robert Irland, a Scotsman, for nearly sixty years professor of law at Poitiers.

and accomplishments and mine were complementary. He had gone far in ways which I had not even entered upon; for example, he not only knew modern history, especially American history, quite well, but he also bent all the powers of his mind towards *understanding* it, towards making interpretations of it which were thoroughgoing, competent, reasonable. I, on the other hand, had been well drilled to an understanding of ancient peoples and their collective doings, and when he would expound this-or-that modern incident or tendency in public life, I could match it with parallels, elucidations, interpretations, drawn from earlier sources. We met at what was, for me, precisely the right time; my debt to him is incalculable. After a very few years of unambitious, undemanding, innocent life, he suddenly died, carried off by some unsuspected affection of the heart. His end was strange and shocking, for he was a man of uncommonly strong physique, a great fisherman, hunter, sailor, and never known to be out of health. The world has not seemed quite the same to me since his death; I have not looked upon his like again.

It is a vain and superficial reflection that such a man would have fared but ill against the blighting east wind of the twentieth century, and that he was therefore fortunate in escaping it. This is not so; he would have fared well, for he was beyond the reach of disappointment or injury. His immense wisdom and penetrating humour, untouched by any taint of cynicism, would have kept him in the spirit which appears throughout all Greek literature; the spirit which finds its noblest expression in the *Phaedo*, and its more special and restricted expression in the verse of the later elegiac poets. He would have had Aeschylus and Sophocles always at hand to remind him that the order fixed by human destiny is not to be coerced or dissuaded, and he would have watched the hopeful little meddlings and strivings of the human comedy with an eye of amused tolerance, even as they ran off into inevitable tragedy. *Omnia orta cadunt.* His was the lucid Greek sense, "born of considering the flux of things and the tyranny of time, that man plays a losing game, and that his only success is in refusing to play. For the busy and idle, for the fortunate and unhappy alike, the sun rises one morning for the last time; he only is to be congratulated who is done with hope and fear. How short-lived soever he be in comparison with the world through which he passes, yet no less through time Fate dries up the holy springs, and the mighty cities of the old days are undecipherable under the green turf. It is the only wisdom to acquiesce in the forces, however ignorant or malign in their working, that listen to no protest and admit no appeal; that no strength can check, no subtlety elude, no calculation predetermine."[2]

II

When in my mid-twenties my eyes first opened on the American scene, I surveyed it with the naïve astonishment of Rip van Winkle. One would hardly believe that a boy could grow up to manhood in such complete unconsciousness of the social and political movements going on around him. My only experience of politics had been with the unpleasant doings generated in the Wigwam, when we lived in Brooklyn, which now seemed long ago; they had prompted a few childish questions, and then their memory had become overlaid. Since then I had heard no mention of politics; nor do I think I was exceptional in this. My notion is that the honest and decent among our elders had pretty generally thrown over any concern with public affairs, and given them up as a hopeless bad job. They had lived through the Civil War, seen the unconscionable knaveries practiced on all sides during the post-war period, frauds on a scale so colossal that they amazed a world which had presumably become pretty well used to such exhibitions of business enterprise. They had seen the fraudful looting of the public domain, the abject villainies of "reconstruction," the Crédit Mobilier, the star-route frauds, the wholesale raiding and looting of railway-properties, the operations of the South Improvement Company, and so on. Not only had they seen this

[2] J. W. Mackail: introductory essay on the Greek Anthology.

alliance of business with politics in the general government, but they had seen it also as busily at work in state and local governments throughout the country; they had watched the Tweed Ring making hay in New York City and Albany, and the Pennsylvania Railway's field-hands diligently harvesting in Harrisburg. As I said, my belief is that seeing no chance of any practicable improvement, they had simply lost interest, and their children had grown up, more or less as I had, in ignorance of politics; or when not quite so ignorant as I, regarding politics as something remote, disreputable and infamous, like slave-trading or brothel-keeping. There is much to be said for our elders' attitude, if I am right in supposing that such was their attitude; their instinct was sound, though their interpretation of that instinct was doubtless uninformed and superficial. The view communicated to their children was also correct in principle, as I came to learn much later; at this time I noticed only that such was pretty generally their view. In our own little coterie of graduate students, for example, three were probably as ignorant of public affairs as I, and certainly quite as incurious. C. J., with his bent for philosophy, his passion for "the reason of the thing," was the one exception.

My first observations put me into the way of working backward through American political history instead of forward; and from that to working through the history of other modern nations in the same way. I am not sure but that for the non-professional person, the amateur of history, it is a good procedure. Observing some turn in public affairs which is before one's eyes, then going back through accounts of antecedent turns apparently related, reasoning out one's inferences, conclusions and generalisations as one goes along,—perhaps in this way one gets the clearest perception of history's force and continuity. On the other hand, perhaps this way came easiest to me because all the history I knew was ancient history, and many commonplace incidents in modern life would suggest some similar happening in the ancient world. Today, for example, I never think of the tremendous fires we used to have in our northern lumber-town without recalling Plutarch's most amusing account of the way Marcus Crassus founded his fortune. But whether the habit I gravitated into be good or bad, there it was, and there it still is.

In the period I speak of, the Spanish War and its consequences in the Caribbean, the mid-Pacific and the Far East were before the public. I was looking at our first full-blown adventure in overseas imperialism, and a most amazing and repulsive sight it was. To my unaccustomed eyes the war itself seemed a dastardly affair, and the attendant hypocrisies indulged in by those who were promoting it, from the President down, seemed utterly contemptible. I could make nothing of the seizure of the Philippines but an unprovoked act of particularly brutal highwaymanry. Years afterward, during our next military adventure, when I saw Americans in hysterics of pious horror over "enemy atrocities," I marvelled at the convenience of a memory which had so quickly granted oblivion to Hell-roaring Jake Smith and the "water-cure." The great doctrine of Manifest Destiny reappeared, freshened up by a well-earned rest from hard service in the decade 1840-1850. Now it was our manifest destiny not only to exercise a hegemony over the whole hemisphere, but also to raid and steal whatever desirable possessions we could wrest with impunity from poor and weak peoples anywhere in the world.

Newspapers especially, and popular literature generally, served up this doctrine with a snuffy sanctimony, wholly Kiplingese, which made a most disagreeable impression on me. We were out to take up the white man's burden in a conspicuously large and exemplary way; we would free the oppressed, lift up the fallen, and distribute the blessings of a higher civilisation with a prodigal hand. Mark Twain wrote a scorching satire on these loathsome pretensions, addressing it To the Person Sitting in Darkness; but his voice, like that of Howells and those of many other distinguished men who were outraged by the whole disgraceful performance, was lost in the clamour of a synthetic patriotism. In the country's journalism, led by Hearst and Pulitzer, I found a most plausible reason why I had never seen a newspaper in my parents' home. Like their successors today, the papers of that period had undergone changes in style and manner from those which Dickens described in *Martin Chuzzlewit*, but none in essential character; they were very filthy. I often thought of Sir Henry Wotton, back in the sixteenth century, saying that "an ambassador is a man of virtue sent to lie abroad for his country; a news-writer is a man without virtue who lies at home for himself." For many years I wondered how people could be got to serve the trade of journalism, but never really understood it until some eighteen or twenty years ago I read Count Tolstoy's analysis of the prostitute Máslova's view of her trade, in the novel called *Resurrection*. I have known a few journalists, not many, and have regarded their attitude attentively, finding them curiously like other folk in general, just as Máslova was astonishingly like other women; and their view of their execrable profession was precisely like Máslova's view of hers.

My observation of the Spanish War and the rape of the Philippines led me to consider the character of our minor adventures in Samoa and Hawaii; and there I found the same record of chicanery and fraud, implemented by violence. In both instances the United States had acquired possession through revolutions made to order by its official agents. Then I went on to take stock of our continental adventures in the same line. I knew what imperialism meant in former times, what its springs of action were, and what its customary modes of procedure were. My classical studies had thoroughly acquainted me with these phenomena of the old days around the Mediterranean, and I had as yet seen nothing to suggest any essential difference between modern imperialism and the imperialism which I had studied and understood. Thus I was able to read between the lines of standard American historical writing, even such as was dished up for the young in our educational institutions. It was clear to me that our acquisition of Texas was a matter of sheer brigandage, and that force and fraud played approximately equal parts in our acquisition of California. I carried on my survey of American imperialism through the Mexican War, our systematic extermination of the Indians, and so on back into the colonial period; and I emerged with the conviction that at least on this one item of imperialism, our political history from first to last was utterly disgraceful.

The last decade of the century gave one an extraordinary opportunity for studying national imperialist activities in all parts of the world. In 1895 Japan gathered in tremendous profits from a raid on China; in the following year Italy came off second best in an attempt to seize Abyssinia. While the United States was consolidating its territorial gains in the Philippines, England was taking over South Africa, the Sudan, and was also acquiring highwayman's rights of various kinds in China, as Russia, France and Germany were likewise doing. No such enormous burst of imperialist energy had ever before been set off in so many divergent directions at once; but, as far as I could see, the only thing that differentiated it was its volume. Other than that it showed me nothing new or strange. I could discern no feature of the imperialism of London or Paris, Berlin or Tokyo, at the end of the nineteenth century, which I could not find exactly reproduced in miniature in that of Corinth in the fifth century B.C., or for that matter, in the imperialism of the great empire-builder Sargon's Akkad, in the thirty-seventh century B.C. It was mainly this unvarying persistence of pattern that gave me such keen interest in studying the phenomena of latter-day imperialism. Here were alliances made and repudiated, federations formed and dissolved, all on precisely the same basis of *Realpolitik* which underlay the Delian League or the Peloponnesian League of the sixth century B.C. or the almost prehistoric coalescence of wild shepherd raiders in Egypt. Moreover, it seemed to me that any one who understood the collisions of imperialist interest which took place between Rome and Carthage twenty-three centuries ago could have no trouble about foreseeing those which were being generated by identical conditions in Africa and the Far East. I soon came to see that all such collisions are reducible to their lowest terms under one and the same formula, the formula of Count Tolstoy's peasant-proprietor Yashvin: "He is after my shirt, and I am after his shirt." Stripping off the sleazy pretexts knaved up by what Ernest Renan so well calls *la bassesse de l'homme intéressé*,—pretexts of religion, morality, humanity, civilisation, democracy, or what-not,—stripping these off, I have examined the actual ground of a great many such collisions of interest, in the hope of some day finding one which Yashvin's formula would not fit as neatly as if made to order; but I have as yet found none.

The foreign policy of McKinley and Secretary Hay was the means of my making some instructive observations on statesmanship. I had already got it through my head that all sound political practice is *Realpolitik*. Ancient practice attested this without exception,—I was sure of that,—and modern practice, as far as I had gone with its history, bore witness to the same effect. This being so, it seemed to follow that the two luxuries which a good statesman must rigorously deny himself during business hours are conscience and sentiment; and the incident of the Philippines impressed this on me with peculiar force.

British imperialism did not want either French imperialism or the newer imperialism of Germany to get into a stronger position in the southwestern Pacific by taking the Philippines. At the moment, however, England had its hands full with preparations for plundering the Boers, and could not very well do much about it; so the architects of our foreign policy obligingly put themselves at England's convenience. They declared war against Spain, took the Philippines; and thereby, for all that one could see, committed the United States to follow the fortunes of British imperialism in perpetuity. Joseph Chamberlain, who, with Cecil Rhodes, represented the ultimate in militant British imperialism at that time, said in a public speech which was reported at large in this country, that the Spanish War was well worth while "if in a great and noble cause, the

Stars and Stripes and the Union Jack should wave together over an Anglo-Saxon alliance."[3]

Our seizure of the Philippines did not by any means command unanimous approval in America. Certain special interests, with no eye for anything beyond a prospect of immediate money, were in favour of it; and, as always, the medley of ignorance and prejudice which goes by the name of public sentiment was all for keeping the spoils of war. I observed with satisfaction, however, that wiser minds were looking below the surface of things and perceiving that in the long run the adventure, with its attendant commitments, was likely to cost a great deal more than it could ever possibly come to. They thought that as far as American participation was concerned, Mr. Chamberlain's Anglo-Saxon alliance was nothing but an eleemosynary receivership in bankruptcy for British imperialism; and moreover, as a matter of settled British policy, it was meant to be just that. They believed, therefore, that Mr. Hay's statesmanship was almost treasonably bad, and they made no bones of saying so.

I could not be quite sure of that. I was sure that the outcome would be ruinously bad, but whether as the result of bad statesmanship or a bad gamble, I was not sure. In the matter of alliances, a good statesman will think twice about leaving a bone for a shadow. As a diplomatist, Mr. Hay was a rank amateur, easily impressible, and during his year of ambassadorship in London, no doubt the official set had put its best foot forward. He may therefore have plumped a gamble on the chance of British imperialism having a longer lease of life than it actually had. One hardly sees how this could be, for there were plenty among the best unofficial minds in England who

[3] I have been interested to hear lately that highly-placed Englishry now speak openly of these two gonfaloniers as "that wretch, Chamberlain" and "that arch-villain, Rhodes." *Sic transit.* Yet Matthew Arnold, who died ten years before the Boer War was launched, prophesied that the dissolution of the British Empire would begin in South Africa. Arnold, however, was a man of letters, with no pretensions to statesmanship, and therefore could not be presumed to know what he was talking about.

could have set him straight. Aside from that, moreover, the historical pattern invariably traced by the rise and decline of national imperialisms would have been enough in itself to suggest serious doubt. A Metternich would not have risked a brass farthing on any such gamble, nor yet would a Bismarck, a Cavour, or a Leo XIII; but Mr. Hay was no Metternich.

I took it as axiomatic that when a good statesman,—a sound *Realpolitiker* who kept his conscience and his sentiment securely locked up in the safe until the day's work was done,—when he confronted a forced choice between two rival imperialisms he would make terms with the one which was on its way in rather than with the one which was on its way out. In 1908 it had looked for some time as if England's was certainly going out and Germany's quite possibly, but as yet by no means certainly, coming in. Good statesmanship on Mr. Hay's part therefore, it seemed to me, would have handsomely accepted Spain's amends, which were ample and sincere, abstained from war, and let the Anglo-German rivalry mull along for another ten years or so until it became more clear which way the imperialist cat would jump. A Jefferson or a John Adams would instantly have reminded Mr. Hay of Prince Kutusov's maxim, *Dans le doute, abstiens-toi*; but Mr. McKinley was no Jefferson. As for the other energetic young imperialism on the Pacific, the situation was still more unclear. No one thought much about Japan, notwithstanding its foray in China in 1895; it attracted little attention until nine years later when it gave so startling an account of itself in the Russo-Japanese war of 1904; and even then it was regarded as weak enough to be rather easily manageable in a diplomatic way. In the Far East as well as on the Continent, therefore, another ten years of salutary self-imposed isolation would have enabled American statesmanship to see its way more clearly and to far better purpose.

But whether Mr. Hay botched his statesmanship through a precipitate and unwarranted commitment, or merely made an unfortunate gamble through being led up the garden by those whom he termed "our English friends,"—and either view is admissible,—the consequences were the same. If the Philippine Islands were made of gold sown broadcast with diamonds, our seizure of them could never meet its cost, whether that cost be measured in terms of blood or of money or of civilisation, let alone of all three together.

So ended my first lesson in modern imperialist statecraft. It was an invaluable aid in constructing the criteria which I was ever afterwards to apply to the conduct of public affairs in general. Yet it was a disappointment, in that it represented no essential advance whatever on what I already knew. Reincarnate any first-class *Realpolitiker* of the ancient world, from 3800 B.C. to 1500 A.D., put him in charge of the foreign office in any modern imperialist capital, and he would have hard work to convince himself that he was not still doing business at the old stand.

III

A strange spirit of uneasiness and depression was abroad in the Western world at the turn of the century. Apparently it affected all peoples and classes alike, though not all in the same way. Three months after I had left college with my bachelor's degree, and had gone forth into the outer world looking for what I might find there, I read a remarkable work called *Degeneration*, written by the able Hungarian Jew, Max Nordau. In it he described this contemporary spirit as "a mixture of febrile restlessness and defeatist discouragement, of fear for the future and sulking resignation. The prevalent sense is one of impending destruction and extinction. . . . In our time the more highly-developed minds have been visited with vague forebodings of a Dusk of the Nations, in which the sunlight and starlight are gradually fading, and the human race with all its institutions and achievements is dying out amidst a dying world."

This put the spirit of the period very well, very correctly. The one description of it which is incomparable in its perfection, however, was accidental; its application was not intentional. It is found in the dream of Aratov, in *Clara Militch*, Tourgueniev's last and greatest work:

> He dreamed that he was in a rich manor-house, of which he was the owner. He had lately bought both the house and the estate attached to it. And he kept thinking, 'It's nice, very nice now, but evil is coming!' Beside him moved to and fro a little tiny man, his steward; he kept laughing, bowing, and trying to show Aratov how admirably everything was arranged in his house and his estate. 'This way, pray, this way, pray,' he kept repeating, chuckling at every word; 'kindly look how prosperous everything is with you! Look at the horses; what splendid horses!' And Aratov saw a row of immense horses. They were standing in their stalls with their backs to him. Their manes and tails were magnificent; but as soon as Aratov went near, the horses' heads turned towards him, and they showed their teeth viciously. 'It's very nice,' Aratov thought, 'but evil is coming!' 'This way, pray, this way,' the steward repeated again, 'pray come into the garden; look, what fine apples you have.' The apples certainly were fine, red and round, but as soon as Aratov looked at them they withered and fell. 'Evil is coming!' he thought. 'And here is the lake,' lisped the steward. 'Isn't it blue and smooth? And here's a little boat of gold,—will you get into it?—it floats of itself.' 'I won't get into it,' thought Aratov; 'evil is coming!' but for all that he got into the boat. At the bottom lay huddled up a little creature like a monkey; it was holding in its paws a glass full of a dark liquid. 'Pray don't be uneasy,' the steward shouted from the bank. 'It's of no consequence. It's death. Good luck to you!'

For the great majority, the last decade of the century seemed to offer every encouragement to complacent hopefulness. All the institutional voices of society were blended to form the sycophantic reassurances of Aratov's steward. Indeed, what more could one ask? Everywhere there was steady progress in all departments of science, in invention, in improving the mechanics of existence, and in the production of wealth. The ancient doctrine of progressive evolution, brought out and refurbished by Darwin,—and run into the ground by Darwin's more adventurous disciples,—copper-riveted the comfortable confidence that progress would go on indefinitely, harmoniously, automatically. Man himself had risen from the primeval slime in a straight line to his present place in nature as *Homo sapiens,* thus giving earnest of his ultimate perfectibility; and now progressive evolution, helped on by science, might be trusted to bring forth in not too long a time a race of saints and sages to dwell together in a society truly perfect.

There was ground for high hopefulness, too, about the more immediate future. The business of the nineteenth century had been to establish the individual's right to liberty and to self-expression in politics. This now, presumably, had been done. A great measure of personal liberty had been effected, and republicanism had gone far enough to call its future assured. The business of the twentieth century would be to create circumstances for improving the emancipated and enfranchised masses, and everything was ripe and ready for that. The applications of science were so many, so easy and practical and so prodigally fruitful, that the new century's task seemed simple. With schools, colleges, universities, free for all; with libraries, technical institutes, museums, and countless other means of self-improvement standing wide open; with fatigue and monotony decreased, labour lightened, and leisure for self-improvement enlarged,—with all this, the twentieth century seemed to have the most brilliant prospects of any since the world began.

Moreover, international affairs appeared to be fairly stable, and peace was in the air. The sensational calling of a peace-conference in 1899 by Alexander III had produced a great effect, even though the gesture was obviously not made in good faith and the conference itself came to nothing. In 1906, not to be outdone by a Muscovite autocrat, Andrew Carnegie gave ten million dollars towards forwarding the cause of peace by way of a "foundation," and five years later a rich Bostonese publisher followed suit with another foundation of the same order. In the wake of these, innumerable international peace-societies appeared everywhere. These manifestations all fell in with the prevailing temper of the peoples in both hemispheres; they bolstered their shaky optimism and therefore were acceptable at their face value.

So, what with progressive evolution approved as *de fide*; with new wonders of science being disclosed and put in service every day; with the production of wealth going on at top speed; with new comforts, conveniences and pleasures steadily multiplying, and their accessibility steadily increasing; with a fair prospect of peace predominating, perhaps permanently;—with all these assets in hand, one might regard the future with complacency. The Western world's estate was rich and prosperous. The horses' manes and tails were magnificent, the apples were fine, red and round. "It's nice, very nice now"; and yet,—and yet,—the vague undefined sense of impermanence and instability persisted. The civilisation wrought out by the application of these assets was felt to be somehow incomplete, dissatisfying, untrustworthy. "The more highly-developed minds" in all countries were saying plainly that the social product of these forces was utterly unworthy to be called civilisation; and they were predicting that soon, very soon, the passenger in the golden boat would hear the perfidious steward shouting, "Pray don't be uneasy. It's of no consequence. It's death. Good luck to you!"

My course of reading, initiated by Nordau's work and supplemented by observation of current affairs as well as by my conversations with C. J., impressed on me the basic fact that western society was entirely given over to economism.[4] It had no other philosophy; apparently it did not know there was any other. It interpreted the whole of human life in terms of the production, acquisition and distribution of wealth. Like certain Philippians in the time of St. Paul, its god was its belly, and it had no mind for anything beyond the ἐπίγεια. I learned that as far as American society was concerned, this had been so ever since the days of Columbus. Michel Chevalier, the most

[4] This word is not in any dictionary, as far as I know. I use it because my only alternative is *materialism*, which is ambiguous and inexact.

acute observer among the many who had visited America in its youth, said that American society had the morale of an army on the march. It had the morale of the looter, the plunderer. In my boyhood, those who had made the best success with it were held up in the schools, the press, and even in the pulpit, as prototypal of all that was making America great, and hence as *par excellence* the proper examples for well-ordered youth to follow. *Go and get it!* was the sum of the practical philosophy presented to America's young manhood by all the voices of the age.

When in those days or a little later I had been considering, more or less idly and fitfully, what I should do with myself through life, what life had to give me, and what demands I should make upon it, I sometimes thought of the rich lumbermen whom I had known so well, and on the whole had rather liked. Now I was looking at the great avatars of their practical philosophy, the Carnegies, Rockefellers, Fricks, Hills, Huntingtons, of the period. I asked myself whether any amount of wealth would be worth having if,—as one most evidently must, —if one had to become just like these men in order to get it. To me, at least, decidedly it would not; I should be a superfluous man in the scuffle for riches. I observed their qualities and practices closely, considered the furniture of their minds, remarked their scale of values, and could come to no other conclusion. Well, then, could a society built to a complete realisation of every ideal of the economism they represented be permanently satisfactory to the best reason and spirit of man? Could it be called a civilised society? The thing seemed preposterous, absurd; I recalled Teufelsdröckh's simile of "an Egyptian pitcher of tamed vipers, each struggling to get its head above the others." After wealth, science, invention, had done all for such a society that they could do, it would remain without savour, without depth, *uninteresting*, and withal horrifying.

I found that the few "more highly-developed minds" in America were well aware of this. Thoreau was; and Emerson,

Lowell; C. F. Adams and his sons, Brooks and Henry; Curtis, Mark Twain, Howells; all these made record of their apprehension and repugnance. Whitman lapsed from his "barbaric yawp" of faith in economism to the desponding observation that the type of civilisation which economism had produced was, "so far, an almost complete failure in its social aspects, and in really grand religious, moral, literary, and æsthetic results. . . . It is as if we were somehow being endowed with a vast and thoroughly appointed body, and then left with little or no soul." Even Henry Cabot Lodge, who did some good service to economism, said in real distress, apparently, that society's exclusive acceptance of it as a practical philosophy was "the darkest sign of all." Even John Hay, who had incontinently dumped a moribund alien imperialism into the lap of the United States to be nursed and pap-fed there indefinitely, and who had glorified the extreme of economism as a practical philosophy by writing *The Breadwinners*, languidly complained of "the restless haste and hunger which is the source of much that is good and most that is evil in American life."

Turning to French literature, I found that the Goncourts, Mérimée, Halévy, de Nerval, Chevalier, Flaubert, de Musset and many others had marked the direction which French society was taking under the spur of economism, and had declared their fixed conviction that "evil is coming." Their writings also reflected the great general feeling of uneasiness. Mérimée, in his last days, testified that "everybody is afraid, though nobody knows of what." In Germany, two giants of the century saw what was coming; these were Goethe and Niebuhr. I found that in England also the most highly-developed minds had long been obsessed by a like apprehension. As far back as 1811 Mrs. Barbauld seems to have seen the approaching cloud of economism, then no bigger than a man's hand, and to have anticipated Macaulay in drawing the gloomy picture of an outlander surveying a scene of lifeless desolation from the ruins of London Bridge. It is all very well for economism to boast of progress and enlightenment; so said Wordsworth, Carlyle,

Kingsley, Arnold,—his *Friendship's Garland* is as fresh today as if written yesterday,—Butler, Ruskin, FitzGerald, Morris, Hardy; it is all very well, it's nice, very nice now, but evil is coming!

There was good reason for this, and the reason was clearly visible even on the surface of things; there was nothing recondite about it. The outbreak of the Spanish War had caused me to doubt that the century's net gains from republicanism were substantial, or that its achievement of personal liberty was at all valid. If two men, one an abject political hack and the other a jobholder of dubious quality,—if these, with the power of patronage in their hands, could manœuvre a nation of eighty million people into an imperialist war, I should take it as pretty good evidence that absolutism can flourish about as luxuriantly under republicanism as under an autocracy. Thus, while considering the phenomena of economism and modern imperialism, I was also led to observe the concurrent growth of what long afterward I learned to call Statism. Within the last half-century in England, France and Germany, the State had been continually absorbing through taxation more and more of the national wealth, continually assuming one new coercive, regulative or directive function after another. In the United States the same process had begun to be speeded up to a headlong rapidity. Everywhere these wholesale confiscations of social power were going on; everywhere social power was being depleted, and everywhere State power being increased at its expense.

Along with this tendency went a curious tacit rationalisation of it, under the dogma of Statism as propounded by the German idealist philosophers of the eighteenth century. C. J. introduced me to the basic political theory of these gentry, and the closeness of its correspondence with the popular belief now everywhere prevailing rather took my breath away. In brief, what it came to was that the State is everything; the individual, nothing. The individual has no rights that the State is bound to respect; no rights at all, in fact, except those which the State may choose to give him, subject to revocation at its own pleasure, with or without notice. There is no such thing as natural rights; the fundamental doctrine of the American Declaration of Independence, the doctrine underlying the Bill of Rights, is all moonshine. Moreover, since the State creates all rights, since the only valid and authoritative ethics are State ethics, then by obvious inference the State can do no wrong.

Such was the view with which the peoples of the Western world had become indoctrinated. To save my life I could not see a shilling's worth of practical difference between this and the old theory of *jure divino* rulership which republicanism plumed itself on having ousted. I saw no reason why John Cowell and Sir Robert Filmer might not shake hands cordially with Hegel over the latter's dictum that "the State incarnates the Divine Idea upon earth," or forsooth with Fichte over his declaration that "the State is the superior power, ultimate and beyond appeal, absolutely independent." Given a people imbued with this idea, the republicanism of the nineteenth century seemed to me only what the Scots call "cauld kail made het again,"—absolutism warmed up and rebaptised. In France, the strong common sense of many like Horace Vernet and Halévy had openly scorned it, and the far-seeing Guizot contemptuously called it the kind of republicanism "which begins with Plato and necessarily ends with a policeman." In England, Herbert Spencer had written the immortal essays subsequently put together in a volume called *The Man vs. the State*, in which he demolished the doctrine of the omnipotent State, and predicted accurately what would take place if that doctrine continued to prevail; but his work, like that of Stuart Mill and others, had little effect. In July, 1898, he wrote in a letter to Grant Allen, ". . . I said, just as you say, that we are in course of re-barbarisation, and that there is no prospect but that of military despotisms, which we are rapidly approaching."

One could hardly wonder that the more highly-developed minds of Europe had been "visited with vague forebodings of a Dusk of the Nations." I was in Europe for a long time at the turn of the century, visiting Italy, Russia, France, Germany and England, and it was plain that for all the talk of peace and liberty, no other upshot was consistent with the general acceptance of Statism as a philosophy, and the consequent prodigious growth of State power at the expense of social power. Any economic dislocation, natural or fabricated, any collision of State interest, actual or pretended, would at once everywhere open the way for a sharking political adventurer, a modern Cleon, to come forward and under some demagogic pretext of "emergency, the tyrant's plea" to commandeer *all* social power, reduce the people to unconditional State-servitude, and use them for his own purposes.

I was reminded of these observations one day in the autumn of 1940, when I unexpectedly met an old friend whom I had not seen for years, a very wise and experienced man of about my own age, Mr. Darwin J. Meserole. Some one had just approached him in a great state of mind, saying that the world had gone clean crazy. Mr. Meserole replied, "You have watched this coming for forty years, and now that it's here, you say the world has gone crazy!"

CHAPTER SEVEN

Le monde est inepte à se guarir. Il est si impatient de ce que le presse qu'il ne vise qu' à s'en desfaire sans regarder à quel prix . . . le bien ne succede pas necessairement au mal; un autre mal luy peult succeder, et pire.

—MONTAIGNE.

HAVING a good deal of leisure at this time, I employed some of it in looking over the various projects that were on foot for political and social reform. There seemed no end of them. Counting in the smaller schemes for reform in city and county politics, they came to a bewildering lot. Some of the larger schemes were aimed at corrupt state legislatures; but the projects which interested me most were those having a national scope, like the movements for direct Federal taxation, popular election of senators, women's suffrage, control of commerce, and control of trust-monopoly.

What first attracted my attention was the astonishing extent to which these latter were animated by hatred of the rich. There was some ground for this. These great fortunes were made by means which were outrageously unfair, and were felt to be so. Their owners were in control of the State's machinery, and were using it to their own advantage by way of land-grants, tariffs, concessions, franchises and every other known form of law-made privilege. In the view of simple justice, this was shocking bad. Yet I could not help seeing that it was in full accord with the dominant social philosophy. Economism, which interprets the whole sum of human life in terms of the production, acquisition and distribution of wealth, must necessarily fashion its gods after its own likeness. Economism must not conceive of the State as an instrument of justice, a social device set up, as the Declaration says, "to secure these rights." On the contrary, it must be what Voltaire called it, "a device for taking money out of one set of pockets and putting it into another." With this conception of the State and its functions accepted everywhere, prevailing everywhere, what could be expected but a continuous struggle to get at the State's machinery and work it to one's own advantage?

Then too, the owners of these great fortunes flaunted their allegiance to economism in ways so brazen and assertive as to amount almost to savagery. Their porcine insensitiveness made them easy targets for those who had marked them out for spoliation. Not long ago I noticed in the bar-room of one of New York's older hotels a line of forty-two cabinet photographs of representative rich men of that generation. They ran all the way from Daniel Drew and Jay Gould down to Henry Ford, the only one of the lot now living. In their totality, those pictures tell an impressive story; a student of physiognomy would be well repaid for giving them careful scrutiny. Such were the men of whom Charles Francis Adams left record that he had known them, many of them tolerably well, "and a less interesting crowd I do not care to encounter. Not one that I have ever known would I care to meet again, either in this world or the next; nor is one of them associated in my mind with the idea of humour, thought or refinement." So, while hatred may be never justifiable, perhaps seldom reasonable, a great popular hatred of such men, under such circumstances, is at least understandable.

The reformers of the period put me off, in the first instance, by their careless superficial use of abstract terms. They talked about the oppressiveness of capital, the evils of the capitalist system, the iniquities of finance-capitalism, and so on, apparently with no idea of what those terms mean. To me, therefore, most of what they said was sheer nonsense. I knew that no society ever did or could exist without employing capital, and my notion was that wherever capital is at work, there of necessity is capitalism and a capitalist system. As I saw it, there was nothing in the nature of capital that was unjust or oppressive, but quite the contrary. I could see that injustice and oppression were likely to follow when great capitalists were in a position of State-created economic advantage, like Mr. Carnegie with his tariffs or the "railway-magnates" with their land-grants; but the same results seemed as likely to follow where small capitalists or non-capitalists were in a similarly privileged position. Spencer's *Social Statics*, published in 1851, had shown me that under such a government as he contemplated,—a government divested of all power to traffic in economic advantage,—injustice and oppression would tend to disappear. As long as the State stood as an approachable huckster of privilege, however, there seemed no chance but that they must persist, and that the consequent social disorder must persist also.

The measures of the reformers took no account of all this which seemed to me so obvious. The reformers themselves apparently did not see that the State, as an arbiter of economic advantage, must necessarily be a potential instrument of economic exploitation. In fact, these are but two ways of saying the same thing, for, as Voltaire saw so clearly, advantage to the State's beneficiaries means disadvantage to those who are not its beneficiaries. By putting a tariff on steel, for example, the State simply took a great deal of money out of the pockets of American purchasers of steel, and put it in Mr. Carnegie's; it acted *ad hoc* as Mr. Carnegie's instrument of exploitation. Neither did the reformers see that those who would profit most by State-enforced exploitation must always be, and would be, those to whom nature has given the largest endowment of that peculiar, instinctive, and unerring sagacity for finding the best ways of access to the State's machinery and the most fruitful ways of operating it. They would personify the highest aims and ideals of economism. In other words, they would be exactly like those Mr. C. F. Adams knew, the very ones whom the reformers were proposing to hamstring and despoil.

The actual situation confronting the reformers, as I saw it, was nothing new or strange. The sum of it was that the American State had always been controlled by those whom I learned shortly afterwards when I came to read Nietzsche, to call mass-men. It was so controlled throughout the colonial period, so in 1789, so in 1890. In sharp contrast with the doctrine of the Declaration, the doctrine of the Constitution was mass-man's doctrine; the document itself was a lawyer's digest and charter of economism. The men of the forty-two photographs were rich mass-men, to be sure, but mass-men, every mother's son of them; unintelligent, ignorant, myopic, incapable of psychical development, but prodigiously sagacious and prehensile. If I had been asked for a definition at that time, measuring by the standards of civilised man,—the standards set by a Plato, a Dante, a Marcus Aurelius,—I should have put it that the mass-man is a digestive and reproductive mechanism, gifted with a certain low sagacity employable upon anything which bears upon the conduct of those two functions. If he is overgifted with this sagacity and has a measure of luck, he becomes a rich mass-man; if not, he becomes a poor mass-man; but in either case he remains a mass-man.

None of the reformers proposed reducing the State's power to distribute economic advantage; on the contrary, every one of their principal measures tended to increase it. Therefore when all came to all, I could not see that these measures ultimately contemplated anything more than prying the State's machinery out of the rich mass-man's control, and turning it over to the poor mass-man. I could imagine no benefit accruing to society from that. The control would again be taken over by the most sagacious among the poor mass-men, they would become rich, the same abuses, jealousies and dissatisfactions would recur, the same contest would again take place, with the same result. I was immensely interested in reading John Adams's clear forecast of the scrimmage I was witnessing, and his prophecy that "the struggle will end only in a change of impostors." One afternoon in 1900 I listened while a young Jewish Socialist was breathing out threatenings and slaughter against the rich. I had asked him just what it was that he proposed to do when he had got them all properly killed off. "We have been oppressed," he said, "and now we shall oppress." I thought he put the matter very well, for I could see no other prospect.

When one brushed aside the reformers' verbiage, the situation was perfectly clear. I was not witnessing a "revolt of the masses" against an alien power; nor yet a war between labour and capital; nor yet a struggle to break up big business; nor yet an attempt to abolish capitalism. What I was looking at was simply a tussle between two groups of mass-men, one large and poor, the other small and rich, and as judged by the standards of a civilised society, neither of them any more meritorious or promising than the other. The object of the tussle was the material gains accruing from control of the State's machinery. It is easier to seize wealth than to produce it; and as long as the State makes the seizure of wealth a matter of legalised privilege, so long will the squabble for that privilege go on. As John Adams had so correctly foreseen, the few more sagacious mass-men will be continually trying to outwit the many who are less sagacious, and the many will in turn be trying to overpower the few by sheer force of numbers.

So I was sceptical about the reformers' projects, and the more they were trumpeted as "democratic," the less good to society I thought they boded. Now and then I was asked to lend a hand with some of them, but I knew I should be out of place or even worse, a mere wet blanket. I knew many of their promoters, some very well; the elder Lafollette, Lincoln Steffens, Newton Baker, Joseph Fels, Frederic Howe. Some of them died in the faith of reform, while others seemed finally to slack off into a vague consciousness that something had somehow gone wrong, and that the realisation of their visions was farther off than they had thought it was. All those I knew, perhaps twenty-five or more, showed less power of detachment and reflection than I should have looked for, and very little sense of history. Their acceptance of the State as a social institution amazed me, since its anti-social character was so plainly visible, and their idea of mankind's leading qualities and motives seemed as unrealistic as Juvenal's observations on boars and tigers. I used to ask one after another to tell me just what reason he had for supposing that a society or an individual could be improved through political action. History was against it, observation and common sense were against it,— just what made him think he was not putting the cart before the horse? I never got an answer; they all took it as if the question had never occurred to them, as I dare say it never had. Once I said I thought that in his sense of statesmanship and his sense of history Thoreau was miles ahead of the whole tribe of reformers, and had proved it by his one saying that the State had never yet done anything to help a good cause along, except by the alacrity with which it got out of the way.

Thus I never quite understood these men, nor they me, though they were always kind, true friends. I think they regarded me as a more or less agreeable person who had been altogether born in sin and could not be expected to do much about it; and as I recall the spirit and temper of my ancestry, I wouldn't go so far as to say they might not be right. But they were always kind, tolerant, lovable. Once when I complimented Robert Lafollette on some *coup* that he had brought off at the "Thyesteän banquet of clap-trap" in the Senate, he said with a rather sad expression, "Yes; but the trouble is, you don't believe what I'm doing amounts to a damn." It was true enough, and I was sorry; yet I was not obstinate, I had no pride of opinion, and certainly no prejudices, but quite the contrary. Aware that I was but a youngster, green as grass, trying only to get my bearings on a straight course of thought, all that moved me was the old Platonist desire to "see things as they are." I could not, nor can I now, make out that these friends ever brought themselves to see the State as it is, or mankind as it is; and the event has abundantly proved that they did not.

There were two exceptions, hardly to be called reformers, Herbert Quick and Brand Whitlock. Quick was always, I believe, on the extreme outer fringe of the reforming party, and centrifugal force soon threw Whitlock as far out. Quick clearly saw the State as an anti-social institution; he saw that as primarily the arbiter of economic advantage and a potential instrument of exploitation, both its initial intent and function are anti-social. He was the only person I knew in that period who drew the line of distinction sharply between the idea of *government*, as set forth by Mr. Jefferson in the Declaration and amplified by Paine and Spencer, and the idea of *the State* as demonstrated in the historical researches of Gumplowicz and Franz Oppenheimer. I owe him a great deal, for our conversations helped me vastly to arrange my thought in an orderly way. One recollection of him, however, is annoying. We used to talk for a while after dinner, and then play billiards. I was no end a better player than he was, and yet the wretched man always beat me, I don't know how. He used to say that when I took him on he played ten times better than he could, which seemed to be so. Once at the Cosmos Club in Washington I vowed I would stick at him until I beat him, if it took a week. We did play nearly all night, but he always managed to nose me out, and I finally quit in disgust. I get hot all through whenever I think of it.

Whitlock had made a tentative start on the path of reform in the days of Altgeld, Eugene Debs, Pingree, Golden Rule Jones. His education and early influences had done little to help him towards a quick and accurate judgement on the worth of their endeavours, but having a reflective mind and a true Platonist instinct towards "the reason of the thing," he soon found his bearings. The war confirmed his worst suspicions; he had felt some "vague forebodings of a Dusk of the Nations," but had not expected this particular prelude to calamity to come on so soon. He was greatly depressed. I remember well one forlorn grey Sunday afternoon in the winter of 1914 when he and I were walking on the deserted outer boulevards of Brussels. Suddenly he stopped and faced me with the question, "Have you any hope *at all* of the human race?" I replied cannily, "As much as I ever had, no less, no more." As we walked on, I told him I was like the darky nurse-girl who had never seen a railway-train until she and her mistress boarded one that presently went into a tremendous smash-up. When her mistress pulled herself together, she looked around for the girl, and saw her sitting where she had evidently been thrown, some fifty feet from the track, unhurt and composedly crooning to the baby in her arms. "Weren't you terribly frightened?" her mistress asked. "No, ma'am," the girl replied, "I thought it done had to stop dat way." Whitlock smiled a little mournfully, and said he wished he might have had half that darky's foresight.

II

Herbert Spencer's essays, published in 1884, on *The New Toryism* and *The Coming Slavery* left me with an extremely bad impression of British Liberalism. Since 1860, Liberals had been foremost in loading up the statute-book with one coercive measure of "social legislation" after another in hot succession, each of which had the effect of diminishing social power and increasing State power. In so doing, the Liberals were manifestly going dead against their traditional principles. They had abandoned the principle of voluntary social coöperation, and embraced the old-line Tory principle of enforced coöperation. Not only so, but they had transformed themselves into a band of political Frankensteins. By busily cutting down the liberty of the individual piecemeal, and extending the scope of the State's coercive control, their work was reaching the point where a few easy finishing-touches would reduce the individual to a condition of complete State-servitude; thus bringing forth the monster of collectivism, ravenous and rampant.

When I saw what American Liberals (for so they called themselves) were doing in this line,—chiefly in their support of the movement for an income-tax and an inheritance-tax,—I got up a distaste for Liberals which soon ripened into horror. For years I have "sweat with agony" at the sight of a Liberal, as Commodore Trunnion did at the sight of an attorney. I had rather encounter rattlesnakes,—far rather,—for the rattlesnake is a gentlemanly fellow who can be relied on to do the right thing, if you give him half a chance. I have had dealings with him in my time, and also with the Liberals, and I speak from knowledge.

I have respect for the old-style Tory, and could always get on with him, because I knew what he would do in a given situation, and above all, I knew what he would not do. There were some things to which he would not condescend even for the Larger Good. Once in a conversation with Chief Justice Taft, he mentioned pressure put on him while President, in behalf of something legal enough and probably ethical, but smelling of sharp practice,—"dam' low, in any case," as an old-school Englishman would say. I so well remember the almost childlike look of embarrassment on Mr. Taft's face as he said, "Why, I couldn't do that." Speaking after the manner of men, you got a play for your money with the old-crusted Tory, as at the other end of the scale I think you would with the honest outright uncompromising radical. But one never knew what Liberals would do, and their power of self-persuasion is such that only God knows what they would not do. As casuists, they make Gury and St. Alfonso dei Liguori look like bush-leaguers. On every point of conventional morality, all the Liberals I have personally known were very trustworthy. They were great fellows for the Larger Good, but it would have to be pretty large before they would alienate your wife's affections or steal your watch. But on any point of intellectual integrity, there is not one of them whom I would trust for ten minutes alone in a room with a red-hot stove, unless the stove were comparatively valueless.

Liberals generally,—there may have been exceptions, but I do not know who they were,—joined in the agitation for an income-tax, in utter disregard of the fact that it meant writing the principle of absolutism into the Constitution. Nor did they give a moment's thought to the appalling social effects of an income-tax; I never once heard this aspect of the matter discussed. Liberals were also active in promoting the "democratic" movement for the popular election of senators. It certainly took no great perspicacity to see that these two measures would straightway ease our political system into collectivism as soon as some Eubulus, some mass-man overgifted with sagacity, should manœuvre himself into popular leadership; and in the nature of things, this would not be long.

Liberals were also prominent in the fast-growing movement for women's suffrage. I could see that in this they had logic with them; the women's contention was valid. I never read a counter-argument that I thought was worth the paper it was printed on. If you are going to have universal suffrage, it should include women, since,—at least presumably,—women are folks, as men are. Practically, I thought it would turn out as it has done; I thought it would do no good and no harm. The only effect it could have would be to increase the preponderance of the mass-vote, and that preponderance was already so overwhelming that doubling it, or even trebling it, counted for nothing in a practical way. So, if all the mass-men were voting, I saw no reason why the mass-women should not. I was beginning to have grave doubts about universal suffrage, however. A political system which, as Dean Inge says, merely counts votes instead of weighing them, began to seem unpromising. Hence I remained inactive in the women's-suffrage movement, regarding its comical antics as a source of diversion. Still, on occasion when I was asked for an opinion, I always declared myself in favour of it, though I was minded to hold my nose when I did so.

One reformer of the period presented himself in a double capacity. He was a very great social philosopher who had trained himself into a first-class polemist, crusader, campaigner; a strange combination, the strangest imaginable. I do not recall another instance of it. This was Henry George. I never saw him, though I might easily have done so, but his days were ending just as I was emerging from the academic shades. C. J. once spoke to me of his philosophy, saying with a nod of his wise head, "That's the real thing." He never mentioned it again. Undoubtedly, as I discovered later on, it was the real thing. As Robert Lafollette said to me, George's social philosophy and his fiscal method, taken together, made a system "against which nothing rational has ever been said, or can be said." As a social philosopher, George interested me profoundly; as a reformer and publicist, he did not interest me, though I tried hard to make the best of him in that capacity.

George and his followers carried on a tremendous country-wide campaign to force George's fiscal method into politics. I knew many of his disciples, some of them quite well; among them were Louis F. Post, C. B. Fillebrown, Bolton Hall, Daniel Kiefer, Charles D. Williams, George Record, A. C. Pleydell. Outside the movement, or on the fringes of it, some of the ablest men in the country were "under conviction," as the old-time Methodists used to say. Newton Baker and Whitlock were in this group; also Lawson Purdy and William Jay Gaynor, who impressed me as by far the ablest man in our public life. Few know that he might have had the Presidency instead of Wilson if he had consented; he was mayor of New York at the time. The story of the approach to him is most amusing, but it would be out of place in this narrative, like so many other amusing matters which I am always being tempted to drag in. I have often wondered what course the country would have taken after 1914 if he had been in Wilson's place.

I did not follow George's campaign attentively, and was neither astonished nor disappointed when it came to nothing. George's philosophy was the philosophy of human freedom. Like Mr. Jefferson, Condorcet, Rousseau, and the believers in progressive evolution, he believed that all mankind are indefinitely improvable, and that the freer they are, the more they will improve. He saw also that they can never become politically or socially free until they have become economically free, but if they gained economic freedom, the other freedoms would follow automatically; and he offered his fiscal method as the most natural, simple, and effective means of securing them in economic freedom. All this appeared to me sound enough,[1] but the attempt to realise it through political action seemed the acme of absurdity. The only result one could expect was that the philosophy would be utterly lost sight of, and the method utterly discredited; and precisely this was the result.

Socialism and one or two other variants of collectivist Statism were making considerable political progress at the time. When I met some of their proponents, as I did now and then, I would put the one question to them that I always put to George's campaigners. Suppose by some miracle you have your system all installed, complete and perfect, it will still have to be administered,—very well, what kind of people can you get to administer it except the kind of people you've got? I never had an answer to that question. In a society of just men made perfect, George's system would be administered admirably and would work like clockwork. So would Socialism. So would any other form of collectivism. In such a society "the dictatorship of the proletariat" would be a splendid success for everybody all round. The trouble is, we have no such society,—far from it. Although I was,—and am,—a firm believer in George's philosophy and fiscal method, I decided that if progressive evolution was to make them practicable in fifty thousand years, it would have to step a great deal livelier than there was any sign of its doing.

[1] True at the time. As will be seen hereafter, I have since given up the environmentalist postulate that the masses of mankind are indefinitely improvable. This does not invalidate George's reasoning for me, however, for his method would enable them, if they cared to do so, to improve themselves up to the limit of their psychical capacity, whatever that may be; which now they are unable to do.

So in the ranks of the militant single-taxers, as they were called, I knew I should make a poor soldier. Convinced that the surest way to lose that war, like all other wars, was to win it, I should be a superfluous man. Now and then I published a line or two by way of showing that I was on the side of the angels, but took no further part. To console myself for my shortcomings I pondered the example of the great social philosophers of the past who had never crusaded for their doctrines or presumed upon mankind's capacity for receiving them; not Socrates, not Jesus, not Lao-Tze, of whom Chi-Yen had said that "he was a superior man who liked to keep in obscurity." What wisdom! "If any man have ears to hear," said the *Santissimo Salvatore*, "let him hear." That was all there was to be expected. I admired the reformers, George in particular, for the splendid intrepidity which one admires in the leader of a forlorn hope. Yet I could not resist reminding myself of Montaigne's great saying, that "human society goes very incompetently about healing its ills. It is so impatient under the immediate irritation which is chafing it that it thinks only of getting rid of this, careless of the cost. . . . Good does not necessarily ensue upon evil; another evil may ensue upon it, and a worse one."

Taking stock of my disorderly array of political and social ideas, I saw that I was becoming a poor sort of republican. As far as the individual was concerned, all State systems seemed to tend about equally towards the same end of State-slavery. In rich countries, as Mr. Jefferson had noticed, they reached that end a little faster than in poor countries, but I could make out no other difference. I was much impressed by France's remarkable experience; it seemed to me one of the most exhibitory experiences in history, though I did not find any one who was taking it as such. In a single century after 1789, France had tried every known kind of State-system, some two or three times over; three republics, a couple of monarchies, two empires, now and then a dictatorship, a directory, a commune—every system one could think of. Each shift brought about the same consequences to the individual, and they all alike bore testimony to the truth of Paine's saying, that "the trade of governing has always been a monopoly of the most ignorant and the most vicious of mankind." I often wondered why this sequence of systems in France had not given rise to more speculation about the actual net value of any one political system over another. If it had given rise to any, I did not hear of it.

I began to think there was a good deal in William Penn's observation that "when all is said, there is hardly any frame of government so ill designed by its first founders that in good hands it would not do well enough; and story [i.e., history] tells us the best, in ill ones, can do nothing that is great or good." The triumph of republicanism was supposed to be a tremendous achievement, yet the republican State, or "democratic," as Americans had begun to call it, (perhaps Andrew Carnegie set the fashion with his Icarian flight of genius in *Triumphant Democracy*) was giving no better account of itself than the autocratic or monarchical State had given. Like theirs, its coercive incursions upon the individual, its progressive confiscations of social power, were limited only by close calculation of what the traffic would bear. Like theirs, its controlling mass-men never lost a chance at what James Madison contemptuously called "the old trick of turning every contingency into a resource for accumulating force in the government." Looking at it from the individual's point of view, I could not see that the republican system had much to commend it over any other. In theory, the republican State existed for man; in practice, man existed for the republican State.

While I was wondering whether progressive evolution had as yet brought mankind within gun-range of a practicable republican system, I ran across Horace Vernet's witty observation made when the revolution of 1848 had ousted the July Monarchy and brought in the Second Republic. "*A la bonne heure*," he cried gaily, "give me a republic such as we understand it in France, all rulers, all natural-born kings, gods in mortals' disguise who dance to the piping of the devil. There have been two such since I was born; there may be another half-dozen like them within the next two centuries, because before you can have an ideal republic you must have ideal republicans, and nature can't afford to fool away her most precious gifts on a pack of jack-leg lawyers and hobnail-booted riffraff. She condescends to make an ideal tyrant now and then, but she will never make a nation of ideal republicans. You might as well ask her to make a nation of Raphaels, Michelangelos, Shakespeares or Molières."

There it was, precisely. I could see how "democracy" might do very well in a society of saints and sages led by an Alfred or an Antoninus Pius. Short of that, I was unable to see how it could come to anything but an ochlocracy of mass-men led by a sagacious knave. The collective capacity for bringing forth any other outcome seemed simply not there. To my eyes the incident of Aristides and the Athenian mass-man was perfectly exhibitory of "democracy" in practice. Socrates could not have got votes enough out of the Athenian mass-men to be worth counting, but Eubulus easily could, and did, wangle enough to keep himself in office as long as the corrupt fabric of the Athenian State held together. As against a Jesus, the historic choice of the mass-man goes regularly to some Barabbas.

III

I have said that my ideas about all these matters were disorderly, fragmentary, for so they were. In trying to make a very long story short, I must have given the impression of having put in a great deal more serious sustained work on forming them than was actually the case. All I did in that way was quite casual and planless. For one thing, I was having too good a time, and had too many pleasanter trivialities to attend to. What actually happened was that some turn in public affairs would attract my notice, and I would "see it as it was," more or less by a kind of reflex;—the Platonist habit of looking for "the reason of the thing" had become almost automatic. Often I let it go at that, and thought no more about it. Sometimes I would be reminded of something apposite which I had read, and I would look that up. Sometimes I got a suggestion that would set me at reading something which was new to me. Sometimes I would follow through to a provisional generalisation, but usually not. In these ways the raw material of ideas gradually got itself together in rough shapes, like a scattered mess of fagots, which I seldom took the trouble to put in order.

In such circumstances, one of the most animating experiences one can have is to come suddenly on something which acts as a binder, putting an armful of these fagots together and tying them in a neat, tight, orderly bundle. One is exhilarated beyond measure at seeing how big the bundle is, how beautifully the fagots are matched and fitted,—and all so unexpectedly. Sometimes it is a chance word or two in a book which does this, sometimes a chance word or two which one hears or overhears. Several times in the course of my life this has happened to me, and twice it has happened with such profound effect as to influence the whole course of my thought. In the one instance, this effect was due to a casual sentence dropped by a friend at a lunch-table; in the other, it was due to an article in a popular magazine which I had idly leafed over while waiting for something somewhere, I have forgotten what or where. I might as soon have expected to find a Koh-i-noor in a limestone-quarry as an article of that character in that publication.

The first incident was this: I was at lunch in the Uptown Club of New York with an old friend, Edward Epstean, a retired man of affairs. I do not remember what subject was under discussion at the moment; but whatever it was, it led to Mr. Epstean's shaking a forefinger at me, and saying with great emphasis, "I tell you, if self-preservation is the first law of human conduct, exploitation is the second."

This remark instantly touched off a tremendous flashlight in my mind. I saw the generalisation which had been staring me in the face for years without my having sense enough to recognise and identify it. Spencer and Henry George had familiarised me with the formula that man tends always to satisfy his needs and desires with the least possible exertion; but they had given me no idea of its immense scope, its almost illimitable range of action. If this formula were sound, as unquestionably it is, then certainly exploitation would be an inescapable corollary, because the easiest way to satisfy one's needs and desires is by exploitation. Indeed, if one wished to split hairs, one might say that exploitation is the first law of conduct, since even in self-preservation one tends always to take the easiest way; but the question of precedence is a small matter.

In an essay which I published some time ago, having occasion to refer to this formula, I gave it the name of Epstean's law, which by every precedent I think it should have. In their observations on the phenomena of gravitation, Huyghens and Kepler anticipated Newton closely. It was left for Newton to show the universal scope of an extremely simple formula, already well understood *in limine*, and hence this formula is known as Newton's law. As a phenomenon of finance, it had long been observed that "bad money drives out good," but Sir Thomas Gresham reduced these observations to order under a formula as simple as Newton's, and this formula is known as Gresham's law. So for an analogous service, more important than Gresham's and, as far as this planet is concerned, as comprehensive as Newton's, I thought that the formula, *Man tends always to satisfy his needs and desires with the least possible exertion*, should bear the name of Epstean's law.

I was indescribably fortunate in getting, as early as I did, a clear sense of the bearing which three great laws of the type known as "natural" have on human conduct. I say fortunate, for it was by good fortune alone, and not my own deserving, that I got this sense. By luck I stumbled on the discovery that Epstean's law, Gresham's law, and the law of diminishing returns operate as inexorably in the realm of culture; of politics; of social organisation, religious and secular; as they do in the realm of economics. This understanding enabled me at once to get the hang of many matters which far better men than I have found hopelessly puzzling, and to answer questions for which otherwise I could have found no answer.

For example, I have already shown in these pages how the current value of literature is determined by the worst type of literature in circulation—Gresham's law. Is not the value of education determined in the same way? I think there can be no doubt of it. Why did the projects of the reformers fail? Why did George's air-tight proposals fall by the wayside? What brought ruin and desolation in the wake of the "social legislation" championed by the recreant Liberals? Why was it impossible to improve society or the individual through political action? Simply because all such well-meant enterprises ran hard aground on Epstean's law. Something like republicanism or "democracy" will work after a fashion in a village or even a township, where everybody knows everybody and keeps an eye on what goes on. Why not, then, in a county, a state, a nation? Simply because the law of diminishing returns is against it. Will political nationalism, as we understand it, ever be made satisfactory or permanently practicable? Not as long as Epstean's law and the law of diminishing returns remain in force, for no one yet has ciphered out a way to beat them.

Once in the early nineteen-twenties some influential Russian friends who knew I had seen Russia to the best advantage under the old régime, quite pressed me to go there again and see what the new government was doing. They would make my way easy, get me every facility, introduce me to everybody, and so on. I vamped up some sort of excuse, and declined. My notion was that any one who knew the course of our republic's political history, and knew the incidence of the laws which turned us into that course and kept us to it, had no need to go to Russia to see the same laws in operation there. I may say that subsequent events in Russia have given me no reason to change my mind or regret my decision.

A week or so ago I spent the best part of a day with an extremely clever, interesting and delightful man who said he had put in two years of work on a plan for a political redistribution of power and territory after the present war. He described his plan in full detail; it took him about three hours. At each successive point he asked if I agreed; I said I did *ex animo*. When he ended, I told him I could find no flaw in his plan; it was complete, perfect, unassailable, as far as it went. "There is only one more little matter," I added. "If you can find some way to suspend the operation of Epstean's law, the whole thing is in your hands, and your plan will give us a magnificent new world. I hope you won't ask me how to do that, however, for truly I don't know."

With the exception of John Adams, who was the most profound student of government that this country ever produced, Chief Justice Jay always seemed to me the soundest and most far-sighted statesman of his time. Ten years after the Constitution was drafted, he wrote this (the italics are his):

> I do not expect that mankind will, before the millennium, be what they ought to be; and therefore, in my opinion, every political theory which does not regard them *as being what they are*, will prove abortive.

But a theory which regards men as being what they are must surely take into account the three laws which so largely determine their thought and conduct. No political theory does this. Beyond any peradventure it seemed to me that the theory of republicanism which overspread Western society after 1789 was about as far away from the Chief Justice's sensible requirement as it is possible to get. Hence I saw nothing for it but that a republican society must follow the historic pattern of gradual rise to a fairly high level of power and prestige, and then a rather sudden lapse into dissolution and displacement in favour of some other society which in turn would follow the same pattern. And so it was that at the age of thirty-five or so I dismissed all interest in public affairs, and have regarded them ever since as a mere spectacle, mostly a comedy, rather squalid, rather hackneyed, whereof I already knew the plot from beginning to end. I have written a little about them now and then, but from the standpoint only of a critical spectator, and as far as possible from any controversial or propagandist intent. Seven years ago I gathered up the substance of what I had to say, and published it under the title, *Our Enemy, the State.*[2] As for the predictions which I made at the end of this volume, I did not expect to live long enough to see them realised. In the short space of seven years, however, they all came true except the final one which seems even now to be in course of realisation.

IV

My adventure with the magazine-article was this: The article in question was an essay by the eminent architect Ralph Adams Cram, whose professional reputation is so great that it has unfortunately obscured his merits as a philosopher and man of letters. The essay's title, *Why We Do Not Behave Like Human Beings*, attracted me at once. This was just what had mystified me all my life; it was the one thing above all others that I wanted to know. I had read a good many theological disquisitions on the rationâle of human conduct, and had found them dissatisfying. If Mr. Cram had anything better to offer, if he could throw any light on that egregious problem, he was distinctly the man I wanted to see. The essay has been reprinted in his excellent book called *Convictions and Controversies*,[3] which deserves the highest recommendation to careful readers.

Mr. Cram's thesis is that we do not behave like human beings because the great majority of us, the masses of mankind, are not human beings. We have all along assumed that the

[2] Published by William Morrow and Co., New York, 1936.
[3] Published by the Marshall Jones Co., Boston.

zoölogical classification of man is also a competent psychical classification; that all creatures having the physical attributes which put them in the category of *Homo sapiens* also have the psychical attributes which put them in the category of human beings; and this, Mr. Cram says, is wholly unwarranted and an error of the first magnitude. Consequently we have all along been putting expectations upon the masses of *Homo sapiens* which they are utterly incapable of meeting. We have accepted them as psychically-human, dealt with them on that assumption, and expected a corresponding psychical reaction, when actually nothing of the sort is possible. They are merely the sub-human raw material out of which the occasional human being is produced by an evolutionary process as yet unexplained, but no doubt catastrophic in character, certainly not progressive.[4] Hence, inasmuch as they are the raw material of humanity, they are inestimably precious.

All this upset me frightfully. In my view of man's place in nature I was still a good disciple of Mr. Jefferson. I still believed that the masses of mankind are indefinitely improvable. Yet all the time I could see clearly that this view presented difficulties with which I could do nothing. How was it, for example, that I could find no shred of respectable evidence that psychically the masses of mankind had budged a single peg in six thousand years? Again, what about the enormous psychical "spread" between Socrates, Confucius, Marcus Aurelius, on the one hand, and on the other hand the Akka, the Australian bushman? This spread was prodigiously, almost infinitely, greater than the spread between the Akka and the anthropoid. What about those borderline forms whose classification either as *Homo sapiens* or as anthropoids is debatable? I still stuck to my view more or less mechanically, but I could

[4] With a poet's insight, the late Don Marquis had a glimpse of this theory. In his delightful *Chapters For the Orthodox*, he suggests as an analogy that in the days of *Pleiohippus* there may have been now and then a horse or two wandering around, regarded with distrust and disfavour by the sub-equine masses. The late Dr. S. D. McConnell, in his *Immortability* also brushed elbows with Mr. Cram's theory, but did not work it out in full.

not help thinking that progressive evolution had the devil's own job on its hands to straighten up matters like these, even granting its postulate of indefinite time.

What was one to do? When somebody comes along with a theory which accounts for everything otherwise unaccountable and answers all questions otherwise unanswerable, the chances are that he has the right pig by the ear. I held to my Jeffersonian doctrine for a long time, meanwhile trying my best to pick holes in Mr. Cram's theory, but with no success. I even published two essays, a year or so apart, one in Harper's and the other in the Atlantic, telling my troubles to the anthropologists and asking for help, but I had no answer. This seemed strange, for Dr. Carrel was just then bringing out his remarkable book called *Man, the Unknown*, and Mr. Hooton was making the welkin ring with demands for a closer study of the animal man. Left in the lurch as I was, I ended by striking my colours as gracefully as possible, parted company with the theologians, with Mr. Jefferson, with Price, Priestley, Condorcet, Rousseau, Mme. de Staël, and went over to the opposition with head unbowed and withers still unwrung.

My change of philosophical base had one curious and wholly unforeseen effect, though it followed logically enough. Since then I have found myself quite unable either to hate anybody or to lose patience with anybody; whereas up to that time I had always been a pretty doughty hater, and none too patient with people. So my change of base certainly brought me into a much more philosophical temper, and I suppose I might even say it brought me nearer to some sort of ramshackle Christian spirit. One can hate human beings, at least I could,—I hated a lot of them when that is what I thought they were,—but one can't hate sub-human creatures or be contemptuous of them, wish them ill, regard them unkindly. If an animal is treacherous, you avoid him but can't hate him, for that is the way he is. If cattle tramp down your garden, you drive them away but can't hate them, because you know they are acting up to the measure of their psychical capacity. If the mass-men of the forty-two photographs were not human beings, you couldn't hate them for not behaving like human beings. The mass-men who are princes, presidents, politicians, legislators, can no more transcend their psychical capacities than any wolf, fox or polecat in the land. How, then, is one to hate them, notwithstanding the appalling evil that they do?

My acceptance of Mr. Cram's theory also caused me for the first time really to like people-at-large. Before that I had frankly disliked people in the mass, though never unkindly. I was often amused by their doings, often interested, but with no feeling of affection. Now I find myself liking them, sometimes to a degree which I should have thought impossible. Flaubert found that *le seul moyen de rester tranquille dans son assiette, c'est de regarder le genre humain comme une vaste association de crétins et de canailles.* Unquestionably so; they are all of that. But when one gets it firmly fixed in one's head that they are living up to the measure of their own capacities and can not by any conjuration increase those capacities to the point of marking themselves as human beings, one comes at once to like them. At least, to my great surprise, I found myself doing so.

One has great affection for one's dogs, even when one sees them revelling in tastes and smells which to us are unspeakably odious. That is the way dogs are, one does not try to change their peculiar *penchant,* one knows the attempt would be futile, yet one likes them. The other day I saw a group of handsomely-dressed, well-kept women, most of them I think older than I am, in a huddle over a loathsome spread of "news from the front." At the moment of my glancing at them they were gloating with expressions of keen delight over some lurid account of the "huge piles of enemy dead" left by some dust-up in Russia. I did not dislike them, indeed I dare say I should have found the bloodthirsty old harpies quite likable if I had known them. That is the way they were, and they were living up to the best they knew. I thought of the women of Paris in October, 1789, I thought of Deborah and Jael, and of Fulvia driving her hairpin through the dead Cicero's tongue. I might have found them quite likable creatures if I had once for all consciously accepted them for what they were.

Of course, what the soldier said isn't evidence. No amount of sentiment goes any way at all in establishing Mr. Cram's theory of man's place in nature. Nevertheless, the fact does remain that on any other theory than his it is impossible for a reflective mind to regard our species otherwise than with disgust and loathing and contempt.

CHAPTER EIGHT

Peggio assai che l'averla perduta
Egli è il dir; la mia gente è caduta
In obbrobrio alle genti ed a me.

—BERCHET.

IN EUROPE, almost as soon as I had got my bearings there, I discovered that food can be interesting. I had been brought up on food that was good and abundant, but nothing to stir one's imagination. One excellent result of this was that I have always preferred a simple diet. Fortunately, any kind of good food agrees with me perfectly and I can eat it with relish, but I prefer the simpler sort, and in Europe I found out for the first time how much can be done with the simplest dishes. What is simpler than potato soup, casserole of veal, fish chowder, stewed chicken, partridge-and-cabbage? Yet in the country where I lived, these were works of art. Another good result of my being brought up in the unimaginative Anglo-American tradition of the table, is that I am no great stickler for variety. My appetite is not flighty. The Greeks never showed their wisdom better than when they said, "Let's have a fine thing two or three times over,"— Δὶς ἢ τρὶς τὰ καλά. If a dish pleases me, I hardly care how often I have it; I can pretty well eat it day in and day out. This monogamous habit clung to me when I was amidst the foods and wines of Europe, so no doubt I missed many confections which I should have looked into, but as I was not setting up for an epicure I did not mind.

What article of diet is more unpretending than Block Island turkey, otherwise known as salt codfish? We have three or four ways of dealing with it, all good, all fair-to-middling palatable, all profoundly unexciting. The Portuguese have forty-one; I think I must have sampled most of them. The way of it was that an altogether lovely and charming young Lisbonienne told me she knew the whole forty-one and could do nearly all of them herself, and among her family and friends the rest might be easily managed. If I could stay in Lisbon long enough, she would mobilise all her reserves and put me through the entire docket. This was impracticable, however, for I was going up through the country and would not return to Lisbon until the time came to take a steamer for Rotterdam. She compromised by giving me a list of dishes to pick from wherever I might be able to get them on my way; so, for a matter of two months or more I found myself subsisting mainly on salt codfish. Like a gallant girl who believed in her country's cause, she offered to forfeit a kiss for each dish I should report unfavourably when I came back to Lisbon. I was pretty sure there must be a chance for me somewhere in a list as long as that, but none turned up; so, being on my honour, I regretfully did the right thing, and never harvested a single kiss.

Thinking to do my American friends a good service, I brought over some cook-books which turned out to be useless. The trouble was that Dutch and Flemish and French cook-books are written for people who already know how to cook in those traditions. They are silent about all sorts of little matters which a native cook would attend to without being told, and which make all the difference in the world with the product. There seems to be even more to it than that, according to a pretty broad hint I got one day from the proprietor of my favourite restaurant in Brussels; a hint which made me think of Opie's famous answer, "With brains, sir," when some one asked him how he mixed his colours. I had screwed up my courage to ask this virtuoso if he would give me directions for making his type of stewed chicken, which was not quite in the mode of Mechelen or of Gand, and was far better than either. To my surprise he said he would do it with pleasure,—delighted,—if I could stop by next morning he would have the recipe for me in full detail. "But," he added, after a moment's reflection, "you can't make it."

"I can't make it after your directions?"

"Oh, no,—quite impossible. If you went into my kitchen and I stood by you all the time telling you what to do, even then you couldn't make it."

I got the recipe next day; it was all he said it would be. I still have it; but there the story ends.

It seems rather odd that after all my experience with European food I should have had to come back to the United States to find the one food which is not only the best in the world from the standpoint of dietetics, but also æsthetically the most interesting and (to me) the most palatable. Up to that time, sheer provincialism had kept me away from Chinese cookery in New York and San Francisco. I may have thought vaguely that birds' nests and rats were the staples of it; some silly quirk of fastidiousness, anyway. Once when I had come back from Europe for a three months' stay, however, my friend Mr. Chan Pak-Sun put me through a course of it to cure a villainous run of nervous dyspepsia, which it did in astonishingly short order. Since then I have stood by it consistently when I have been in this country, and have given it as careful study as I could. When I asked Mr. Chan to explain my remarkable cure, he said in his polite, deprecating way, "You must remember that my people had brought the science of cooking to practical perfection when your ancestors were eating their food raw." When one looks into the matter and puts a little thought on it, one sees how this is so.

It is a commonplace that a country's food is a reliable index to its degree of civilisation, and my experience has convinced me of its truth. Where I found the most interesting food, as in the Low Countries, Denmark, France, Norway, there I found the soundest idea of what civilisation means, and the clearest understanding of the discipline necessary to produce it. On the other hand, where I found the dullest appreciation of food, as in America and the British Isles, there I found the idea of civilisation standing at the lowest level, and there also by consequence I found its discipline most persistently disparaged and disallowed. The contrast gave me a lively notion of what existence would be like if the Anglo-American conception of civilisation should prevail in the world, as it then seemed likely to do, and now seems even likelier. Its chief representatives in those days were repulsive enough, but their successors today are men—and women—whose very names make one shudder.

II

In my early thirties I perceived that I could get on better outside my native land than in it, so I decided to put in as much as possible of my lifetime in some other part of the world. I had nothing against America or American society; nothing whatever. The author of the *Imitation* says acutely that "the fewer there be who follow the way to heaven, the harder that way is to find." My trouble was that hardly anybody was going up my street, which made the street hard to find and harder to keep to. Vandals had broken down most of the traffic-signs, and knaves of every description had so defaced the rest that they turned you off in the wrong direction at almost every fork and cross-road. Moreover, I knew I had nothing to contribute to our society that it would care to accept. The only contribution it would care for was something that might helpfully fall in with its doctrine of economism, and I had nothing of that sort to offer. The whole sum of it was that I was like a man who had landed in Greenland with a cargo of straw hats. There was nothing wrong with Greenland or with the hats, and the man might be on the best terms with the Greenlanders in a social way, but there was not the faintest chance of a market for his line of goods.

Economism was rampant in Europe, but it had not yet made a clean sweep of the survivals, the vestiges, of an opposing philosophy, nor had it yet obliterated all traces of traditional respect for that philosophy and for those who represented it. Not for nothing had Europe gone through its long, intensive experience of the doctrine that man does not live by bread alone, that the whole content of human life can not be summed up in the production, acquisition and distribution of wealth. America had no such fund of experience. Knowing only the philosophy of economism, it respected none other, made place for none other. One who represented any other was clearly superfluous in its society. His philosophical existence must be a hole-and-corner affair which he would carry on as a sort of spiritual Robin Hood. The prospect looked rather bleak and benumbing on the whole, so I decided that I had best pack up my philosophical straw hats as soon as might be, and go where there seemed to be a little more doing in my line.

This decision brought me in sight of the curious notion which Mr. Pearsall Smith observed as prevailing in American society, that a person who leaves America for reasons like mine is somehow unpatriotic and disloyal. I could not understand this, and the more I reflected on it the more mechanical and unintelligent this view of patriotism appeared to be. What is patriotism? Is it loyalty to a spot on a map, marked off from other spots by blue or yellow lines, the spot where one was born? But birth is a pure accident; surely one is in no way responsible for having been born on this spot or on that. Flaubert had poured a stream of corrosive irony on this idea of patriotism. Is it loyalty to a set of political jobholders, a king and his court, a president and his bureaucracy, a parliament, a congress, a *Duce* or *Führer*, a *camorra* of commissars? I should say it depends entirely on what the jobholders are like and what they do. Certainly I had never seen any who commanded my loyalty; I should feel utterly degraded if ever once I thought they could. Does patriotism mean loyalty to a political system and its institutions, constitutional, autocratic, republican, or what-not? But if history has made anything unmistakably clear, it is that from the standpoint of the individual and his welfare, these are no more than names. The reality which in the end they are found to cover is the same for all alike. If a tree be known by its fruits, which I believe is regarded as good sound doctrine, then the peculiar merit of a system, if it has any, ought to be reflected in the qualities and conditions of the people who live under it; and looking over the peoples and systems of the world, I found no reason in the nature of things why a person should be loyal to one system rather than another. One could see at a glance that there is no saving grace in any system. Whatever merit or demerit may attach to any of them lies in the way it is administered.

So when people speak of loyalty to one's country, one must ask them what they mean by that. What is one's country? Mr. Jefferson said contemptuously that "merchants have no country; the mere spot they stand on does not constitute so strong an attachment as that from which they draw their gains." But one may ask, why should it? This motive of patriotism seems to me perfectly sound, and if it be sound for merchants, why not for others who are not merchants? If it holds good in respect of material gains, why not of spiritual gains, cultural gains, intellectual and æsthetic gains? As a general principle, I should put it that a man's country is where the things he loves are most respected. Circumstances may have prevented his ever setting foot there, but it remains his country. If Mr. Ford and Mr. Rockefeller had been born in Burma and lived all their lives there, America would still be their country, their spiritual home, with the first call on their every patriotic sentiment. They would, as we say, "belong here," because here is where the things they love are devoutly, nay, exclusively respected. Then if they came here in person, one would envy them their emotion at finding themselves spiritually in step with an enormously numerous society whose sole basic philosophy was theirs. What could be more exhilarating than the sense of complete spiritual unity with more than a hundred million of one's fellow-beings? After all, as Dumas said, "man is man's brother."

Burke touches this matter of patriotism with a searching phrase. "For us to love our country," he said, "our country ought to be lovely." I have sometimes thought that here may be the rock on which Western civilisation will finally shatter itself. Economism can build a society which is rich, prosperous, powerful, even one which has a reasonably wide diffusion of material well-being. It can not build one which is lovely, one which has savour and depth, and which exercises the irresistible power of attraction that loveliness wields. Perhaps by the time economism has run its course the society it has built may be tired of itself, bored by its own hideousness, and may despairingly consent to annihilation, aware that it is too ugly to be let live any longer.

Yet I have always a regard for the America I had known in my earlier years. In those days the ineffectual impulse which moved my friends the reformers and "progressives" was at least understandable. One could think of American society as Bishop Warburton thought of the English Church, that like the ark of Noah it "is worth saving, not for the sake of the unclean beasts that almost filled it and probably made most noise and clamour in it, but for the little corner of rationality that was as much distressed by the stink within as by the tempest without." Nevertheless, with America's basic philosophy what it was, and is, how could the thing be done?

In Europe I watched the slow relentless suffocation of life's amenities as the various peoples were forced closer and closer into the pattern set by economism. Brussels was Brussels when I first saw it; amenity still existed in its society, the whole organisation of its life was amiable. Its pleasures and diversions were amiable, unmechanised, satisfying. They gave the sense of being taken as a wholesome and regular part of life. One was as much at home in the museums, the concert-hall, the theatre, the opera, as in one's own house. Going to the opera was not a laborious and costly job, and it gave one no sense of being let in on a purely professional occasion. I would get a light, unhurried dinner at the Trois Suisses or the Pourquoi Pas, and then when the bell rang I would leave my hat and overcoat in the restaurant, walk twenty steps to the Monnaie's side-entrance, and join in a performance of high professional excellence pervaded by the spirit of the highly-gifted, highly-cultivated amateur. I say "join in" advisedly, for one felt that one belonged there, one was a participant, not an auditor, an outsider. Then when the performance was over, I would retrieve my hat and coat, stroll over to some near-by resort for a taste of steamed mussels and Spatenbräu beer while I listened to some energetic discussion, perhaps of the opera, perhaps of any other subject under the sun, and then if the night were pleasant I would walk home.

All this is perhaps a small matter, but it will pass as an illustration showing how the aggregate of many such small matters combined with some that were larger to make up the total of an amiable life. In my years there, however, I saw the curious phenomenon of great continuous improvement in the mechanics of civilisation going on *pari passu* with deterioration in the quality of civilisation itself. Economism kept bringing in a steadily increasing volume and variety of the apparatus of civilisation, its comforts, conveniences, devices to save time and labour, devices which if used intelligently would promote amenity; but with a curious constancy, the larger this volume of apparatus grew, the fewer and scantier the amenities of life became, and the faster the general standards of civilisation declined. One remarked the progress of this deterioration wherever one looked, in the current ideals of taste, manners, education, culture, religion, morals and art.

In Belgium I observed also that as the material benefits of economism increased and multiplied, not only did the quality of civilisation deteriorate, but also the quality of happiness.

One of the things which mainly attracted me to Brussels in the first instance was the evidence of happiness I saw there, notwithstanding the slightness of the material basis on which they rested. An American who had some business connexion there,—this was in 1911,—said to me one day, "It's a queer place. From our point of view everything in the country is dead wrong, and yet they seem to be the happiest people I ever saw." This remark made an impression on me, for I had just returned from America where I could not see that as a people we were happier than we were in the bad old times before economism had given us so much apparatus. What I saw in both countries convinced me that like the task of civilising a society, the task of making it happy is beyond the power of economism, quite as the religionists and moralists have said it is.

When the war of 1914 broke out, I was not prepared to attribute more than a purely casual significance to it. Having its roots in the philosophy of economism, it served only to accelerate a degenerative process which had been steadily going on since first that philosophy overspread Western society. In my view it was a mere incident, more or less spectacular, in the general "course of rebarbarisation" which Herbert Spencer in 1898 so clearly saw Western society taking. Its antecedents being what they were, it was a consequence inevitable at some time or other, and the time happened to be then. With this view of the war I naturally had no interest in it. What I saw of its action, which was not much, has so far passed out of my memory that I doubt I could recall any of it accurately. I kept no track of it, read no newspapers, heard few reports. When one has known for forty years precisely how a society's course of rebarbarisation must turn out in the long-run, one does not waste one's attention on day-to-day incidents of its progress.

I have often thought it might be amusing to write a humorous essay on how to recognise the Dark Ages when you are in them. Did the average European in the last half of the fourth century know that the Dark Ages were closing in on him? I rather doubt it. Probably he took the overspreading of ignorance, corruption, violence and bestiality as being pretty much the regular thing, and evading or warding off their impact was merely so much in the day's work. Probably many of them took this state of things as a challenge, as the world's normal dare, and barged in ruthlessly to beat it on its own terms, at anybody's cost but their own. People are like that now, and doubtless were like that then. In all likelihood the man of the Dark Ages did not recognise symptoms, or know what they meant, or pay any attention to them. Indeed, how could he? Knowing no history, he could not understand history, and so he had no rule of comparison by which to measure the quality of his civilisation and determine whether it was changing for the better or the worse. The tide-gauges set up by Lucilius, Juvenal, Horace, Persius, Tacitus, may as well not have existed, as far as he was concerned.

Since 1914 I have been watching social symptoms, especially in the United States where economism has had everything its own way and has done its best. Here again the neolithic masses of the present day have no historical measure of their own society; virtually no one knows anything of what has gone before him, still less could understand its interpretation. Virtually all accept economism's word for it that where you have "prosperity," railways, banks, newspapers, industry, trade, there of necessity you have civilisation. One who hinted that a society might have all these and yet remain uncivilised; or that a society might have almost nothing of any of them, and still be quite highly civilised;—anyone hinting at this would be laughed at. Since 1914 the only virtues that I have seen glorified with any kind of sincerity or spontaneous acclaim are barbaric virtues, the virtues of the jazz-artist and the cinema-hero, tempered on occasion by the virtues of Jenghiz Khan, Attila, Brennus. The ideals I have seen most seriously and purposefully inculcated are those of the psychopath on the one hand; and on the other, those of the homicidal maniac, the plug-ugly and the thug. In a book published three or four years ago, an able and experienced observer of social symptoms, Dr. Alexis Carrel, says:

> Moral sense is almost completely ignored by modern society; we have, in fact, suppressed its manifestations. All are imbued with irresponsibility. . . . Robbers enjoy prosperity in peace; gangsters are protected by politicians and respected by judges; they are the heroes whom children admire in the cinema and imitate in their games. . . . Sexual morals have been cast aside; psychoanalysts supervise men and women in their conjugal relations. There is no difference between wrong and right, just and unjust. . . . Ministers have rationalised religion; they have destroyed its mystical basis. They are content with the part of policemen, helping in the interest of the wealthy to preserve the framework of present society; or, like politicians, they flatter the appetites of the crowd.[1]

Turning then to another order of social symptoms, Dr. Carrel says further:

> In the state of New York, according to C. W. Beers, one person out of every twenty-two has to be placed in an asylum at some time or other. In the whole of the United States, . . . each year about 68,000 new cases are admitted to insane asylums and similar institutions. If the admissions continue at such a rate, about one million of the children and young people who are today attending schools and colleges will sooner or later be confined in asylums. In the state hospitals there were in 1932, 340,000 insane. There were also in special institutions 81,580 feeble-minded and epileptics, and 10,930 on parole. These statistics do not include the mental cases treated in private hospitals. In the whole country, besides the insane, there are 500,000 feeble-minded; and in addition, surveys made under the auspices of the National Committee for Mental Hygiene have revealed that at least 400,000 children are so unintelligent that they cannot profitably follow the courses of the public schools. In fact, the individuals who are mentally deranged are far more numerous. It is

[1] *Man, the Unknown*, ed. Harper, p. 153.

estimated that several hundred thousand persons not mentioned in any statistics are affected with psychoneuroses.[2]

I suppose one might add to this the testimony of a prominent alienist who told me lately that while the secrecy of the drug-habit makes it impossible to get accurate statistics, a conservative estimate would put it that more than two million of our population are to some degree dependent upon drugs. Perhaps it might also be remarked that in the spring of 1941 the Selective Service System reported that forty per cent of the men examined for the draft had been rejected as physically unfit for service.

The quality of civilisation attested by these symptoms does not appear too much unlike what one would have expected to find prevailing in the Dark Ages. In the face of it one can only smile at all the current sublimated drivel about the preciousness of "democracy." Yet it is nothing to get stirred up about, to arouse resentment, or to evoke the pestilent meddlings of what Mr. H. G. Wells calls the Gawdsaker. Mere hopeful fiddling with these symptoms by devices of political quackery does nothing but aggravate the radical disorder which gives rise to them. The widespread corruption of a society which has committed itself root and branch to the philosophy of economism is to be regarded *sub specie aeternitatis* as simply an example of cause and effect. "Things and actions are what they are," Bishop Butler said, "and the consequences of them will be what they will be." There is no known way in the nature of things for well-meaning persons to play the part of deputy-Providence and cut in on the acceptance of a social philosophy to make it bring forth any social consequences save those it must bring forth.

During the last twenty years I have often thought it would be rather a grim joke on our pretentiousness and gullibility, if some pukka historian of, say, A.D. 2942 should decide that the apprehensions of Max Nordau's "more highly-developed

[2] *Op. cit.*, p. 154.

minds" were well-founded, and that a second Dusk of the Nations had set in on Western society about A.D. 1870. I am not at all sure but that he might make out a pretty plausible case for that date, when the time comes.

III

Living in Brussels in the years before 1914 was to me curiously like living with one's best girl in the days of chivalry and romance. You liked to visit other cities, look them over, perhaps make up to them a little, maybe chuck one or two of them under the chin, but when the train rolled into the good old North Station and you came out on the Place Rogier into the dear creature's arms, you would not trade her off for a whole haremful of what you have seen. Her ways and manners, her unpretending grace and charm, her feel of stability and soundness, are all just as you have been impatiently expecting to find them, and her face wears a jolly Flemish smile as you whisper in her ear the phrase of pure contentment, *Oost west, t'huis best.*

She has a pair of attractive sisters, Antwerp and Liége, and doesn't care how much you philander with them; in fact, she rather likes it, for it is all in the family and she isn't above a wicked sisterly satisfaction in putting their noses out of joint. She is not even jealous of her shoe-string cousin Luxemburg, a raving beauty, but encourages you to go over every spring for a long flirtatious visit. She herself is perhaps a little on the plain side when you think of the opulent handsomeness of Paris or Kiev, although her city-hall square is the finest single-group object in Europe. One of the pleasantest ways to spend an idle morning is to sit in front of a café on the north-west corner of the square with some beer and a field-glass, and pick out the ornamental details of the city hall and the guild-houses. As often as I did this I never failed to find some spot of beauty that I had not noticed before. Knowing that the spire of the city hall was completed exactly fifty years before Columbus sailed gives rise to many reflections. One thinks there may be something in Artemus Ward's idea that it would have been better for the world if the savages had given Chris a warm meal and sent him home again ore the ragin Billers.

Aside from this one feature Brussels has little to take the eye of the sightseer or casual visitor. Her points of beauty and interest are disclosed only gradually to her intimates, which is as it should be. The street-names in the old part of town were a matter of unending diversion to me in my hours of idleness. Those which marked the street as a seat of some occupation, institution, or personage, were easy,—Chicken-market Street, Hospital Street, Bishop's Street. So were those named for some physical peculiarity, like One-person Street, so narrow that two can hardly pass without "scrooging." But many streets have names whose significance is completely lost. In my dalliance with them I did not really wish to know what their significance was, nor would I have thanked any one for telling me. I believe some Belgian archivist has done something with the subject, but I never cared to look up his findings. Aware that a street is the most nearly permanent of all human institutions, my satisfaction was only in musing over them, guessing, contemplating the retrospect over the long course of busy life which they had witnessed.

Stoofstraat,—there almost certainly was the site of a public bath in the Middle Ages when, strange as it may seem, people did more bathing than they did in the Renaissance and afterwards. Krakeelstraat, the street of the Quarrel,—what quarrel, and when, and why? One would say it must somehow have been a pretty distinguished affair, for quarrels were never uncommon here in the old days. The little street not a pistol-shot long, called Eclipse,—was a tavern or some sort of rendezvous by that name located there? The street of the Virgins, —what virgins and what was the connexion? I heard the vague legend that a mediæval fountain stood there, three naked girls in stone *à croupetons*, delivering water after the naïve manner of the Manneken-Piss. It may have been so; this bit of naturalism was not an uncommon design for fountains in the Middle

Ages. Zespennigenstraat, the street of the Six Counters, what we now call poker-chips,—a large building, extremely old, stands here, which by all appearances was once an inn. I thought that in mediæval times it might have been one called the Six Counters, and the street took its name from that. There was considerable business going on in that neighbourhood; the street called Navets suggests a vegetable-market or herb-market, and the Potbakkersstraat testifies that the flourishing earthenware-industry had its headquarters there; so probably an inn thus conveniently situated would get some trade.

But life in Brussels was not all dreams and visions, nor yet was it all beer and skittles. Brussels was always a hard-working, busy town, and in that atmosphere I did more and better work,—if one can call it work,—than I ever succeeded in doing anywhere else. One could read and study with unruffled attention and think with undisturbed concentration. Oddly enough, one would say that my immediate surroundings were anything but conducive, especially in my last habitation. My living-room was an immense affair, nearly fifty feet long by thirty wide, with a handsome parquetry flooring, probably once a ball-room. It was full of authentic Second Empire furniture, with mirrors galore, and large oil-paintings in gilt frames. My landlord told me that once when the old queen was having her portrait painted, she chose to come here for her sittings in order to get the real thing in background and surroundings. I do not vouch for this, for the old gentleman's tongue hung in the middle, and some instinct told me he was not always reliable. Still, I must say that the queen could not have chosen better for her purpose, so the story may have been true. A humble student might expect to feel lost and addled in the midst of all this gorgeousness, but I found it inspiring and delightful. My improvised work-table was a tiny thing with a heavy top in brown mottled marble, but it served me, as I said, for the best of what little literary work I have ever done.

In Brussels one passed one's days in the rich, balanced, intelligently-organised sort of life that I had vaguely felt must exist somewhere, if only one could find it. One could work at one's best as long as one liked, then stroll out, sure to find pleasures that were intelligent, diverting, restful, the kind from which one always learns something. On almost any summer evening a concert would be going on in the city-hall square. There were more musical societies in Brussels than there were black cats, and a more deadly spirit of rivalry among them than cats ever knew. It is an inspiring sight to see the Amphion Society (or whatever its name might be) march around the square and into the stand, full of grim determination to make the Arion Society, who are to play there tomorrow night, sound like fish-pedlars. I heard Meyerbeer's *Struensee* played there one evening by some amateur group in a way that I have long hoped to hear again, but never have. In the fifteenth century the Low Countries taught music to the whole of Europe, as Rabelais bears witness in the incomparable prologue to his Fourth Book, and they still can do it. The Belgian musician has all the scholarly correctness of the German, and he adds to it an unfailing superiority of intelligence, an elegance of finish, a style and grace, which I have never found elsewhere.

My club was the most interesting in Europe, I believe, and I would wager incidentally that it set the best table of any. It was made up largely of the official set, endlessly experienced, hard-baked, devoid of illusions, who discussed the rationâle of public affairs with Bismarckian frankness. I so well remember the wily old stager Baron X, as he sat with me for long hours one evening five years ago, dissecting "the European situation" like a surgeon, and telling me precisely what would come of it, and why. Again, in conversations on trains or street-cars or in cafés one would get the talk of mature, experienced people. Belgians have a good deal of the Americans' gregariousness and affability; they enjoy passing the time of day with strangers. Once in a chance talk about political theory under the new régimes in Russia, Italy, and Germany, my fellow-gossip said impatiently, "Oh, that's all the same thing, that's Statism. We know all about that, we went through it years ago." He was one of the plain people, not a student; I gathered that he had some sort of commercial agency, for he seemed to be familiar with various kinds of machinery. I wonder how many such men in America would know that Communism, the New Deal, Fascism, Nazism, are merely so-many trade-names for collectivist Statism, like the trade-names for tooth-pastes which are all exactly alike except for the flavouring.

Then again of an evening there might be the chance of an hour's chat with Mme. B. after one had watched her spit fire at Filena in *Mignon*; or a discreet making-up to Filena herself when she had laid aside her stage-trappings, a charming person and a great beauty. Or perhaps one might make up a little more seriously to another charmer, then about at the end of her student days, full of hope and ambition, ready to shine brilliantly in *Les Noces de Jeannette*. A truly lovely young woman, and the most bewitching of soubrette singers, her career was ruined by a strange disability. After three years of heroic struggle at the Opéra-Comique, she was driven off the boards and almost into insanity by incurable stage-fright. I do not know what became of her, except that she survived the war. I met her accidentally about fifteen years after her retirement, and spent two or three days with her at her home in a suburb of Paris. Our talk often took a nostalgic turn, which made my visit rather a sad one, on the whole. Her first reminiscence was of going over in the old days to eat *moules-frites* on the Beenhouwersstraat, after the opera. Odd, I thought, that such a trifling matter should have been the first to rise to the surface of her memory.

Tout s'en va, tout passe, l'eau coule, et le cœur oublie. That is how life is, and one should be thankful for it, as Flaubert goes on to say, for the soul could not bear the whole weight of accumulated experience that piles up day by day. Yet one is thankful, too, when some trifle of sentimental recollection has unexpectedly escaped oblivion. One of the great historic scenes which I would give much to have witnessed took place in front of a café opposite the Comédie Française. George Sand passed by, a dowdy, musty old woman, making her way against a driving rain, and collided with a little old man who wore a decoration in his button-hole. Untangling their umbrellas, they both lost their temper and blackguarded each other venomously for several minutes. One of a group inside the café said, "Gentlemen, there is something worth seeing. That man is Jules Sandeau." Once they had lived together, perhaps married, and had collaborated in literary work for some time. Now neither had recognised the other. Better so, no doubt. It seems unnatural and harsh, but *telle est la vie. Les nœuds les plus solidement faits se denœuent d'eux-mêmes parce que la corde s'use. C'est une grande misère, mais. . . .*

IV

Several times I have spoken of my luck. Good fortune has indeed followed me with strange persistency, up to the last three or four years. Previous to that, to the best of my recollection, no misfortune ever befell me but such as I brought on myself. Nor do I recall that I ever had a door closed on me without my subsequently discovering the best of reasons why it should have been closed. I doubt that many can say as much for the impersonal direction of their passage through life. My one piece of bad luck came at the outset, in my being born when and where I was. I do not say this by way of complaint, nor do I hold it as a grievance against the order of the universe, for I have no grievance nor any complaint to make. On the contrary, I feel that with the luck which has attended me, I have done extremely well, undeservedly well. Nevertheless the fact stands; and even so, I count myself lucky beyond expression to have lived through the last sixty years rather than the next sixty.

Probably most reflective persons have now and then looked back desirously on some period, some civilisation as better suited to them than their own. One of my friends was saying to me only the other evening that he would like to have lived in

London of the eighteenth century. Others have spoken of Elizabethan England as their choice, and others again of Athens in the days of Pericles. My choice would be for none of these. If I could have made a deal with an easy-going Providence, I would have elected to be born in the Paris of 1810, and after a year or so of quiet retirement on the island of Port-Cros, slip out of life in the autumn of 1885 and be buried there in the unkempt little cemetery near the manor-house. My only stipulation would be for as good an education as the one I have had, and for money enough to go on with in a reasonable way, without anxiety.

The blight of economism did not settle on all classes in France until long after 1840; indeed, as late as 1860 one did not see the evidences of its contaminating contact on every hand. People stayed where they were, content in the practical philosophy of Candide; an unsettled, nomadic life did not attract them. In 1850 France had barely fifteen hundred miles of ramshackle railways, their ownership parcelled out among twenty-four companies, all virtually bankrupt. When Thiers held the portfolio of the Interior he went over to England to inspect the railway-systems, and on his return said, "I do not think railways are suited to France," thus setting back railway-construction a good ten years. Noble fellow, Thiers!—one can forgive him a great deal for that. Even after 1870, even after the Second Empire had strained every nerve to push the cause of economism, France obstinately remained a country of agriculture, artisanship, crafts and trades, home industries. Paris itself remained a city of small shops which were closed for a couple of hours each noon and for a month or so each summer. The idea that there is something to live for besides the production, acquisition and distribution of wealth—this idea died a slow, hard death in France. One whom fate had cast for the part of a native of Paris in the period 1810-1885 would have had all the best of it.

For never in the world, I believe, have so many great practitioners of the good life, the truly humane life, been gathered together in one place, as in the Paris of that period. In no other society could a humble amateur of the humane life get so effortlessly a clear and complete conception of what that life is, what its philosophy is, and what its rewards are. In no other civilisation, if I may say so, would he find himself less an alien, less a superfluous man.

One reason for my choice, perhaps the main reason, is that among the fourscore names which occur to me off-hand there are so many borne by men whom one would give anything to have known, irrespective of their achievements and proficiencies. This is most unusual. At other times and places there were men whom one admires and respects immensely, but one does not feel attracted to their society. With all one's exalted reverence for Herbert Spencer one would be indifferent to his acquaintance. One is not drawn to Carlyle, Mill, Dickens, Ruskin, Matthew Arnold, Trollope, by what one knows of them, any more than to Thiers, Balzac, Eugène Sue. Works on the social life of Paris in the nineteenth century,—among many others, the memoirs of Véron, Houssaye, Bertaut, Halévy, du Camp, Daudet, Claudin, Scholl and the anonymous author of *An Englishman in Paris*,—these testify that one would hardly know how to choose among those from whom the light of the humane life shone out with such irresistible fascination. To have grown up with Guizot, Cousin, Villemain, Duruy; to have been on friendly terms with Ste.-Beuve. Renan, Scherer, Taine; with the novelists Dumas, Mérimée, Daudet, Tourgueniev; the painters Delacroix and Horace Vernet; the poets de Vigny, Leconte de Lisle, Sully-Prudhomme, de Musset; the musicians Adam, Auber, Meyerbeer, Rossini, Offenbach! The list seems endless.

In the Brussels of the incoming century one lived on remnants, it is true, but they were sound remnants. One could still feel oneself at the centre of things, which was what I needed to clean off whatever spots of provincialism and parochialism might be defacing my philosophy of existence. I had been forming my views of life and mankind on my own, as every dweller in America, where the winds of doctrine blow only one way, is obliged to do. I was uncertain about them, needing reassurance of what in them might be right even more, perhaps, than correction of what might be wrong. For this a larger experience was necessary, an exposure to as many different "climates of opinion" as I could find, and Brussels afforded it. The civilisations of Holland, Germany, Luxemburg, France and Austria were all within easy reach, and ever since the twelfth century Brussels had done as big a trade in ideas as it had done in merchandise.

CHAPTER NINE

Those who can not remember the past are condemned to repeat it.

—GEORGE SANTAYANA.

Man, biologically considered, . . . is the most formidable of all the beasts of prey, and indeed the only one that preys systematically on his own species.

—WILLIAM JAMES.

THE war of 1914 ended in an orgy of looting, as any rational being might have known it would, even if he had never heard of the secret treaties which predetermined this ending. It ended as all wars have ended and must end. Any pretence to the contrary is mere idleness. One can say for Brennus that he was no hypocrite, exuding repulsive slaver about "mandates," "reparations," and the like. He chucked his sword on the scales, saying *Vae victis*, and that was that. Of all the predatory crew assembled at Versailles, the only one for whom I had a grain of respect was old Clémenceau. He was a robber and a brigand, but he never pretended to be anything else, and he was a robber in the grand style. His attitude towards his associates pleased me. He regarded Lloyd George, Wilson, Orlando and their attendant small-fry from a lofty height of disdain, as one might imagine Jesse James or Dick Turpin regarding a gang of confidence men, area-sneaks, porch-climbers. He also took no pains to disguise his opinion of them, which delighted me. If you left your watch and pocket-book at home, you could do business with Clémenceau. He would not poison your rum-and-water or besmear your character, and all his cards were on the table. As highwaymen go, one has a good bit of respect for that sort.

In my view, the most significant and distressing result of the war was one which has gone virtually unnoticed; it completed the destruction of Europe begun by the war of 1870. Before that there had existed a very real European spirit, a community of understanding, a reciprocity in culture, which expressed itself in many common modes of thought and feeling, even of action. One gets probably the most complete understanding of it from the writings of the great *Weltbürger* Goethe. The persistent pernicious meddling of England in Continental affairs had done all it could to check the unifying influence of this spirit on European political organization, and Bismarck, as the architect of the imperial Germany, finished the job. It was after the events of 1870 that the Austrian *Reichskanzler* von Beust made his celebrated remark, "Europe no longer exists." This was strictly true. The European spirit, which was the only Europe worth preserving, the only Europe that held any promise for the future, the only Europe that the student of civilised man cared two straws about,—this spirit was finally asphyxiated in smoke from the guns of von Steinmetz and Frederick-Charles.

Economism then had a clear field. The European spirit was everywhere promptly replaced by the spirit of an unintelligent, myopic, dogged, militant, political and economic nationalism, and the war of 1914 fixed this spirit upon Europe forever, as far as one can see. Wilson's shallow stultiloquence about "self-determination" and "the rights of small nations" rationalised it everywhere to the complete satisfaction of the political mind, and gave it respectability as good sound separatist doctrine. Epstean's law immediately and on all sides swept in an enormous herd of political adventurers, the innumerable Pilsudskis, Horthys, Kerenskys, Masaryks, Beneshes, big and little, and kept them working tooth and nail to provide pasturage for themselves in a mishmash of little twopenny succession-states.

In each of these, strictly according to pattern, they made it their first business to surround themselves with a high-tariff wall and order up a first-class army.

It appeared to me, then, when the war was over, that Western society was an extremely sick patient on the world's hands, and as happens in the case of certain diseases, its condition would have to get very much worse before it could get better. The palliatives and opiates of political empiricism ladled out like Mrs. Squeers's brimstone and treacle every morning of the next two decades turned out to be sheer quackery. The effect of this dosage strengthened my conviction that death alone could rid the social body of the bacteria of economism and Statism. It was a fair presumption that as long as the planet can support a population it will have one of sorts, and that the population will organise itself into some form of society. No doubt, then, there would in time be cobbled up in Europe and America a social reconstruction in one shape or another. But before this could take place there must be a longer or shorter period of death-throes in the existing order, a period like the Dark Ages, when "the casual anonymous forces of dissolution will be supreme." This was what had happened before, and with conditions being what they were, there seemed every reason to believe it was what would happen again.

What puzzled me profoundly was this: The history of all human institutions affords a study which is really very simple, of the operation of three great natural laws in the realm of the spirit. *Homo sapiens* is so remarkably sapient about the incidence of natural law in the physical world, and so resourceful about adapting himself to it—why, then, is he so impenetrably stupid about recognising the incidence of natural law in the spiritual world, and about accommodating his plans and doings to its inflexible operation? When *Homo sapiens* discovered that electricity always follows the path of least resistance, it took him no time at all to perceive that the thing to do was to arrange a path for lightning to follow, and then stay out of that path. The habits of electricity are a recondite matter, but

Homo sapiens was equal to discovering and dealing with them intelligently. Why is he apparently unequal to discovering and dealing intelligently with the natural laws which can bear so disastrously upon the social institutions which he attempts to form?

In response to an urgent social demand, a revolutionary régime was set up in France in 1789. At the outset it was backed and promoted by men of far-seeing intelligence, including a good part of the aristocracy. They charted the revolution's course, and made a good job of it. Taine says truly that the French aristocrats were never so worthy of power as when they were on the point of losing it. The thing to be remarked is that the primary interest of these men and the primary intention of the revolution were *social.*

Then at the moment when the revolution became a going concern, Epstean's law brought in a waiting troop of political adventurers whose interest was not social but *institutional.* Their views of the social demand which brought the revolutionary organisation into being were shaped by that interest. As Benjamin Franklin put it, they were of the sort whose sense of political duty is, first, to themselves; second, to their party; and third (if anything be left over) to society. Their aim was to make the revolution serve this institutional interest, and in virtue of their numbers and peculiar aptitudes they rather easily did so.

Then Gresham's law struck in. As the numbers of this latter group increased, their interest became the prevailing interest, and their view the prevailing view. Social interest was rapidly driven out, and as almost always happens in the case of political revolutions, those who represented it were lucky if they escaped with their lives.

Then finally the law of diminishing returns took hold. As the institution grew in size and strength, as its confiscations of social power increased in frequency and magnitude, as its coercions upon society multiplied, the welfare of society (which the original intention of the revolution was to promote) became correspondingly depleted and attenuated.

These three laws dog the progress of every organisation of mankind's effort. Organised charity, organised labour, organised politics, education, religion,—look where you will for proof of it, strike into their history at any point of time or place. In view of this, the question of collective behaviour which baffled me was the one which baffled Henry Adams. Why, if *Homo sapiens* be really sapient, does he not take these laws into account in designing his institutions? I suppose that in his search for an answer, Adams had encountered as much feeble talk about "poor fallible human nature" as I had, and been as impatient with it. He died puzzled, as I expected to do, and should have done if subsequently I had not been lucky enough to come upon Mr. Cram's theory of man's place in nature, which answered my question at once. There was a stroke of fate's irony in this, for Mr. Cram was on friendly terms with Adams; it was he who got Adams's consent to a commercial publication of *Mont-St.-Michel and Chartres*. Mr. Cram, however, did not broach his theory until a good many years after Adams's death.

So as I surveyed the symptoms displayed by high-pressure nationalism in post-war Europe, my knowledge of these three laws gave me a clear idea of what to expect from it. The furore of jubilation over the spread of "democracy" did not impress me, for I knew as well as Chief Justice Jay that "every political theory which does not regard mankind as being what they are, will prove abortive." The peoples had once more been persuaded, browbeaten, coerced or otherwise bedevilled into the old stock notion that adopting this-or-that political system would make nationalism permanently workable; whereas to make it workable under any system is ludicrously beyond their collective psychical capacities. I did not yet know *why* it was beyond their capacities; I was willing to believe that in course of progressive evolution it would not always be so. The present fact, however, was that by no conjuration could the thing be done.

II

During the decade following the war I lived in New York for four years, engaged in getting out a weekly publication modelled in format and general appearance after the style of the London Spectator. I had no illusions about the enterprise, for I knew it had no prospect of ever even beginning to pay for itself, and therefore it could not last long. Gresham's law had already made hay of our periodical literature. My opinion on this point was not asked, and I did not proffer it; in fact, I believe this is the first time I have spoken of it. The venture did, however, present the chance of what I thought might be an interesting experiment, which turned out to be so, far beyond my expectations.

The idea was, first, to see whether such a paper as we had in mind could be produced in this country. I did not believe it could be; I doubted that there was enough latent literary ability of that grade to supply us with contributors. I was soon proven wrong about that. Then, second, we proposed to see whether the quality and character of the paper could be successfully held up from issue to issue. Jumping three or four hurdles of the same height is perhaps no great feat, but jumping fifty-two at a stretch is another matter. Again I had sturdy doubts that this could be done, and again I was proven wrong. Finally, we thought that the paper's distribution might give us some sort of rough measure of the general level at which the best culture of the country stood. I had my own ideas about this also, and for once I was approximately right. Any one who remembers the state of the public mind in the early 'nineteen-twenties does not need to be told that we launched our experiment under as unfavourable circumstances as could well be imagined; and this made such success as we had all the more satisfactory to me. In my eyes the marvel was, and will always be, that we had any success at all.

We produced what was quite generally acknowledged to be the best paper published in our language. I think it was that. Moreover, its character and quality were maintained at an exact level throughout the four years of its existence. Looking through a volume of any year, one will find each issue precisely as good as those preceding it and those following; precisely the same character of philosophical and literary integrity. No issue had any soft spots or padding, nor did it have any "features" or star contributors. The paper must have made some sort of mark, in a way, for I notice that after twenty years a thin tradition of it still survives. I still see it mentioned once in a while in some connexion, and always with respect, almost always with some little touch of affection.

I feel free to speak thus frankly of the paper's quality because I had far less to do with forming or maintaining it than people think I had. My chief associate was (or I should say is, for he is still living) one of the ablest men I ever knew, far abler than I, and more experienced. He did not live in New York and had less frequent contact with the office, so on this account I gravitated into the status of a *chargé d'affaires*. With the business of the concern I punctiliously had nothing to do. I think an editor should follow the line of William Winter's policy, who throughout his long career as a critic of the drama steadfastly refused to meet an actor or actress or (I believe, but am not quite sure) a stage-director or producer. Our business manager was an old friend and a sensitive gentleman who kept as decorously out of my cabbage-patch as I out of his. Our relations were affectionate and delightful, but we never talked business.

Once only he criticised my judgement. It was at the outset, when we were setting up the office and I had put out bait for a stenographer. After the usual run of unemployable applicants had subsided, Miss A was announced, and a drooping, drawling, slacktwisted creature produced herself and collapsed into a chair. We had a few words, and I told her to be on hand next day, and meanwhile to stop in at the manager's office and tell him to put her on the payroll. The manager was disgusted. "You're a fine one," he said. "That wishy-washy wench you sent down this morning doesn't know enough to come in when it rains. You'd let any pretty red-head with a drawl and a seventeenth-century face wander in here any time and pull your leg." The young lady dawdled in next morning and went to work. A month later she graduated out of stenography, and at the end of four months she had mastered the routine of proofreading, indexing, making up dummies, seeing the paper through the press, and was running the office.

I mention this because it brings me around to my qualifications as an executive. I had only two. I am probably the poorest judge of character now living; none could be worse. A person might be a survivor of the saints or he might be the devil's rag-baby, for all I should know. But I never yet made the mistake of a hair's breadth on a person's ability, one might almost say sight-unseen. If a captain of industry made me his personnel-manager he would find me worth a ducal salary. This gift is no credit to me, so I can speak of it without immodesty; I was born that way. I can smell out ability as quickly and unerringly as a high-bred pointer can smell out a partridge.

My second qualification was the belief that a good executive's job is to do nothing, and that he can't set about it too soon or stick at it too faithfully. In our early days, when some one asked me how something ought to be done, I would look at him in a vacant kind of way, and say I didn't know—hadn't thought about it—couldn't just say, at the moment—how would you do it? So-and-so. Well, probably that's all right—you might take it up with the other people and see if they have any ideas. In this way they soon stopped looking to me for directions. I never gave any directions or orders; sometimes a suggestion but only as the other staff-members made suggestions, provisionally, and under correction from any one who had anything better to offer. I did not assign subjects for editorial treatment. Each of us picked his own, and we all discussed them together, once a week. I did a good deal of writing for the paper at one time and another, but the managing editor treated my copy like any one else's; it was in no way sacrosanct.

This plan of action was practicable because there were three superexcellent editorial minds on the staff, and all of them totally inexperienced. I knew what their abilities were as soon as I laid eyes on them, and I would not let any one who had had any experience come on the premises. Thus these persons had nothing to unlearn, they were not unconsciously bound by any editorial conventions, and when they met a difficulty they would deal with it by the untrammelled application of excellent ability and sound common sense.

My little ways as an executive, however, reacted on me by setting up my reputation in the office as a rather amiable imbecile, and I doubt I ever quite lived it down. It was well along in our second year, I remember, when I overheard one of the girls talking to some woman who had come in with something on her mind which apparently she was proposing to unload on me. "Oh, don't talk to Mr. Nock," the girl said. "He doesn't know anything about that. Mr. Nock doesn't know anything about *anything*. Go in and talk to Miss X." I was so delighted by this that whenever I saw the girl afterwards I could hardly keep from thanking her for the compliment.

Miss X was my secretary for the whole of our four years, barring the first month. When I finally told the lackadaisical Miss A that she was getting too good for me and would have to move on, I commissioned her to scratch me up a substitute. In a day or two she brought in Miss X, smaller and younger than herself, and even prettier. Within a week I began to learn what petticoat government is, and I kept on learning that bitter lesson to the end. Miss X had Scots blood and an idea of domestic discipline which was truly Scottish. I never got up courage to ask her whether she had been reared in the Calvinist persuasion, but she might well have been. I sometimes suspected that her predecessor had put her up to taking me on as a sort of problem-child, but whether so or not, that is what she did from the first day of her sojourn with us. I could do nothing of my own motion; my soul was not my own. She told me what I must do, always something I preferred to put off, and what visitors I must see, usually some one I preferred not to see; and she stood by with sweet, calm, quiet, gentle, cussed persistence to see that I did as I was told. The worst of it was that the wretched girl was always right, so what could one do?

I mention her because she was closest to me, and therefore her attitude towards me was probably the best index of the general estimate which the office put upon my intelligence. I had a pet name for her which I have forgotten, perhaps Lollipop—something of the kind. One day when an eminent and dignified professor and his wife were in my room, talking about an article which he was bringing out in our next issue, I stepped to the door (for I had no push-buttons on my desk, nor yet a telephone, *Gott soll hüten*) and called Lollipop to fetch me a proof. After my visitors had gone, I heard one of the girls say, "I think you ought to tell Mr. Nock to call you Helen when such distinguished people are around." Miss X replied, "No, he couldn't remember that name five minutes to save his life."

In the true and proper sense of the word we were a radical publication, and gave ourselves out as such. That is to say, we struck straight through to the root of whatever subject we discussed. We had no ink to waste on superficialities. We were not taken in by buncombe or clap-trap, and while we were urbane about it, we managed to let our readers know our opinion of those who hawked these commodities. Thus, as Mr. Beard says of us in his history of the period, we scattered acid on many a sacred convention. Once in a while, not often,—we never overdid it,—in a good-natured way we especially enjoyed upsetting some extra-preposterous mare's-nest which our Liberal friends were solemnly exploiting. In an incurably convention-ridden, truth-dreading, humbug-loving society, this could hardly be called giving the people what they wanted, and we took no umbrage when it was found unpalatable. There is some satisfaction in seeing now how very little the test of time has left us to regret or retract; and how much there is which we said was so, and which the people have belatedly found out is so.

In one way, our editorial policy was extremely easy-going, and in another way it was unbending as a ramrod. I can explain this best by an anecdote. One day Miss X steered in a charming young man who wanted to write for us. I took a liking to him at once, and kept him chatting for quite a while. When we came down to business, he diffidently asked what our policy was, and did we have any untouchable sacred cows. I said we certainly had, we had three of them, as untouchable and sacred as the Ark of the Covenant. He looked a bit flustered and asked what they were.

"The first one," I said, "is that you must have a point. Second, you must make it out. The third one is that you must make it out in eighteen-carat, impeccable, idiomatic English."

"But is that all?"

"Isn't it enough for you?"

"Why, yes, I suppose so, but I mean, is that all the editorial policy you have?"

"As far as I know, it is," I said, rising. "Now you run along home and write us a nice piece on the irremissibility of post-baptismal sin, and if you can put it over those three jumps, you will see it in print. Or if you would rather do something on a national policy of strangling all the girl-babies at birth, you might do that—glad to have it."

The young man grinned and shook hands warmly. We got splendid work out of him. As a matter of fact, at one time or another we printed quite a bit of stuff that none of us believed in, but it all conformed to our three conditions, it was respectable and worth consideration. Ours was old-school editing, no doubt, but in my poor judgement it made a far better paper than more stringent methods have produced in my time.

As soon as I saw that the success of our experiment was certain and, if I may say so, that it would be rather distinguished, my interest began to dribble away. For some time I knew I had worked myself out of a job, as I had all along meant to do, and when we stopped publication I felt no regret, but only, like Spencer at the end of the *Synthetic Philosophy*, a sense of "emancipation from a long task." The clear proof that I had become a superfluous man in our enterprise came towards the end of our third year. I abruptly dropped everything and went to Germany, leaving instructions that the paper should not be sent me, and that no one should write me any letters under any circumstances. I was away about three months. When I returned I called for all the issues that had come out in my absence, and went over them line by line. Nowhere could I find a jot of evidence, not even a suggestion, that I had been off duty for as much as a day.

This was precisely as it should be. I once heard a story of Thoreau which by internal evidence should certainly be authentic, though I do not know that it is. When he took up his father's trade of pencil-making he worked at it diligently until he had made the definitive pencil, the pencil which in every respect was beyond his power of improvement. Then he shut up shop and made no more pencils. He was a superfluous man in the pencil-making business. He had shown that the thing could be done, shown how it could be done, he had hung up his achievement in plain sight of any one who wished to look at it, and that was that. One pencil was enough to prove his point, so why make any more?

A month ago I was dining with one of the country's great industrialists when something that was said led up to this story of Thoreau, and I told it. The industrialist promptly said he thought Thoreau was a fool. There I had before me the product of two mutually exclusive philosophies. Economism would insist that having made the perfect pencil, Thoreau should make more pencils and sell them for money with which to buy more material to make still more pencils to sell for money to buy still more material, and so on, because the making and selling of pencils is the whole content of life. Thoreau did not believe it is the whole content of life. It was clear that economism's philosophy was the only one which my companion was capable of accepting. Detach him from his particular specialised practice of it, and existence would have no further meaning for him; and in this he was representative of the great bulk of society in this present age.

I find that I have gossiped at great length about my editorial adventure, perhaps too discursively. Nevertheless, with the aid of a little imagination the reader may easily see that the experience was invaluable in consolidating my views of life and in certifying that my demands on life were rational and sound. The best way to make sure of how much one actually knows of a thing, and especially to find out how much one does not know, is to write about it. When one writes from the standpoint of a certain philosophy week by week one is continually thrown back upon one's fundamental principles and positions to reëxamine them and satisfy oneself that the logic of one's conclusions from them is water-tight. My experience was diversified and searching, and like virtually all of the weightier experiences which luck has brought my way, it came at precisely the right time for doing me the most good.

Four years to a day, or rather to a week, from the date of the paper's first issue, our enterprise closed down. It was on a Friday evening that we of the staff bade one another farewell; and at eleven o'clock next morning, when the Dutch liner *Volendam* moved out of her slip, I was aboard her on my way to Brussels.

CHAPTER TEN

A work of art should express only that which elevates the soul and pleases it in a noble manner. The feeling of the artist should not overstep these limits; it is wrong to venture beyond.

—BETTINA BRENTANO.

One must, I think, be struck more and more the longer one lives, to find how much in our present society a man's life of each day depends for its solidity and value upon whether he reads during that *day, and far more still on what he reads during it.*

—MATTHEW ARNOLD.

IN MY brief career as a sort of jack-leg executive I had seen at close range all I wished to see of Western society's floundering progress towards collectivism. American society's antics in the course of this progress made a spectacle which was immensely amusing for a while, but one soon became weary of it. The absurdities of that decade were exceeded only by those of the succeeding decade, 1930-1940. Before that I could find no match for them in human history. American society had not the faintest idea of what it was doing or where it was going. It simply clung to its inveterate practice of making brag, bounce and quackery do duty for observation, reason and common sense. It had not yet got a glimpse of the elementary truth which was so clear to the mind of Mr. Jefferson, that in proportion as you give the State power to do things *for* you, you give it power to do things *to* you; and that the State invariably makes as little as it can of the one power, and as much as it can of the other. Mr. Harding's famous "return to normalcy" was not a return to anything. It was a mere acceleration of society's lolloping, wallowing advance towards the goal at which it arrived in 1932.

There was nothing to be done about this, even if one had wished to do anything, when I certainly did not, so I reverted to my own pursuits. My editorial work had got me into the habit of writing, occasionally with a view of publishing something I had written; a habit which has gradually slacked off of late. I published two or three little books, none of which attracted any particular attention. The one thing which was a labour of grateful love, and in which I was truly interested, was my share in editing the Urquhart-Motteux translation of the works of Francis Rabelais. The Pantagrueline philosophy had held my chin above water ever since my days with C. J. as a graduate student, and I wanted to do what little I could do in return. I had no idea beyond this, and I was unfeignedly astonished when the firm of Harcourt, Brace and Co. consented to publish so unpromising a work.

But such has been the invariable hospitality of publishers, in my experience. My books have been unrewarding to them, but they have printed them hopefully, without complaint. I think Mr. Harcourt's firm may have made a dollar or two out of my little study of Mr. Jefferson, but I am sure my other books have been published at a loss. I never had any but the most pleasant book-publishing relations. Moreover, besides those who have borne the burden and disappointment of my books, I have become acquainted with other publishers, and there is not one of them whom I have not come to regard with great respect and sincere liking.

Occasionally I contributed essays to periodicals. Mr. Wells, the editor of Harper's, got me in the way of it, and I rather enjoyed it. I wrote a good deal for him at one time or another. After Mr. Wells retired, my old friend Mr. Sedgwick took me on with equal hospitality in behalf of the Atlantic. Mr. Mencken of the Mercury, and his successor, Mr. Palmer, were likewise hospitable; and thus for a long time, whenever I had something on my mind which seemed worth publishing, I would bring out an essay in one or another of these publications, perhaps three or four times in the course of a year.

With these editors my relations were always as pleasant and satisfactory as my relations with book-publishers. They were also as disinterested, for I do not imagine that my essays were ever anything of a circulation-getter. Probably I had some readers, but they were not of the sort that is likely to write in and tell the editor how they felt about what they read. My editors were all of the old style. Mr. Palmer was a young man, but in some mysterious way he had become infected with the old-style tradition, and when he found that Gresham's law had made it impracticable to go on in that tradition, he quietly sold his magazine and gave up editing.

Judged from a contributor's viewpoint, my editors were all one could desire. They respected the contributor, knew his rights, and saw to it that he got them. They had none of the finical "rage for interference" which George Borrow complained of in his London publisher. On the contrary, they let me express myself as I chose to do. Never that I can remember did Mr. Wells, Mr. Mencken or Mr. Palmer tamper with my copy in any way, and only once or twice did Mr. Sedgwick find some insignificant expression which he besought me to modify. I found him a very able and lovable man, a delightful friend. Under a queer feminine mask of fussiness and indecision he concealed a great deal of resourceful courage. When I proposed a subject to him he would groan and sigh, and vow I was bound to lose him his last subscriber, but in the end he would tell me to go ahead and write the essay. All these men had the power of mature and seasoned judgement; they were able to deal as justly with what they did not like as with what they did like. I remember once when some subordinate relucted at something I was publishing in Harper's, Mr. Wells jerked his thumb towards him as he was passing by, and said to me in an undertone, "I'd print lots more stuff like that than he would—you see, I've got to stand for it, and he doesn't." An editor who insists that a contribution should in every way be a weak reflex of his own opinions or idiosyncrasies, or that it must conform to some set pattern of his own devising, seems to me an extremely poor, incompetent affair.

I have had very little chance to observe editors of the newer style. From what I have seen of them, they impress me rather as misplaced journalists and salesmen than as editors. It is true that the editor was always a salesman, but it is also true that there are salesmen and salesmen. A salesman for the great house of Bagstock and Buggins, wine-merchants in the City ever since Charles I was beheaded, is a very different breed of cats from a high-pressure salesman of mass-produced gimcrackery. Bagstock and Buggins have always had about as much trade as they can carry comfortably, and their clients are their old hereditary friends, whose tastes and wishes they know as well as they know their own merchandise. So, when the salesman goes out he is aware that the House is distinctly less interested in his drumming up new clients than in his taking proper care of those he has. The old-style editor seemed to me to stand in much that same relation of salesmanship with his readers, while the new-style editor seems to stand more in the cutthroat-competitive attitude of Marks Pasinsky, Moe Griesman and Hymie Salzman towards potential buyers in the heyday of the cloak-and-suit trade, forty years ago.

In a society given over to the philosophy of economism, this is inevitable; and therefore I must not be taken as disparaging the more modern type of editor. The old-style editor is merely one of the casualties of economism. Gresham's law has driven out his conception of the editorial function and has replaced it by that of the go-getter, just as in Brussels I saw it drive out the old-style restaurateur's conception of his function and replace it by that of the mass-producer. Brussels was known the world over as a city of little restaurants providing the most consummate artistry in food. Two of them had been going concerns for something over three hundred years. One after another they disappeared under my eyes. First, the Stielen went; its site was taken over for an extension of a department-store, and when I first saw Brussels one could almost say there was no one there who knew what a department-store was. Then the Leyman went, then the Écrevisse, the Charlemagne, and so on, until when I finally left Brussels hardly any of the higher amenities of food were surviving, save in private kitchens.

So when, as in the case of Mr. Palmer, the modern editor is young, able, possessed of some literary standards and would do better if he could, so far am I from disparaging or finding fault with him that I feel he is much to be pitied. In the nature of things it is presumable that not many are of that character,—Gresham's law would take care of that,—but no doubt some of them are. They have professionalised themselves, and considerations of one kind or another, usually economic, keep them in the groove of their profession. With only one life to live, they must continually feel their existence as cramping and dissatisfying, for as Paul Bourget says, every disused or misused faculty becomes a source of uneasiness.

Some years ago I was in company with half-a-dozen men when the talk somehow turned on the odd question of what are the three most degrading occupations open to man. When the question got around to me, I said I thought the first was holding office in a modern *soi-disant* republic, the second was editing an American metropolitan newspaper, and as for the third I was of two minds whether it would be white slave-trading or keeping an assignation-house. Every one laughed, though I had spoken quite seriously, and one gentleman whom I had not met before said he thought I ought to find a place somewhere in my categories for his job, since he was the chief fiction-editor or tripe-editor (for so he called it) of one of our leading popular mass-produced weekly publications.

He told us interesting things about his occupation. He amazed me by saying that notwithstanding the immense volume of trade-writing that is being done, publications like his are sometimes at their wit's end to get enough printable tripe to fill their space. So this, I thought, is what Mr. Jefferson's cherished principle of universal literacy has come to! The editor said further that in choosing material his aim was constantly at what he judged to be the lowest common denominator of intelligence, taste and style among his actual and prospective readers. Moreover, his sole official measure of the merit of a piece of fiction was its nearness to hitting the mark of this lowest common denominator, as indicated by the volume of sales. "A few weeks ago," he said, "we featured a story that was a bit above the average, and that week our news-stand sales fell off sixty thousand."

This editor was a pleasant, companionable man of good taste, considerable ability, a lively sense of humour, in all ways very far above his distressing occupation. I felt extremely sorry for him; he seemed a poor miserable wretch. I hope God will have mercy on his soul.

II

While living in Europe I almost completely lost the run of literary produce in England and America. This was not deliberate. It was due somewhat to indolence, largely to preoccupation with other literatures, but chiefly to the fact that there was hardly any English print available where I was, and what there was of it was slight and poor. This was especially true of Brussels in my earlier days there. The Belgian is one ahead of the Swiss in the matter of native languages. The Swiss rubs along on German, French and Italian, while the Belgian has to wrestle with Flemish, French, Walloon and German. These tongues, however, are pretty sharply localised. Brussels is the only place in the kingdom where Flemish and French meet, so a person living there can get on with either. To the north and west is solid Flemish, Walloon begins at Liége and runs to the French line, while over on the Prussian border there are about fifty thousand Belgians who speak German. I got the impression that there was less English spoken in Brussels, and less English print available there, than in any other Western European capital I visited, except Lisbon. I found a considerable amount of colloquial English going on in Antwerp, and for some reason that I could not make out there was also a little of it here and there in Bruges; but in Brussels I went for months on end without sight or sound of my native tongue.

So it was that in my four years as an amateur editor in New York I brought a fairly fresh eye to bear upon the post-war literary doings which had taken place without my knowledge. In the field of creative art, if one can call it that, the field of ποίησις, *Dichtung*, whether prose or verse, they presented a remarkable sight. In a way I was prepared for something of the kind, because I had already seen evidence, especially in France, that the current practice of music, painting and sculpture had become a *tohu-bohu*, a chaos of confusion, and one would expect the current practice of literature to be in even worse case because naturally a larger number of ill-assorted aspirants would be trying their hand at it. The period presented a curious phenomenon, one that I think may have been unique. Writing is an occupation, and up to the period I speak of I believe it is the only one, in which a person who knows nothing whatever about it can engage and quite often achieve a popular success; so the success of incompetent writers in this period was not exceptional. I do not know of any other time, however, when it has been possible for a person who knew nothing whatever about painting or music or sculpture to make any kind of success, popular or otherwise, in the practice of any of those arts. Yet I had seen it done; I had seen, for example, a great vogue of French painters, a whole school of them, who (with one exception) did not even know how to draw; and I had also seen a considerable popular interest extended towards French and German composers who clearly lacked even the most elementary discipline to fit them for what they were trying to do or wanted to do. I had furthermore nibbled with long teeth at some specimens of "modernity" in French and German writings, and saw in them no sign of anything more promising than unwarranted ambition. So, with what I had seen, and with my knowledge of what American society's critical insight and judgement were worth, I was, as I said, .in a way prepared to encounter the astonishing cultural extravagances that awaited my return to America.

I was amused by them, and still more amused by the effort to create a vogue for them and glorify them as permanent enrichments of art and culture, but I did not give them any serious attention, for I expected them shortly to succumb to asphyxiation in the atmosphere of their own inanity and peter out, as in fact they did. To tell the truth, I was rather inclined to encourage certain of these promoters of literary absurdities when it fell in my way to do so. They were mainly young persons, ardent, bungfull of self-consciousness, not doing much actual harm,—probably not even much harming themselves in the long-run,—and they seemed to be having such a glorious, disorderly, irresponsible good time out of tousling our poor old austere alphabet that one could not be stepmotherly with them, even in one's heart. Was life given us for any purpose but that we should get a good time out of it? Surely I think not. The sound Pantagruelist and Rabelaisian remembers that his *maistre et seigneur Pantagruel* never tried to reform Panurge or wean him from his amusing deviltries, though he himself took no part in them. That is the way Panurge was, Pantagruel took him as he was, loved him as he was, did not wish him to be other than he was, always countenanced him even when he entered on paths which he himself was disinclined to tread. According to the great Pantagrueline philosophy, the only reform that any one is called upon to attempt is reform of oneself. One notices that Pantagruel was extremely strict about that, for all that a precisian moralist might call his culpable laxness towards Panurge.

So I often, sincerely enough, gave a friendly word to breathless young literary innovators, though I did it more or less in the spirit of a professor under whom I sat for a time as a graduate student. He was a big rawboned Irishman with a gorgeous brogue, a graduate of Trinity in the great days of Mahaffy and Tyrrell. He had also been ordained in the Anglican Church by Whately, the redoubtable archbishop of Dublin, who was a tremendous fellow in all his ways, and moreover probably in some respects the most cantankerous old cuss that ever filled an episcopal chair. My professor—his name is immaterial, so let me call him Murphy—was a man exactly after Whately's own heart. I remember him once shuffling into his lecture-room, glaring around at us from under his bushy red eyebrows, and saying, "Look out f'r ye'erselves this mornin', gintlemen. Mrs. Murphy an' I have had a disagreement!" Whately might well have done just that.

He had a son named Jimmy, an exemplary fine fellow and a good student in the class next below ours. After leading a sober, righteous and uninteresting life for twenty years or so, as the Book of Common Prayer prescribes, Jimmy suddenly broke out on a roaring spree one night and came home in a state of advanced decomposition, thinking he could make his way to bed without arousing anybody. As he was half-way upstairs, creeping on all-fours, the old man appeared on the stair-landing in a long cotton nightshirt, with a nightlamp in his hand. They considered each other in silence for a minute or two, and then the old man said, "Go it, Jimmy! Go it! Ye're very young. Ye have plinty iv time befure ye to diskiver what a fool ye ar're. So, go it!" With these words he turned back into his bedroom, closing both the door and the incident in one magisterial motion.

In many ways the youthful dabblers in literature, painting and music kept reminding me of Jimmy, especially when I contemplated the upshot of their efforts. The other day I blew the dust off a volume of their productions in verse, and remarked once more how strongly symptomatic their aberrations were; and looking back upon the parallel aberrations which I had observed in Europe, I saw how right Menander was in saying that evil communications corrupt good manners.

A second Max Nordau of the 'twenties, tracing his way down from Baudelaire, Mallarmé, Rimbaud, Verlaine, to our young American aspirants, might well have conceived a *Degeneracy* as a sequel to his predecessor's *Degeneration*. The unmistakable mark of degeneracy which stood out on the period's attempts at artistic production was an intense and conscious preoccupation with the subjective. As Goethe remarked, all eras in a state of decline and dissolution are subjective, while in all great eras which have been really in a state of progression, every effort is directed from the inward to the outward world; it is of an objective nature. I have always believed, as Goethe did, that here one comes on a true sense of the term *classic*. Work done in the great progressive eras,—the work of the Augustan and Periclean periods, the work of the Elizabethans, of Erasmus, Marot, Rabelais, Cervantes, Montaigne,—one accepts these as classic, not at all because they are old, but because they are objective and therefore strong, sound, joyous, healthy. Work done in an era of decadence is subjective, and therefore with the rarest and most fragmentary exceptions pathological, weak, bizarre, unhealthy. Indeed as Goethe suggested, in the interest of clearness one might very well make a clean sweep of all terms like *classic*, *modernist*, *realist*, *naturalist* and substitute the simple terms *healthy* and *sickly*.

Hence it was the symptomatic character of artistic practice both in Europe and America that chiefly interested me. In Europe I saw a good deal of "modernist" French painting, done in the 'twenties by Pascin, Soutine, Picasso, de Segonzac, de la Fresnaye, Metzinger, Dufy and others. In literature I also nibbled gingerly at specimens of subjectivity *in excelsis* furnished by Proust, Laforgue, Dujardin and practitioners of the "stream of consciousness" principle. One's presumptions upon any society from which such work could emanate and get itself accepted, were inescapable. At Gastein nine years ago, in talking with a member of the old German General Staff, I spoke of a possible attack on France. He opened his eyes wide with astonishment, and said, "We shall not attack France. We have no idea of attacking France. Why should we? Why should any one attack France? Let her alone, and she will collapse." I had occasion to remember this six years later, for certainly the passage of von Reichenau's forces from Sedan to the seacoast could hardly be dignified by the name of an attack. It was a promenade.

But at the end of an era of unmitigated economism, what else could one expect? How otherwise could a society dominated by this philosophy express itself, whether in literature, music, the graphic arts, politics, or any other mode of its collective life? All these manifestations seemed to me purely exhibitory, and therefore quite in the order of nature. So also seemed to me the character of the ephemera who appeared in the rôle of chief exhibitors, star performers. Not long ago I heard a Frenchwoman say, "I dislike Hitler heartily, I dislike everything he does and says, but the fact remains that Hitler is only the result of *us*"—and she made a wide sweeping circular gesture which brought the whole of Western society within the scope of her indictment. An analyst like Nordau would find the heads of our collectivist governments in both hemispheres, all of them without exception, as wholly in the order of nature, as purely exhibitory, as were the Rimbauds, Verlaines and Gauguins of the last century. Revolting as they are, they are nevertheless precisely the forms of organic life which one must expect to see, and does see, if one insists on turning over the social plank which has so long lain rotting in the muck of economism.

III

During my four years in New York I found our amateurs of creative literature largely touched by the strange spirit of desperateness which seemed to rest on a whole generation of youth in that period. Putting it roughly, I should say that it rested heaviest on those who were approaching adolescence when the war ended and were in their early twenties when

I first noticed them. In respect of their malady they were exactly like Misha in Tourgueniev's marvellous piece of analysis called *A Desperate Character*. As I observed them carefully they kept reminding me of Misha at every turn; if I had not known his story I believe I could not have understood them. Desperate characters is just what they were. I saw them everywhere here, and when I returned to Europe I saw many who had transferred themselves to Continental centres, mainly to Paris, existing as mere wastrels. The peculiar thing about them was that their desperateness, like Misha's, was directed only against themselves. Depraved, they were not; no one could say so; they were simply obsessed by Misha's almost insane passion for self-destruction. They were unwilling to hurt any one but themselves, and never consciously did so, though through ignorance and thoughtlessness no doubt they often did. Towards others their impulses were generous, kindly, simple-hearted, affectionate. They were truthful, and with Misha's ill-assorted type of courage, they were very brave. Some of them had all Misha's power of attraction and his genius for friendship. Like Misha, they had frankly given themselves up for lost, and were wretched, dissatisfied, desperate. With all their good qualities which marked them sometimes with a certain touch of nobleness, and with all their fine loyalty to anomalous social codes of their own devising, they were desperate characters; no other name describes them.

When such as these take to expressing themselves in literature, as some did, not much in the way of good art can reasonably be expected. They have little to express but an overdeveloped and disorderly self-consciousness, and this is a most refractory material for art to manage. *Il dit tout ce qu'il veut,*—so runs the terrible sentence of a French critic,—*mais malheureusement il n'a rien à dire.* Yet sometimes the Not-ourselves shoulders its way to the front of most unpromising circumstances and produces a work of art. John Reed, a desperate character who threw away his life on the Russian revolution, addressed an absent sweetheart in a few lines of pure and exquisite lyric verse which might well have been written by a Herrick or a Lovelace. Only a trifle, it is true, and it stands alone for its merit in the thin volume in which it is printed; but there it is.

As I read it my mind turned to thoughts of Villon, a desperate character of the old days, from whom a philosopher might draw a fairly clear line of resemblance down through Misha and Reed to the desperate characters of the 'twenties. One never knows when or where the spirit's breath will rest, or what will come of its touch. "The spirit breathes where it will," [1] said the *Santissimo Salvatore,* "and thou hearest the sound thereof, but canst not tell whence it cometh and whither it goeth." Out of the slums of Paris, out of the lowest depths of wretchedness and desperateness, came the voice which celebrated the *belles dames du temps jadis* in immortal verse. A lowlived drunken tinker lying in Bedford gaol conceived the *Pilgrim's Progress.*

The only certainty I could arrive at concerning the literary produce of the 'twenties was the one which I had already long entertained, that art goes rancid when *as art* it becomes consciously this-or-that; and that the one invincible and implacable enemy of art is the writer's self-consciousness, his preoccupation with the subjective. Writers sometimes produce a work of art, perhaps great art, with no intention of doing anything of the kind, and every intention of doing something else. They do it in pursuance of some purpose, but the relation of that purpose to art is fortuitous, and in their pursuance of it they do not deliberately bind themselves to making their work illustrative of any wire-drawn formula or theory of art. One writer wrote in haste, oppressed by terrible grief, under great pressure for immediate money, and produced *Rasselas.* Another wrote avowedly to entertain the boarding-school *Back-*

[1] Τὸ πνεῦμα ὅπου θέλει πνεῖ, John III, 8. There can be no doubt about this reading. The Vulgate has *Spiritus ubi vult spirat.* I do not know what led King James's translators to give the reading which appears in the Authorised Version.

fisch and women of the lower-middle class, and produced *Evalina*. This was pure market-writing, as far as the authors' intentions went; in point of art, they were not concerned to show themselves as representing any school or sect or theory. They simply went ahead and did the best they could in behalf of the object they had in view.

My reading of current novels and poetry at that time, however, was desultory and not extensive. I was impressed by the enormous amount of market-writing that was being done. On the one hand, the wide spread of a frail and futile literacy had set up a great demand for a frail and futile literature to match. On the other hand, publishing had become one of the country's major industries, and the ensuing competition was so sharp that each house had to keep its presses going at full speed in order to live. It was a case of "print or die" with all of them, in an effort to capture a share of the market furnished by the faintly literate, and the operation of Gresham's law set the general standard of what was printable. As some one put it, a good book, from a publisher's point of view, was a book as nearly as possible like another book which had sold a great number of copies.

In consequence, the great mass of writing produced to meet this demand bore a curiously stereotyped character. As art, it was nothing; and in point of workmanship it all stood at the same level of mediocrity. For all one could discern, the whole of it might have been done by the same hand. The hall-mark of individual authorship had disappeared. One could not possibly tell from reading this-or-that popular work which one of the authors who were prominent in public favour had written it. The dearth of imagination, of inventive power, manifested in these productions was also remarkable. In some cases one could hardly escape the conviction that an author had merely changed the names of his characters and their locale, and then written the same story over and over again. The same state of things appeared to prevail in British market-writing, judged by the specimens of it which were reproduced here by the thousand; though as a rule the British writers' workmanship was better than ours.

Yet "the spirit breathes where it will." In Montague Glass, whose work lived well over into this period, America produced one of the greatest delineators of character that ever held a pen; and in Glass's contemporary, Finley Peter Dunne, it produced the soundest and most perspicacious of all critics of American society, with the single exception of Artemus Ward. The fate of these two men was interesting to me, as furnishing perhaps the most conspicuous proof that Gresham's law has destroyed the last hope of literary criticism's resurrection in America. It has created circumstances whereby in literary criticism as well as in social and political criticism "the test of a great mind is its power of agreement in the opinions of small minds." In other words, it has effectively arranged matters so that there shall never be at any one time in America more than a corporal's guard of persons capable of recognising and identifying a work of literary art if they saw one.

Both Glass and Dunne were market-writers. Their work had a wide vogue, it was eagerly accepted, and it furnished amusement to millions. But in their respective fields they were also great artists, and as such they were never recognised. So I saw their vogue pass, leaving no mark to show their true position and status in the country's literary history. I saw this with especial regret in the case of Glass, for his work turns attention steadily upon a social asset of immense value, which is rapidly disappearing from among us; I refer to the authentic Hebrew culture and tradition. America opened its doors wide to this Oriental people, and Jews have made many important contributions to our civilisation; and Gresham's law has seen to it that the most important are those for which they get the least credit. Readers of Arnold's *Literature and Dogma*, if any still exist, will have no trouble about getting the point of this observation. But among other powerful incentives, our silly notion of the "melting-pot" and our sillier conception of its function, encouraged them in a preposterously superficial and impracticable attempt to Occidentalise themselves; and this attempt entailed a self-chosen disparagement and sacrifice of their culture. Our society has lost incalculably by this, and aside from the cultural damage to the Jews themselves, I believe the social consequences of this attempt will be most unfortunate for them.

In Europe also, during the post-war period when literature was almost as deep in the doldrums there as it was here, I had occasion to see how nature pursues her own free way, regardless of the formulas and prescriptions which purblind men devise. I came upon two works of excellent art where, under the circumstances, one would hardly expect to find them. One was *Les Thibaults*, by Roger Martin du Gard. It was published in sections appearing at intervals of some length. I read about half of it in French, and the rest of it lately in an uncommonly good translation. I had a high opinion of it. The second work was one mailed to me in Brussels by an American friend who was travelling in England. It was a *tour de force* of pure creative fancy, and of an art unexampled in any work of the period which I had seen, or in any I have seen since then in the literature of any country. It was Bruce Marshall's *Father Malachy's Miracle*. I should not know where to look for a power of character-portrayal superior to that which is applied everywhere, to all sorts and conditions of men and women, throughout this small volume. With equal precision, completeness and convincing force it exhibits what goes on in the mind of subjects as diverse as a Benedictine monk, ballet-girls, dancers, a Scots bishop, a jovial Scots rounder, an Italian cardinal, a pair of raw Irish priests, a precious brace of British theatrical promoters and their hard-boiled wives, and an ultra-modernist British Protestant parson. I have looked industriously for something to match this achievement within the same limit of proportions,—for as I said, the book is small,—but I have not as yet found anything.

IV

A few months ago I re-read two or three of William J. Locke's earlier novels, to see how well the opinion I had formed of them twenty years ago was holding up, and whether I still felt the attraction of one special interest in them. Locke was a prolific market-writer, extremely popular and successful. His later pre-war work ran somewhat on momentum, but even so it was good strong momentum. Perhaps, like Thackeray, he may have "taken too many crops out of his brain" at too short intervals. The war impaired his powers, as it might well have done, and by comparison even with *The Glory of Clementina* his post-war work is probably negligible. Locke was a man of sensitive artistic instincts and fine culture, who observed closely and wrote charmingly. One would say he had been educated in the bad old way, as I was, for the mark of "the grand old fortifying classical curriculum" was clearly visible on his estimate of life and on his conception of his task.

It was by this latter aspect,—his idea of what true fiction is and what it is for,—that his work had a special interest for me. He seemed to have got his idea pretty straight from Hesiod and Aristotle, and had probably considered with some care what had been done with it in the romances of Apuleius, Heliodorus, Longus, Achilles Tatius. At all events *Septimus* and *The Beloved Vagabond* took me back as promptly as when I first read them, years ago, to Aristotle's profound analysis of the difference between history and fiction; and I thought at once how admirably, how delightfully, Locke's work exemplified Aristotle's critical dictum on the true and proper nature of fiction. History, Aristotle says, represents things only as they are, while fiction represents them as they might be and ought to be; and therefore of the two, he adds, "fiction is the more philosophical and the more highly serious."[2]

My impression is that *Septimus* and *The Beloved Vagabond* come up to Aristotle's specifications beyond cavil or question.

[2] Φιλοσοφώτερον καὶ σπουδαιότερον. I hope I have not made too free with Aristotle's νδια γένοιτο,ἂ but I think the implication is certainly there.

There is not an implausible character in them, or an implausible situation; they all "might be," might easily be. Moreover, I believe the normal ordinary run of opinion, uninfluenced by any hard-and-fast literary formula, would agree that they "ought to be." Locke takes title as an artist, I think, not only by presenting his characters and situations as they might be and ought to be, but also by doing it without communicating to the reader any sense of strain or affectation. The reader assents to them at once; and this assent completes the establishment of Locke's work as a work of art. I repeat that I am speaking of his earlier work. Here and there *Clementina* stirs a sense of strain, and what I have read of those which follow,—true, I have read but two,—pretty well keep that sense alive throughout.

For many years, indeed ever since first I had mulled over Aristotle as a student in college, I had been in the habit of applying his dry analytical remark as a test of whatever creative literature came before me. Nothing in my experience or observation during the 'twenties weakened my faith in that procedure, but on the contrary everything tended to confirm it. This test enabled me to put my finger firmly on the reason for my disinclination towards most of the fiction current at the time, especially the *Tendenzschrift*, the sociological novel, and the "novel with a purpose." I was reminded that with all my respect for Flaubert's ability I could get nowhere with *Madame Bovary*. Not all my regard for the valour and industry of Zola, for the fine literary qualities of the Goncourts, could keep my nose to the grindstone of *La Terre* or *Soeur Philomène*. These are not works of fiction, but of history; and if I wanted history I preferred getting it from historians. There was a wealth of sound criticism in the French musician's remark on Honegger's imitation of the sounds of a locomotive; he said that if he wanted to listen to a locomotive he went down to the railway-station. The vigorous young American publicists who are constructing novels around the various social and political phenomena of the moment aim only at presenting things as they are. Their work, as far as I have seen it, is not fiction, it is history. It may be sound history or bad history, inaccurate history, but in either case it is history. It has neither the philosophical character nor the high seriousness which distinguish true fiction, and it lacks them because it presents things only as they are, and not as they might be and ought to be.

So Aristotle's remark has stood always as my first canon of criticism applicable to creative writing. For me, it determines in every case the answer to the question whether this-or-that work is or is not true fiction, and if it is or is not, why. My second canon bears on the question: What is fiction for, what is its true intention, its proper function? This second canon was very well put in terms by Prince Alexander Kropotkin when he advised his brother to read poetry. He said, "Poetry makes you better." I imagine that Prince Kropotkin would have made no difficulties about including prose as well as verse under his term, as the Greeks did and the Germans do; indeed, if Russian has an inclusive term like *Dichtung*, he may have used it; I do not know. He put the fact exactly, however. A work of the creative imagination which makes you better fulfils the true intention of such literature, and one which fails to do this fails of its true intention.

There is an important distinction here. The Goncourts spoke scornfully of a certain type of literature as an "anodyne." They had something on their side, no doubt, but they were undiscriminating, as our readers and reviewers often are when they lump off certain works under the general stigma of "escape-literature." Any creative work which one reads with attention will make one forget one's troubles for the time being, as will a hand at bridge or billiards or watching a lively comedy on the stage. Some works do this and do no more; in the reaction from them their total effect comes to nothing. Others do this, and their total effect is enervating. Others again do this, but they are so conceived that the reading of them elevates and fortifies the spirit, they are spiritually dynamogenous, they make one better. The Goncourts missed this distinction as completely as the degenerate realism and naturalism of the 'twenties missed it; and in the absence of anything remotely resembling a sound and authoritative criticism, the true function of creative writing, as well as its true character, is everywhere lost sight of at the present time.

I have no idea of pressing my two canons of criticism upon any one's acceptance, nor am I disposed to argue for their usefulness to all in general. I can say only that they are fundamental to the development of the literary and cultural element in my philosophy of existence. Culture is knowing the best that has been thought and said in the world; in other words, culture means reading, not idle and casual reading, but reading that is controlled and directed by a definite purpose. Reading, so understood, is difficult, and contrary to an almost universal belief, those who can do it are very few. I have already remarked the fact that there is no more groundless assumption than that literacy carries with it the ability to read. At the age of seventy-nine Goethe said that those who make this assumption "do not know what time and trouble it costs to *learn to read*. I have been working at it for eighteen years, and I can't say yet that I am completely successful." In the course of the rigorous discipline which learning to read imposes, I have found that with regard to creative literature the canons of Aristotle and Prince Kropotkin together make the most efficient sieve for a preliminary straining-out of what may be worth reading, and separating it from the prodigious mass of what is not.

Again, the effect of keeping good company in literature is exactly what it is in life. Keeping good company is spiritually dynamogenous, elevating, bracing. It makes one better. Keeping bad company is disabling; keeping indifferent company is enervating and retarding. In literature one has the best company in the world at complete command; one also has the worst. One has a social conscience which dissuades one from harbouring unprofitable company in life, and I find that my two canons are a great aid and support for an analogous literary conscience which speaks up against consorting with unprofitable company in literature.

Literary art is appreciable only by a minority, as indeed all art must be. This minority are capable of exercising a literary conscience and of keeping themselves under its direction. They are unable to make its intimations prevail at all generally, nor are they called upon to attempt this obvious impossibility. They can, however, make them prevail in the development of their own culture, and with that their responsibility ends. The task of enlightening the literary conscience and enforcing its decrees upon oneself is difficult enough to make one glad of any substantial help that one can get; and (though, as I said, I speak only for myself) I have had more substantial help from my two basic canons of criticism than from any other source.

CHAPTER ELEVEN

Si sine uxore pati possemus, Quirites, omnes ea molestia careremus; set quoniam ita natura tradidit ut nec cum illis satis commode nec sine illis ullo modo vivi possit, saluti perpetuae potius quam brevi voluptati consulendum est.

—SPEECH OF THE CENSOR METELLUS NUMIDICUS, 102, B.C.

I thought love had been a joyous thing, quoth my uncle Toby. 'Tis the most serious thing, an' please your honour, that is in the world, said the corporal.

—LAURENCE STERNE.

During the post-war period I was interested in seeing how frankly the whole output of English and American creative literature,—novels, verse, drama,—dealt with sex-relations, conventional as well as unconventional. This in itself did not seem to me at all objectionable; on the contrary, the social fashion of obscurantism with regard to sex-relations, and the literary fashion which reflected it, always impressed me as silly and irritating. The factitious and obtrusive decencies of earlier writers ran to indecency, like the ridiculous performances of Anthony Comstock and the various organisations for the "suppression of vice." For example, when one looked over the literature designed especially for women, one could hardly resist the harsh suspicion, probably in a measure unjust, that Mrs. Slipslop was right in telling Lady Booby that the gentle ladyfolk's ears were the most modest things they had about them. But the matter seemed a small one, either way you took it. I did not regard either of these literary fashions as symptomatic or as having any influence on conduct. In the nature of things one would expect the average of sexual irregularity to run about as high in a society which followed the fashion of obscurantism as in one which follows the fashion of frankness; and I believe that it did run as high in pre-war American society as it does now. So, like most fashions, neither of these seemed anything to be taken seriously, or to get up a great pother about. To me, the one seemed somewhat more infantile than the other,—if there be degrees in infantilism,—and therefore somewhat more annoying; and that was all.

On the score of art, however, my distaste for the fantastically exaggerated literary exploitation of sex, sex-attraction, sex-relations, soon ripened into utter disgust. My complaint was primarily that writers acting under this obsession were attempting an impossibility; they were trying to make too grotesquely much out of too pathetically little. The standard English novel of the period, according to a disgruntled English critic, consisted of two hundred pages of smooth and easy prose leading up to an act of adultery, and then eighty pages more of smooth and easy prose leading down again. This statement strikes one as perhaps a little fanciful, but taken by-and-large it is really not excessive. I think that Pharaoh, king of Egypt, was a pretty generous fellow compared with a public taste and fashion which could even dream of getting a work of art from a writer after giving him only such exiguous and sleazy stuff as this to work with. The point is that the males and females of the period's fiction were creatures of purely physiological reactions, responsive only to raw sensation; and literary art can do nothing with such as these, or with the situations which they arrange for themselves.

For this reason: What Panurge whimsically calls "the act of androgynation and the culbatising exercise" is something so extremely undifferentiated, so undiversified, that in an objective view it is bound to appear extremely prosaic. With respect to all its demands and fulfilments, one man is seen to be exactly like another, one woman exactly like another, one pair exactly like another. Evidence of its commonplace character is found in the fact that a disinterested view of it always excites a sense of incongruity with its sentimental associations, and therefore excites derision. Hence with the stark act of androgynation as his *pièce de resistance* the literary artist can do simply nothing. Proof of this, if one cares for it, may be had by reading half-a-dozen of de Maupassant's short stories at a sitting. An hour devoted to this exercise will be found to leave one with nothing but the sense of a viscid and sticky monotony. The utmost that the artist can do with this piece of literary property is something occasional and special, by way of pointing up some incident or topic, usually of a humorous turn, as Rabelais uses it in his story of the deaf-and-dumb Roman lady, or in his account of the nun's misdoings at Brignoles; or indeed wherever he chooses to employ this property.

In a word, the fiction of the period specialised in presenting sex-attraction, sex-emotion, consistently at their lowest level. This was understandable, and I for one saw no reason to complain of it on any score but that of art. The neolithic masses of mankind are psychically incapable of experiencing the emotions of sex at any but the lowest level, and having become dimly literate, they would naturally require the level of depicted experience to be not above that of the actuality with which they are acquainted. This being so, the objections raised on moral and social grounds seemed exorbitant, and did not interest me. In the austere old Chief Justice's phrase, those who raised them apparently did not "regard mankind as being what they are," and were unaware that there is nothing in the vast overwhelming majority of mankind which could be made to feel the force of those objections, or even to understand them.

The fashion of frankness did perhaps tend to overmagnify the importance of crude sensuousness in our society's scheme of life, and to give the impression that it has a larger place there than it actually has. I am not sure that this is so, but it may be. Purely libidinous sex-adventures are, as the Greek philosopher said, "the occupation of those who have no other occupation," and certainly the intimations of magazine-covers, advertisements of apparel, the cinema-screen, the illustrations in our newspapers and periodicals, all would reinforce those of our fictional literature in suggesting that our society has little else to do in its hours of leisure and less to think about. When one considers our collective life by its serious side, one probably finds some degree of misrepresentation here; and as for its lighter side, one would hardly venture an opinion either way. One gets, however, a distinct impression that when sex-attraction does operate, it is presumed to function only on the plane of stark sensuousness, and that sex-relations rest ultimately on no other basis.

As a matter of observed fact, this is not the case. It is no doubt uniformly so with the neolithic man and woman of today, as it has always been, and therefore the sales-policies of economism are unquestionably right in shaping themselves by the rule and taking no account of the exception. While it may sometimes also be the case with the psychically-human being, it is almost invariably not. Sex-attraction often operates powerfully and fruitfully in instances where its sensuous side is in complete abeyance, and again sometimes where its sensuous side makes a belated appearance at the end of a long period of intimate association. Here I think one might find some ground for believing that the physical lure of sex-attraction, especially in view of its evanescence when alone and unsupported, is in its nature essentially casual and incidental, as one finds it generally throughout the animal world; and that the importance which society has put upon the act of yielding to it is monstrously exaggerated. As I have already remarked somewhere in these memoranda, one may well believe that the only court of competent jurisdiction in the premises is that of taste and manners. The idea of sex-relations on which the mediæval Courts of Love were instituted,—the idea which

Rabelais worked out in detail for the moral architecture of Friar John's abbey of Thélème,—appears most reasonable and most in accord with truth of experience. Far from disregarding or disparaging the physical lure of sex-attraction, this idea merely ranges it at its proper degree in the scale of importance; the response to it is in no sense an end-in-itself. As between persons experiencing the immense power and beauty of reciprocal sex-influence, if this element presents itself as an ancillary part-and-parcel of this experience, well and good; if not, well and good. In either case the rational rule of conduct is the one which the psychically-human being will naturally and instinctively follow for the cogent reasons which Rabelais assigns: *Fay ce que vouldras.*

Everyone knows that the spiritual energies of psychically-human men and women are vastly enhanced by the aid of appropriate sex-relations. It is observable also that among psychically-human beings there are some who are so little automotive that they can hardly turn a wheel without this aid. Back in the 'twenties, when "realistic" fiction was set in a stereotyped pattern inimical to art, I often wondered why some one did not try his hand at a work of true art made up around the sex-experience of a couple whose mutual reactions were not physiological. It would be an interesting thing to do, and a good artist could make something very fine of it, as good artists have done in the past. Such a novel moreover, as far as I can see, might be kept quite strictly answerable to all the tenets and prescriptions of realism. If realism means the representation of life as it is actually lived, I do not see why lives which are actually lived on a higher emotional plane are not so eligible for representation as those lived on a lower plane. It must be said, however, that while a love-story consistently carried out on the higher emotional plane might be a work of art, even great art, a publisher's reader would almost automatically report it as "not of general interest"; and considering the circumstances to which I have alluded, he would be quite right in so doing.

Nevertheless there can be no doubt that sex-relations of a most intimate, profound and satisfying character do persist on the higher emotional plane and are susceptible of artistic literary treatment, not only in the fictional form but in other forms as well. Not long ago one of my friends asked me what I thought of an idea he had for a book which should analyse and discuss the sex-motive in the careers of some eminent Aspasias, ancient and modern. I told him that this ground had been gone over pretty thoroughly already, but if he wanted a clear field he could make a very fine enlightening analysis of the sex-motive in the instance of certain hand-picked Egerias where physiological reaction did not come in play. Again for reasons sufficiently obvious such a work would have no great sale, but from any competent hand it would be interesting, and from the hand of a Sainte-Beuve it would be superb. My friend agreed with me fully, but did not feel that his powers of analysis were equal to the task. I also mentioned the idea to a lady who already at my suggestion had published a very acceptable book on some of the less well-known women of the French Renaissance, but she too thought her analytical equipment was hardly up to the mark, and I dare say she was right.

One might be content to touch lightly on the *loci classici* among one's examples. A word or two would be enough to make clear what everyone knows already, that the world of letters owes an incalculable debt to the sex-attraction of Beatrice Portinari and to that of the none too well identified Laura of the *Canzoniere*. Modern opinion, especially that large section of it which is shaped by neolithic culture, may have it that these sex-associations were not in any sense love-affairs; or indeed, putting it generally, that any sex-association which does not culminate in Panurge's act of androgynation and the culbatising exercise is not to be classed as a love-affair, but as an affair of simple friendship. Yet since the sex-element is so clearly there, and since it sets up such far-reaching differentiations in both the character and the spiritual product of the relationship, this classification seems to me purely arbitrary. If the association of Voltaire with Mme. du Châtelet; of Joubert with Pauline de Montmorin; of Montaigne with Marie de Gournay; of Goethe with Bettina Brentano; of Wilhelm von Humboldt with Henriette Herz;—if these were not love-affairs I do not know what to call them. Such associations are a matter of abundant record, and I believe they would prove rewarding under analytic literary treatment.[1]

I found that the fashion of extreme frankness prevailing in post-war literature prevailed also in social conversation; so, moved by curiosity, I took advantage of it. Whenever an appropriate occasion came about, which naturally was not often, I would bring up one or two instances of the working of sex-attraction, such as I have just cited, to hear what people had to say about them. By keeping up this practice for several years and in several countries, I amassed a considerable number of accounts of experiences confirmatory of my own conclusions. Case-histories are rather boring, so I shall here mention the salient points of only three. One man had maintained for twenty years what he described as the one and only true love-affair of his life by correspondence with a woman whom he had never seen, and from whom he had always been separated by great distances. Another similar love-affair had gone on for seven years, and was still going on, between two persons who had seen each other but once; their mutual sentiment took root at first sight. An interesting fact in this case was that neither knew the other's language; their communications were carried on in a third language, common to both but native to neither.

The account I got of a third experience is especially noteworthy as proving my point beyond peradventure. The man was deeply in love with the young wife of one of his friends, and she with him. Both were extremely able, brilliant, highly

[1] A striking contemporary instance appears in the association of Mr. G. B. Shaw with Miss Ellen Terry. This is described at length in the recent biography of Mr. Shaw, by Hesketh Pearson. Since the account of the relationship was authorised by Mr. Shaw I see no indelicacy in citing it.

cultivated; their relation was perfect in all its exquisite sympathies and confidences. He was most personable; his presence and manners were unusually engaging; and she was pretty, graceful, charming. I can bear witness to all this, for I knew them well. Yet the physical indifference obtaining between them amounted almost to repugnance; they seldom shook hands when they met, and then only in a perfunctory way, utterly inexpressive of sentiment. One might imagine just such terms of association subsisting between Turgôt and Jeanne-Julie de l'Espinasse or between Benjamin Constant and Mme. de Staël,[2] or in other historical instances.

Thus I was upheld in my belief that the physiological element in sex-attraction is by no means invariably present, and that one's understanding of the term should be broadened accordingly. When sex-attraction is spoken of, one should ask just what is meant by that. The great Cousin, for example, who all his life had hardly ever even noticed a pretty woman, suddenly discovered that his historical studies had forced him into a state of most lover-like devotion to the charms of Mme. de Longueville, who had been dead nearly two hundred years. The experience was highly animating and energising, as the portions of his work which are referable to it show at once. Was this a valid sex-experience, was the attraction at the root of it a valid sex-attraction? If not, then just what was it? What is one to say?

The sum of my observations led me to believe that society's attempts to canalise the course of sex-association by systems of ethical precept and statutory law do not work well because they rest on a basis of purely factitious generalisation. In ways both positive and negative, these attempts have done, and still do, much more harm than good. The psychically-human man and woman soon become aware that the only sure principles

[2] It is impossible to say how far the current notion that the relations of Constant with Mme. de Staël came to more than this, can be justified. Some circumstances make it seem erroneous, while others admit the possibility, but establish nothing. I incline to the former view. The relations of Turgôt with Mlle. de l'Espinasse have never been under suspicion, as far as I know.

on which their sex-relations can be satisfactorily maintained are those which were laid down for them four hundred years ago by Friar John of the Funnels; and that once these principles are established, Friar John's one simple rule becomes their only rule of conduct in the premises: *Fay ce que vouldras.*

II

Towards the end of my term as an editor in New York I stumbled on a statement that considerably more than half the national wealth of the United States was in the hands of women. This interested me to the point of taking measures to find out if it were true; and it was true, to my surprise. I knew that the dean of St. Paul's had described American society as an ice-water-drinking gynecocracy, but I did not imagine that his view could be borne out by anything so cogent. I immediately formed the reasonable notion that so large an amount of economic control combined with full political equality, full equality of educational and cultural opportunity, and an unprecedented liberation from traditional disabilities,—all this should be showing some distinct and salutary social effects. I not only saw no signs of any such effects being produced, however, but I also saw no signs of any disposition to produce them, still less of any sense of responsibility in the premises; and this excited my curiosity. Considering the great enlargement of opportunity for American women to do what they liked with themselves, I was curious to see what, if anything, they were actually doing; and I made this a matter of observation and inquiry for several years, whenever occasion offered.

Putting the results in a word, I found that they were contenting themselves with doing exactly what men do. Their conception of their new-found liberties and the use to be made of them did not reach beyond this. All the evidence I could turn up tended with unfailing regularity to this conclusion. Women entered the same trades and professions as competitors with men, played politics with the same unscrupulous predacity and mountebankery, shared the same unintelligent habits of mind, accepted the same cultural standards, the same codes of social life and manners. They wore men's dress on occasion, smoked, swore and used loose language as men do, drank and sat around bar-rooms as men do. I was amused at observing that their ideal of general conduct, both good and bad, was not that of doing the same things men do and doing them better or even differently. Apparently they were quite satisfied, rather slavishly as it seemed to me, to do just the same things in just the same ways, and do them just as well.

These observations diverted me immensely, and in the end my amusement was the means of my making a great fool of myself in the public prints. Some six or seven years after I had first noticed the statement concerning the distribution of our national wealth I wrote two essays mildly critical of our women's lack of initiative and enterprise, and sent them over from Brussels to my old friend Mr. Sedgwick, who was kind enough to publish them at once for me in the Atlantic. The story of these essays is worth telling because it shows so well the discouraging way Fate has of dropping the warmth of one's self-esteem down to the zero-point, and keeping it there. I thought uncommonly well of those two essays, and so did Mr. Sedgwick. They covered all the ground, they were written in a good spirit, they were playful enough to be ingratiating, and their logic was burglar-proof if one accepted the implied major premise,—but just there, alas, was where the cat lay down in the pepper.

I had based my essays in all good faith on the premise which I had accepted without question from Condorcet, Rousseau, Mr. Jefferson, Henry George, Herbert Spencer and the rest of the goodly fellowship of the prophets; this premise being that the individual *Homo sapiens*, female and male alike, is psychically human and indefinitely improvable, and by consequence the collective *Homo sapiens* is a human society likewise indefinitely improvable. If this premise were valid, my essays would be sound as a nut. But just as I was congratulating myself on a pleasing success, Mr. Cram produced his hypothesis concerning man's place in nature; it blew my premise sky-high, and made my essays not worth the paper they were written on.

The point of my essays was that while admittedly women can do pretty much anything that men can do, and do it pretty much as well, they can also do something which men do not show, and have never shown, any appreciable aptitude for doing; they can civilise a society. In view of this I ventured to suggest that in their peculiarly privileged position American women might do well to get a really competent understanding of what civilisation is and what its terms are, and then apply themselves to quickening the extremely stodgy dough of American society with the leaven of civilisation. If one were addressing an aggregation of psychically-human beings, this would be all very well. But when Mr. Cram showed that neolithic society is not one whit more truly civilised now than it was six thousand years ago, and in the nature of things will be no more truly civilised six thousand years hence, he reduced all I had been saying to sheer nonsense. What it amounted to was that I had been putting the most fantastically extravagant expectations upon psychical capacities which do not exist, never did exist, and in all probability never will. I had placed myself in the absurd position of one recommending the study of analytic geometry to a flock of more or less attentive ewes.

III

The change in women's economic status helped to bring about a great increase in the number of divorces; and this in turn went far in relieving divorce almost entirely from the weight of social obloquy which had long rested on it. This seemed to me an unqualified good thing. In itself, the growing number of divorces was unimportant; what really counted was the disappearance of a prejudice largely superstitious and wholly unintelligent. With the views I entertained of sex-relations in general, I was glad to see the subject of marriage and the family brought up for some measure of reconsideration, and my only regret was that the reconsideration was not more thorough-going.

I regard marriage in the way that the French have of regarding it, as a partnership effected for certain definite purposes, essentially practical. If sentimental considerations favour it at the outset, or if they make a favourable entry after the partnership is established, that is all very well; but the institution itself, *das Ding an sich*, is of a purely business-like and non-affectional character. This view keeps the issues distinct, separate, clear-cut, thereby avoiding the endless trouble caused by confusion and misapprehension. If Potash and Perlmutter were antecedently fond of each other, no doubt that helped; if subsequently they become fond of each other, no doubt that helps; but the purpose of their partnership is the production and sale of cloaks and suits, and the personal qualities and aptitudes called into play for successful promotion of a sentimental attachment are by no means the same as those called into play for successful promotion of the cloak-and-suit business. Thus it was that notwithstanding the notable tepidity of friendship between the partners Klinger and Klein, they were held together by a perfect community of interest in the conduct of a thriving trade. So in the matter of marriage, whether sentimental considerations make their appearance first or last or not at all, they have only an incidental bearing on the purpose for which the partnership is formed. If I remember correctly, it was Mr. Zudrowsky, of the firm of Zudrowsky and Cohen, who said that "for a business man, understand me, love comes after marriage"; and apparently as many successful marriages have been arranged on that basis as on any other.

What had always seemed to me thoroughly unfair and objectionable was society's merciless insistence on making the marriage-bed a bed of Procrustes, if I may put it so; and on the principle that half a loaf is better than no bread, I was pleased to see this insistence even slightly moderated. Society insisted that persons who wished to realise for themselves the immense benefits of a sex-relationship—and I humbly hope I have made clear just what I mean by a sex-relationship—must subject themselves to the duties, sanctions, responsibilities, changes and chances of a quasi-industrial enterprise before they could be permitted to do so. Any other arrangement, however much more appropriate and satisfactory, was inadmissible. Thus marriage was, most arbitrarily as it seemed to me, interposed as a bar or condition between the individual and one of the main sources of his or her well-being. So arbitrarily were these requirements laid down that they took no account whatever of the individual's ability to meet them; and here is where the sheerly Procrustean unfairness of the matter is apparent.

Regarding marriage as essentially a quasi-industrial partnership, a business enterprise, and then looking over the persons of one's acquaintance who are engaged in it, one must see, I think, that the distribution of natural aptitude for it is about what it is for other occupations. There are many misfits, many who through no great fault of theirs have obviously mistaken their calling. Society's tacit assumption is that all normal persons are qualified for matrimony, and this is not so. Many women are as ill-adapted to a career in matrimony as they are to a career in blacksmithing or steam-riveting; many men are equally ill-adapted. I refer to disability imposed by nature, not by circumstance. When such as these experience a valid sex-attraction of whatever type, and seek to make the most of it by accepting the only terms that society has hitherto presented as admissible, the consequences clearly are bound to be unfortunate. The best they can do is to maintain a position on the bare edge of spiritual solvency through a continuous series of stultifying compromises and makeshifts; and at that, the spiritual deputy-sheriff is always lurking about their dooryard, armed with a warrant of levy-and-distress. Mr. Marquand's recent novel, *H. M. Pulham, Esquire*, bears upon these difficulties, and illustrates them admirably.

Again, one may observe if one be candid about it, that polygamy and polyandry are phenomena as common among mankind as they are elsewhere in the animal world, and are therefore to be regarded as natural; though here once more I express the hope that this statement will not be interpreted with exclusive reference to Panurge's *acte mouvent de belutaige.* On the stage in the *Beggar's Opera* we have Captain Macheath declaring roundly that "a man who loves money might as well be content with one guinea as I with one woman"; and I believe that if intelligent men and women examined their hearts without prejudice they would find there the question: Well, just why should he be content with one woman? Why should Polly Peachum or Lucy Lockit be content with one man? Why should any man or woman be so content? Goethe found that question not easy to answer. He gives the institution of marriage a rather shaky leg-up by saying it deserves respect as one of the triumphs of culture over nature, but he leaves one doubting whether this may not be a Pyrrhic triumph after all, for he adds that "marriage, properly speaking, is unnatural."

It is unnatural for the reason, among others, that it tends to interfere with a free association of men and women, such as Friar John of the Funnels contemplated in the design for his abbey. One remarks the interesting fact that Rabelais, who never made a mistake in his interpretations of the spirit of man, has no married couples in Thélème, though he makes no rule against such being there. He says that if for any reason a man wished to leave the abbey and go out into the world, taking his declared sweetheart with him,[3] they would then marry and live happily ever after. Not to put too fine a point on it, there seems here a distinct intimation that however appropriate marriage might be to conditions prevailing in society-at-large, it was inappropriate to those prevailing in the abbey; and by testing one's own reactions to the story one can see how this would be so. The abbey's tenants were such as on Mr. Cram's hypothesis would be classed as human beings, and when one considers their character and qualities one is conscious of considerable violence in any attempt to associate the idea of marriage with them.

[3] Celle laquelle l'auroit prins pour son devot.

After Mme. de Staël had eased her rather plantigrade husband out of the reckoning, she lived on the freest terms of intimacy with such men as Talleyrand, A. W. Schlegel, de Sismondi, Benjamin Constant, travelled with them on occasion, and on occasion occupied the same premises with them. Each of these had something peculiarly his own to contribute towards the enrichment of her cultural life, and she to theirs; and among them all, in virtue of this free association, they contrived to add a fairish bit to the resources of European civilisation. She had great gifts and a great power of sex-attraction, though by all accounts not much on the physiological side; but she had no more natural faculty for partnership in the quasi-industrial enterprise of marriage than she had for handling a steam-shovel. Manifestly, then, any social pressure tending to hold her to an occupation for which she had no aptitude, and interfering with her advancement in activities for which she had great aptitude, would result in loss and damage, and therefore must, at least by me, be regarded as pernicious.

One often sees great loss traceable to this cause, if one keeps an eye out for it. I saw notable loss incurred in the instance of sex-relation cited in my third case-history a page or two back. The lovers in question seldom met, though there was no definite agreement not to meet, but merely a tacit understanding. The lady had no fears or scruples, and her husband was not one to make any difficulties about the intimacy; on the contrary, he understood it perfectly and was glad to encourage it. But her social and domestic responsibilities frittered her time and energies, and her lover had the spirit of the *preux chevalier*, unwilling that the lady should run the least chance of being exposed to suspicion or her husband to embarrassment. So their romance went undeclared, and they got but little out of each other; which was a profound misfortune for them and a loss to all who moved in their social orbit.

My survey of these matters left me with the belief that in the view of a sound practical philosophy, marriage should be reduced to a footing with other respectable industrial enterprises, and that all discussion of it should leave sentimental considerations aside. For those whose natural aptitudes run that way,—and there are many, both of men and women,—there could be no better upshot to a sex-relation than marriage; and for those whose aptitudes do not run that way, hardly anything could be worse. I think the great majority will always take to marriage, however free they may be to choose their estate. Pending a régime of complete economic freedom, most women will certainly take to it,—Epstean's law will attend to that,—and I should say the majority of men will also. But of both there will always be a minority who see in marriage something which *for them* is unnatural, disabling and retarding.

In behalf of these I think the unintelligent opprobrium of impropriety and "irregularity" attaching to relations such as those which Mme. de Staël established for herself should be dissipated. One observes with satisfaction that the large measure of economic independence which American women have gained has already done much towards clearing it away. This is one of many indications pointing to the great truth which apparently must forever remain unlearned, that if a régime of complete economic freedom be established, social and political freedom will follow automatically; and until it is established neither social nor political freedom can exist. Here one comes in sight of the reason why the State will never tolerate the establishment of economic freedom. In a spirit of sheer conscious fraud, the State will at any time offer its people "four freedoms," or six, or any number; but it will never let them have economic freedom. If it did, it would be signing its own death-warrant, for as Lenin pointed out, "it is nonsense to make any pretence of reconciling the State and liberty." Our economic system being what it is, and the State being what it is, all the mass of verbiage about "the free peoples" and "the free democracies" is merely so much obscene buffoonery.

IV

At the time when I was turning over in my mind this matter of sex-relations, a German friend said to me in bitterness one day, "I tell you, the man who invented the family was an enemy of the human race." My poor friend was not altogether without reason. With all the advantages of wealth, social position and high culture, he had led for many years what Mrs. Quickly called "a very frampold life" with a domineering spouse and some unsatisfactory daughters, of whom he had the misfortune to be very fond. I believe that under the régime of economism nearly all men have at one time or another had to face the grievous truth of Bacon's aphorism concerning hostages to fortune. No doubt also many women, especially those who have gone into matrimony under the spur of Epstean's law, sometimes feel that they have let themselves in for a hard bargain. Nevertheless in general the family, regarded as an institution, still seems to work about as well as the rest of our rickety institutions do, since the majority of people like children, more or less, and therefore may perhaps be said to have some sort of rough-and-ready aptitude for it. On the other hand, a very respectable minority have not even the most attenuated aptitude for it. In my opinion, the most prolific source of misfortune lies in taking a strong biological urge towards procreation as evidence of this aptitude. Women are peculiarly liable to this error, but even the standard jokes in our comic papers show that men also fall victims to it. Herbert Spencer liked children, but felt that he had no faculty whatever for family life, and God wot he was right. So, like the resourceful man of science which he was, he used to borrow batches of children from the neighbours and hob-nob with them in order to keep the springs of his affectional nature from drying up. Mark Twain, whom certainly nature never cut out for a family man,—poor soul!—also did something with this practice; and how bitterly one regrets that the colossal Tolstoy did not confine his affectional excursions to it! I think it is a sound practice, and one to be encouraged in all such circumstances. I would follow it myself if I liked children, but I have a great horror of them.

Where the family chiefly shows itself as inimical to the human race, to borrow my German friend's term, is in its character as the strongest bulwark of whatever economic system may be in force, even the most iniquitous. No wonder the State and the Church unite in coddling the family and hedging it about with all the protective devices that law and factitious ethics can devise! A person with a family does what he must and as he must. Often, like the tripe-editor I spoke of a moment ago, he has to reconcile himself to stultifying and despicable courses of conduct which, if he were free to do so, he would refuse even to consider. He must stay within the economic system and uphold it; and thus the demands of family are responsible for the atrophy of many fine talents, and for the progressive moral dim-out which darkens many lives.

Throughout the post-war period I listened to a vast deal of vague lugubrious talk about the evil of divorce and the ruinous loosening of family ties. I saw nothing in all this but what was to be expected, nor could I make it seem so calamitous as these prophetic voices made it out to be. In the time of an individualist agricultural economy the family was an economic asset; the larger it was, the better. The shift to an industrial economy with mass-production in agriculture converted it into an economic liability. The inflow of women into the trades and professions took up some of the slack, thereby somewhat redressing the balance of loss and gain, with the important difference that the women so employed earned money-wages, which under the old economy they did not do, and they kept control of their earnings. This tended to break up the family as an economic unit, and to leave it held together only by such affectional bonds as might exist on their own merits. This seemed to me quite as it should be, and quite to be expected. As for the increase in divorce, I took it as an outcome of women's altered economic status, quite inevitable, quite to be expected, and suggesting nothing especially immoral or reprehensible. Like the facilities for dissolving other forms of partnership, the facilities for divorce are susceptible of abuse and no doubt are sometimes seriously abused; but once again if one "regards mankind as being what they are," one sees that this also is to be expected; it is inevitable.

I was much impressed by my learned friend Hendrik Willem van Loon's remark that "a sense of the inevitable" is the most valuable thing one can get out of one's classical studies. I have already shown in these pages how steadily from the very beginning my own studies were directed towards an intensive cultivation of this sense; and I can never be thankful enough for the good fortune which brought me that advantage. In speaking of William the Taciturn, who had "absorbed some slight admixture of the old Roman and Greek philosophies with his more formal Christian training," Mr. van Loon shows how almost automatically this saving sense, when it is well developed, gets itself applied to every appraisal of mankind's ways and doings. One may wish they were better and wiser than they are, but the sense of the inevitable gives warning that no force of wishing or striving can make them so; and therefore the less they are meddled with, the better.

It is interesting to see how often the poet's conclusions, arrived at by the light of this sense, are identical with the philosopher's. Goethe's sense of the inevitable made his forecast of mankind's progress identical with Mr. Cram's. "Man will become more clever and sagacious," said Goethe, "but not better, happier or showing more resolute wisdom; or at least, only at periods." Inevitably so. Cleverness and sagacity are traits which the neolithic man shares with his humbler relatives in the animal world; he owes his survival to his immense superiority in combining and managing the two. In respect of the other traits he is devoid of capacity; they characterise the human being. Perhaps the most striking evidence of this is found in the apparent anomaly which so baffled Mr. Jefferson and Henry Adams: that with all man's marvellous ability to invent things which are potentially good, he can always be counted on to make the worst possible use of what he invents; as witness the radio, printing-press, aeroplane and the internal-combustion engine. On the assumption that the neolithic men and women massed in society are human and therefore indefinitely improvable, the problem of conduct here presented is past all resolving. Mr. Jefferson gave it up in despair, saying "What a Bedlamite is man!" On the contrary assumption there is no anomaly, and hence no problem; we perceive at once that all which seemed to be unaccountable is quite in the order of nature and quite to be expected.

V

My meditations on the family and family life hardened me in the sin of cleaving to a most unorthodox idea which I had formed long before. I believe that a mother should have nothing to do with her daughters' bringing-up and should be with them as little by way of companionship as possible; and likewise a father with his sons. I came by this idea originally through noticing the excellent results of this practice in the few instances where I knew of its having been followed. The girl brought up by her mother until she reaches the age of twelve or thirteen gets only the feminine view of life-in-general, into which view she is bound to gravitate in any case. She does not know the male mind well at first-hand, does not know how it works or what its dispositions are, nor can she get a competent knowledge of this as long as she is subjected to a confusing association with the feminine mind. She is equally unable to get a sympathetic understanding of the male character as long as she knows it only through a maternal interpretation. The boy brought up in habitual association with his father is under a like disability at every point.

I might mention also my belief that after children are past the stage of bringing-up, all formal teaching of them in school, college and university should be done by men. I have not examined my grounds for this belief very closely, and I am quite willing to listen to reason in the matter of making room for an occasional Hypatia in post-graduate instruction, but my present strong conviction is that under any circumstances the employment of women as teachers is disadvantageous.

I have sometimes wondered, perhaps rather perversely, whether the fashion of easy divorce might not tend to make the "irregular" type of sex-relation more durable than the conventional type. I must repeat the assurance that I am not speaking of the relation as exhibited by the heroes and heroines of our popular literature, notably by those of Mr. H. G. Wells's latest novel, *You Can't Be Too Careful.* Far from that, I speak of it only as exhibited by psychically-human beings in the instances I have cited. My thoughts were set going in this direction by some words from an experienced married woman in her late twenties. An observant friend had just then been telling me that in his opinion the most moral men in America are actors, "because," he said, "they always marry their wenches." I was amused by this,—it did seem really to have some point,—and I mentioned it to the lady by way of a joke. "I don't quite see that," she said. "The way things are, it's a lot easier to get rid of a wife than a wench."

One can see how this might be so for the general run of mankind, and one can see a special reason why it should be so for the psychically-human being. In the city of Tours one day I looked in on one of the great regional markets where buyers from all parts of France were dealing with peasants for grain. I was astonished to see that every bit of business on the premises was done on parole; no formal contracts, no memoranda, not a pen-scratch or a pencil-mark in evidence anywhere. I was told that this is an invariable custom, because reading and writing were suspect arts with the French peasant from time immemorial. Make an agreement with him by word of mouth, and he would never fail, never was known to fail. Force him to sign a formal contract, if you could, and there was no telling what he would do, but you could pretty well count on its being something you might not like.

It may be that in the psychically-human being there is a streak of this resentment, however larval, against the obligations of formal contract in general. I think there is. It is conceivable also that in the case of a formal marriage-contract this resentment might be heightened by the consciousness that society's assumption of a clear right to barge in and regulate a relation so distinctly personal is open to question. Hence if the relation became unsatisfactory, one would feel no great compunctions about taking any available way out of it. On the other hand, if the relation were established on parole or by tacit understanding, one would have to stick it as best one could, and no doubt all the better for knowing that whatever discipline of spirit may be called for is self-imposed. At the instant when a sentiment of affection becomes authoritative a dry rot sets in on it. When Polly let it out that she meant to marry her dashing captain, Mr. Peachum asked her in great indignation, "Do you think your mother and I should have lived comfortably so long together if ever we had been married?"

But the reader must remember that this chapter, like all my chapters, amounts to nothing but the more or less aimless reminiscences of a superfluous man. It would be vain to pretend that I am wiser about mankind's affectional relations than any one else would be who had watched their tacks and turns as long as I have watched them from my seat in the grandstand. Perhaps at that distance one misses many of the game's most interesting fine points of play, so *que scai-je*? Certainly I do not know so much that I should write out my reflections on these or any other subjects with a view to any one's interest but my own.

CHAPTER TWELVE

"But what do I know of Aurelia, or any other girl?" he says to me with that abstracted air; "I, whose Aurelias were of another century and another zone."

—GEORGE WILLIAM CURTIS.

There is no excellent beauty that hath not some strangeness in the proportion.

—FRANCIS BACON.

WHEN I said a moment ago that I thought all teaching should be done by men, I hope I made it clear that my reference was to formal teaching, institutional teaching. A great deal of informal non-professional teaching is, and should be, done by women,—indeed must be, if it is to be done at all, for only women can do it; and here I am referring not so much to instruction in the nursery or kindergarten as to the invaluable directions, suggestions and spiritual assistances that one gets continually from women throughout one's later life. I must observe, however, that my opinion about women's place in professional teaching is only an opinion. I think that, *ceteris paribus*, women are less well adapted to a career in teaching than men are. Given two persons, a man and a woman whose abilities and attainments are in every respect exactly equal, I believe the student will profit more from the man's instruction than from the woman's. I do not know why this should be so, and I am sure I could not defend my belief to the satisfaction of the intrepid ladies who so nobly fit, bled and died in the cause of feminism some twenty-odd years ago. The matter appears to me as one of the innumerable phenomena of nature which simply are so, and about whose reason, necessity or justification one finds it useless to speculate.

But the enlightenment,—let me say, the education,—which one gets from women is of immense abundance and priceless value. One may easily see how this should be so, for women are roughly one-half of the race, and in studying the special endowments and characteristics of this feminine mass, in observing the ways by which they approach and take hold of life, their particular adaptabilities, their instinctive turns of view upon specific questions, interests, sets of circumstances,—by this means one gets a vast amount of education that is otherwise unobtainable. It is surely unreasonable to think that one can round out a practical philosophy of existence without taking full account of a distinctly differentiated half of the beings among whom that existence must, for better or worse, be spent. For my own part I am free to say that, taking my education as a whole, I am indebted to women for the most valuable part of it; even though, to the best of my recollection, I never got a single line of book-l'arnin' through the instrumentality of any woman.

One of the most fascinating adventures of my life was exploring the literature of the *Querelle des Dames*. What started me on it was Rabelais's account of Panurge's shilly-shallying indecision about taking a wife, which makes up practically the whole subject-matter of the Third Book. One would hardly believe that during the last half of the fifteenth century and well into the sixteenth, a red-hot feminist controversy raged in Europe like the plague, and that virtually all the capable male minds of the time lent themselves to it, some maintaining that woman is by nature an inferior being, properly subject to man, and others maintaining the contrary. The subject had a large literature before the invention of printing; and after that, a great number of books appeared. Even the colossal Erasmus of Rotterdam chipped in with a short treatise, *On*

Christian Marriage, which was probably more or less done to order at the instance of his English friends.

Scholars think that Rabelais published the Third Book as a piece of market-writing, knowing that feminism was a live topic, and hoping that a playful work which touched on it would have a good sale. I disagree with that view. My notion is that Rabelais was wickedly delighted by the spectacle of full-grown men making such a tremendous pother over nothing, and felt an irresistible temptation to stir up the animals. It is clear that nothing pleased him more than a chance of this kind, and he never missed one. Even a careless reader of the Third Book can see that when it got into the hands of people who took all this foolishness seriously, whether they were on one side of the controversy or the other, it would make them madder than wet hens, as in fact it did; and I believe he meant it to do just that. I can see him now, slapping his thigh and roaring with laughter as he turned off one salty paragraph after another at the top of his speed. He was promptly blackguarded as an anti-feminist, for such is the habit of the neolithic mentality under such circumstances; and this despite the exalted view of women which he expressed when writing seriously in his description of Thélème. A few years after Rabelais's death François Billon, who wrote a massive history of the great controversy, renewed the old calumny, and in some quarters it sticks to this day.

It was many years ago, just after I had finished my graduate studies, that I dipped into this literature. I touched on it in a superficial way, as I was reading only for fun, so actually I did little with it beyond sampling it here and there as something would strike my fancy, and I soon gave it up. I got enough out of it, however, so that when the British suffragettes broke loose under the lead of Mrs. Pankhurst, and the American sisterhood dutifully followed suit by going on the warpath, I found I had a complete perspective on their doings. I was on familiar terms with the whole substance of their contention; I had been familiar with it, so to say, for four hundred years; it was good classical fifteenth-century stuff. Perceiving this at once, I saw I was in for a long season of excellent diversion, and I accordingly got myself comfortably squared away to enjoy it.

I remembered one matter which had interested me at the time of my earlier readings. I had noticed that in Rabelais's period the controversy was carried on by men. Men wrote all the books, did all the pamphleteering. Women did nothing. I thought this was rather remarkable, especially as the French Renaissance brought forth any number of women perfectly capable of lending a hand if they had seen fit to do so. They were able, brilliant, successful in politics and literature, and were at the top of the heap in point of social influence and prestige. Those were the days when Louise of Savoy, Marguerite of Angoulême, Anne of Brittany, Renée of France, were distinguishing themselves in public affairs. Some women of the time, moreover, had that rarest of gifts, potent even after the lapse of four hundred years, the power of making one wish mightily that one could have known them. They were not great, no doubt, except for this wonderful gift of imparting, if I may put it so, a delicate and delicious fragrance to their period's literary history. I am unable at the moment to think of any of the great historical female characters of the period, or any period, whom I should much care to meet, but I would cheerfully give all my old boots and shoes if I could have known the *belle cordière* Louise Labé, Anne Tallonne, Sybille and Claudine Scève, and Pernette du Guillet, who must have been the most exquisite of spirits, and who died so young.

Yet out of all this array of feminine ability, no one seems to have got up much steam over the question which was agitating the men-folk: the question whether by nature women are, or are not, inferior beings. I suspect that with good hard common sense they, like Rabelais, thought the whole contention was supremely silly. If the men saw fit to fool away their time on it, well and good, let them do so; it would do no harm, and might tend to keep them out of mischief; but as for themselves, they had better fish to fry. I think that here one can recognise a turn of realism essentially feminine, or should I say French-feminine? It is noteworthy that Marguerite of Angoulême befriended Rabelais, as she did Marot, des Périers, Dolet and other unruly gentry who made the mistake of being too openly sportive about matters which the authorities of State and Church regarded as serious. She wangled a copyright for Rabelais out of her brother Francis I, which was a hard thing to get in those days, and Rabelais paid off the favour by dedicating the Third Book to her in a short flight of shocking poor verse. She unquestionably read the Third Book, for there is a reminiscence of the lively thirty-fifth chapter in one of her own poems; so if she saw any signs of anti-feminism in it, she seems not to have taken them to heart.

So much, then, for the attitude of women towards the earlier controversy. When the storm broke out afresh in the twentieth century I made two interesting observations. The first one was that this time, in both England and America, it was the women who were sweating all the blood and raising all the commotion. They had some men under conviction in both countries, but they were largely of the Liberal persuasion and hence devoid of humour, incapable of recognising the essential futility of causes which for some reason seem always chiefly to attract them. A few others gave a diffident and sheepish sort of allegiance, probably under domestic dragooning of a severe type. Aside from these, the men stood aloof; many of them, especially in England, annoyed by the various arsons, assaults, picketings and general carryings-on with which the ladies were entertaining themselves; and the rest either indifferent or displaying only a sporting interest. In short, the men and women of the twentieth-century cast had simply swapped rôles with the actors in the earlier performance four centuries ago.

I was much interested by this, and far more by my second observation, that in France the women were standing pat, precisely like the women of the Renaissance, and the men had cooled off to the zero-point, so that feminism was distinctly a dead issue. I looked into the matter, and found that French law *prima facie* bore as hardly on women as English law, much harder than American law, yet Frenchwomen seemed to be doing very well under its iniquities, and were quite indisposed to make a fuss about them. Missionaries from England got no results; the Frenchwomen were polite and pleasant, but firmly declined to get stirred up. The result of my investigations convinced me that if they had full suffrage presented to them outright they would not take the trouble to find out when election-day was due. I was pleased by these discoveries. When I contrasted the Frenchwomen's attitude with that of the British and American sisterhood, I was no end delighted at perceiving that the steady-headed, realistic, thoroughly objective spirit of the great Louises, Marguerites and Renées was still to the front and going strong.

As I saw it, the Frenchwomen were toeing the Platonist mark of seeing things as they were; not as they thought they should be, or wanted them to be, but as they actually were. With regard to suffrage, they could see that as long as the State was administered by criminals and psychopaths, their vote would not be worth casting. Moreover, they might know what any one of ordinary common sense would know, that the State must go on being administered by criminals and psychopaths because in the nature of things none but a criminal or psychopath would take the job, or could get it, or could do anything with it if he had it. France's century of political experience would seem to have drummed a sense of this transcendent truth into the Frenchwoman's head. If by an untoward stroke of fate some one who was neither a criminal nor a psychopath found himself at the head of the State's affairs in a modern republic, he would do about as well and last about as long as Adrian VI at Rome or John Quincy Adams at Washington. The British suffrage was extended to women; the suffragettes won their case,—and look at England's political record of the past twenty years! The American suffragettes also won their case; they have been busily voting, jobholding and saving the country ever since, and now,—God help us all!—just look at it!

I say this not by way of aspersing American womankind or of offloading any undue responsibility on them. As I have already explained, a sense of logic and justice put me on the side of the suffragettes and kept me there. I was, and am, for full suffrage, full rights of property, a "single standard of morals," whatever that is, divorce on demand,—I do not think there is a single moot point on which I would be found tripping. I am interested only in remarking that by the test of practice the contention proved worthless, quite as I knew it would; and that the attitude of the Frenchwomen was far more sensible. They had made France a woman's country, not by voting or jobholding or getting up parades and mass-meetings, organising clubs, and so on, but by making themselves indispensable to the country's welfare. France was a country of small businesses, and women managed them; women managed the household, the family; in fact, there was precious little in the day-to-day life of France that women did not manage, and manage exceedingly well. They knew they were indispensable; the men also knew it, and went very gingerly about interfering with any of their prerogatives, law or no law. When Marianne spoke up, her menfolk listened earnestly and took due notice. Experience, I repeat, must have bred in the realistic Marianne a calm Emersonian disregard of Falstaff's "old Father Antic, the law"; and properly so. If one has an unbreakable grip on the reality of power, why bother to coerce an omnium-gatherum of illiterate blackguards into validating the mere appearance of it?

I saw a delicious exhibition of this spirit only a few weeks ago when I was in company with a lady who was bitterly resentful—and rightly so—of some of our statutes affecting women. It appears that somewhere in the Grand Republic there is a state law permitting a husband to alienate his children from their mother by will. This did not seem so heinous to me (though I did not say so) for I understand that in the state where I am sojourning a man can be put in gaol for kissing his wife on Sunday, though I have not yet heard of its being done.

A case which the lady cited as the *locus classicus* was that of a wife who found under the pillow of her husband's death-bed a scribbled codicil bequeathing his unborn child to another woman, said to be his mistress. Most thoughtlessly (the French strain in me is always cropping out when it should not, and getting me into trouble) I said at once it was no doubt an excellent arrangement, for the man knew both women and knew all the circumstances, and therefore—but I was not permitted to go on. When the smoke cleared away, a French girl in the company quietly said, "A Frenchwoman would just have torn up that paper and said nothing about it."

Precisely so; there you have it! That girl knew her country-women. I was so delighted that I yearned to kiss the hem of her garment, but being new to this country she could not possibly have understood why I should make so much fuss over what would seem to her a very small matter of everyday good sense; so I restrained myself and gave no sign.

By a series of adjustments and understandings, quite elaborate and entirely extra-legal, Frenchwomen had built themselves into a position of power and authority substantial enough not only to make them indispensable to the working of their social system, but also to make them recognised as indispensable; so what the law might say or not say mattered little. While I was on the side of our suffragettes, I could not help thinking that their contention was paltry, as the outcome has shown it to be, and that they might have done better with their energy and devotion if they had taken a leaf out of the Frenchwomen's book. American women had long been in a notoriously privileged position; the fact was known wherever the sun shines; and I wondered why they had not shown the Frenchwomen's sagacity and cleverness in consolidating their advantage. Quite evidently they had not done so, and the exhibitions they have put on since they were legally enabled to cut a larger figure on the public stage gave additional evidence that they neither had nor have any idea of doing so.

On one point of doctrine, perhaps, I was a little heretical.

I was all for equality of the sexes before the law, but the left-wing doctrine of "natural equality" impressed me as profound nonsense. The Tiraqueaus and Bouchards of the Renaissance struck me, as they did Rabelais, as acting like incredible simpletons, and so did their continuators in the twentieth century. Any one capable of seeing what he looks at knows that there is no such thing as this natural equality anywhere in the mammalian world. It is ten to one that neither Tiraqueau nor Bouchard ever kept cats, though such a thing is hard to believe of any Frenchman. Women, like the she-females of any mammalian species, are in some respects superior to their males, immeasurably so, and in other respects are distinctly inferior. These qualities of excess and defect are complementary, and the practical thing is to adjust one's personal sex-relations in correspondence with that natural arrangement. Here again the Frenchwomen, in my opinion, have shown themselves the soundest of feminists, and American women, as I observed in my last chapter, the most unsound.

My belief is that the most unfortunate result of the American *querelle des dames* has been an aggravation of the peculiarly American itch for inquisitional meddling, snooping, prying into all sorts of ill-understood matters, and bustling about in the effort to regulate, re-shape and, *Gott soll hüten*, to improve them; and invariably invoking the very worst and most incompetent agency for the purpose—political action. I do not imply, nor do I believe, that American women are more subject to this odious disorder than American men. I observe merely that for obvious reasons their seizures are usually more violent and longer protracted; also that their change of legal status adds greatly to the epidemic force and spread of this mania. Since the first days of Prohibition, whenever I have visited this country I have found its atmosphere reeking with the "insane smell," familiar to alienists, of *Weltverbesserungswahn*; and in the last ten years its thickening stench has become unbearable. Thus one may say quite justly, I believe, that the New Woman of Anglo-American feminism has contributed much more than her full share to a continuous process of debasement and vulgarisation. As a matter of simple honesty, the first act of our present Administration should have been to take the legend *E pluribus unum* off our currency, and substitute Goethe's phrase, *Was uns alle bändigt, das Gemeine.*

II

Since I began this chapter I have been prodding my memory vigorously to see what I could stir up about the little girls who were in my orbit when I was a little boy. The result is that I have drawn a complete blank, except for the French child who lived next door to us, or it may have been two or three doors away, in Brooklyn. I think my remembering her at all may be due to the fact which would naturally make a considerable impression on a child, that while apparently she knew well enough how to talk, she did not say anything that I could understand, nor could she understand anything I said to her. Aside from this, all I can recall of her is that she was a light blonde and seemed frail. I do not remember her face, her actions, or anything that passed between us except two or three haphazard attempts at making conversation.

Barring this episode, my life up past the age of ten seems to have been completely girlless. There must have been a herd of girl-children loose about our neighbourhood, but I do not remember ever seeing any. I do not recall a single name, face, skirt, pinafore or hair-ribbon. Of the boys I played with, some at least must have had sisters, but if they ever spoke of them I do not recall it. This seems rather strange, now that I think of it, for most men have preserved some little recollection of having been thrown with girls at no later age than ten, playing games with them, fighting them, teasing and bullying them, and being teased and bullied in return. But I have no such recollection. One reason may be that I did not go to school, for I suppose it is usually at school that boys and girls first find themselves mixed up promiscuously. Another reason may be that I had no sisters; all my associations in the family were with men and women around the age of thirty, so my views and impressions of womankind and their relations with men were formed on adults.

In this I was extremely lucky, for the women around me were, without exception, superb specimens of their kind. They were able, gifted, handsome, witty, strong-minded, humorous, and above all they were downright. There was not a grain of humbug or sickly-sentimentalist nonsense in any of them. I was loved devotedly as none too many children are, but I was also respected as far too few children are. No woman ever petted me, took me on her lap, made up to me, gushed baby-talk over me. I should have taken anything of the kind as a low indecency and an outrage. I know this, for I remember one attempt made by a silly old blister who was talking with my mother at our front gate when I happened along. She got as far as patting me on the back, with a maudlin word or two thrown in, when I retired in silent indignation with every feather bristling, and I never went near the sappy old creature again.

Thus my early impressions of women were not of a kind to provoke any curiosity about their nature or their peculiarities; still less, to excite any sense of their inferiority or their superiority. There the women were, and I took them as they were. They were different from the men, different in appearance, dress, interests and occupations, but they did not seem at all superior to men or in the least inferior, but merely different. I liked them immensely, thought they were splendid, and they never amused me more than when they were matching wits with their menfolk; but my affection for them was no deeper than for the men, nor yet any shallower. As for their relations, I saw that in certain well-defined ways the men looked after the women, and in other ways, equally well-defined, the women looked after the men; and this seemed perfectly reasonable and natural.

I noticed also that both the women and men came in for

certain conventional deferences as matter-of-course, and could count on their being punctiliously yielded; but these stirred in me no sense of inequality either way, nor did they seem to betoken any sacrifice of self-respect. I was instinctively all in favour of these deferences, since I saw that both the women and men were far above taking any unscrupulous advantage of the spirit which prompted them. I could understand how they would make things go easier, more agreeably and gracefully, and hence I liked them and more or less unconsciously fell in with them. The two sets of deferences were different, naturally, but they were equally effortless and prepossessing. All this probably did something towards putting me in the way, later on, of appreciating the devoted and undemanding spirit of the *cavaliere servente*, which I have always believed to be the best for men's cultivation, and which I always have cultivated in my relations with all sorts and conditions of women. As well as I can judge from observation, experience, and the reading of history, the *cavaliere servente* has always got the best out of womankind, and hence I think it likely that he always will.

As for the girls in our northern lumber-town, my memory serves me but little better. There were some with whom I was on terms that were friendly and pleasant enough, but all I had to do with them was casual, and I remember almost nothing about them. I suppose I had too much else on hand to get up any great amount of interest in cultivating them. I can recall a few names, but no faces to answer to them. I remember any number of older women well enough, but no girls of anywhere near my own age. Perhaps the doings of a long life among many peoples have overlaid these memories, but I do not think so. I think they have faded out because there was so little of any consequence to be remembered.

I do, however, remember very clearly when I began to take critical notice of youthful female beauty; I believe I have already mentioned somewhere that it was in the period of my being away at boarding-school. The town was brimming with pretty girls, and I took a good deal of interest in studying their looks and making comparisons, as one does when considering objects in a jeweller's window. We boys scraped acquaintance with a number of them; probably some of us flirted with them more or less, and perhaps one or two of us came down with mild cases of calf-love, though this is only a suspicion on my part. I did not get so far as any of this. The girls were always amiable and pleasant with me, and that was all.

Nevertheless I liked to look at them, more than anything for the sake of making out just what it was in which their good looks consisted. I began to consider such matters as bone-structure, facial contour, types of feature. The one whom I put up in my mind as entitled to the blue ribbon had a perfect Roman face, in full and in profile, and she carried herself with somewhat of a Roman bearing; which was rather remarkable, for she was *echt*-German as Dortmund beer, like nearly all the girls in that town. Still, she may have thrown back to some irregular ancestor in camp on the banks of the Lippe confronting the mighty Arminius; perhaps to Varus himself. There is a pleasant irony in the thought of all the innumerable social complexities and dishevelments which the mere lapse of time so quickly irons out.

Somehow I managed to contemplate this kaleidoscopic array of alluring loveliness without being seriously smitten by anything I saw. I liked the girls I knew, liked to look at them, liked to please them and do them what little courtesies were in my power, and was usually ready to chatter small-talk with them till the cows came home; yet, after one had chattered, looked and listened through a session of small-talk, what was there to show for it? Later I discovered the reason why these girls had so little affected my peace of mind. They were stunning beauties, sweet as they could be, and horribly out of luck in being born too soon to make their everlasting fortune in Hollywood or on magazine-covers. But despite all this, there was no denying that their beauty not only betokened immaturity, which was quite to be expected, but also disclosed the certain forecast of a mature being who, in point of perspicacity, imagination and humour, would be more than a little *dumm*. Their good looks gave no promise of ever becoming *ausdrucksvoll* with the irresistible power of attraction which I had seen residing in the faces of the women I had known since first my eyes were opened on the world.

My perception of this was instinctive at the time, but accurate. Ever since then,—or always, in fact, counting in the period during which my preferences were established by instinct,—this quality which I then found undetectable in prospect has been the one to mark the difference between effective charm and the lack of it in determining my reaction to female beauty. Mere regularity in beauty has never interested me, though until it became so filthily vulgarised I enjoyed looking at it with the appreciation of a connoisseur. I soon became aware of the curious magnetic power resident even in certain positive defects, though I do not more than half-understand it; the kind of thing that helped out the astonishing popularity of stage-women like Anna Held, Polaire and Rigolboche. Once at a foreign summer-resort, when I was twenty-six or so, I wasted a great deal of time on putting myself in the way of a pretty-pretty young girl who had one green eye and one brown eye. I had not the slightest wish to meet her or talk with her, but I could see how this strange defect might be a great asset to a face that carried the expression, which hers distinctly did not carry, of high intelligence and refinement. With those eyes a Marguerite or Renée might have made even the inexorable Tiraqueau come to terms. I presume my sense of this magnetic power may account for the rather silly satisfaction I got out of tagging around after the young woman for views of her eyes. I do not know how else to account for it.

III

To me it appears indisputable that out of all peoples, nations and languages, male writers of every sort and size have committed themselves to more damneder fiddle-faddle on the subject of women than on any other subject under the sun. Perhaps in saying what little I have to say on the subject I am merely adding one more to the list. I must take my chances on that, however, in pursuance of the purpose of this book, as I have already explained; withal admitting, as I do, that with so many eminent writers talking nonsense, the chances are heavily against one so obscure as myself. The writers of the French Renaissance, incredible numskulls as Rabelais seems to have thought them, were in my opinion quite as rational in their appraisals of women as writers of the nineteenth century on whose works I browsed. These could be roughly sorted into three schools; the dry-nursing, the analytic, and the lyrical. I have in mind chiefly the French representatives of these schools, because they are the most thorough-going; but they had able competitors in England and Germany whose names will at once occur to any reader, and no doubt in other countries as well.

The school of dry-nursing,—the cult devoted to exploiting the *enfant malade et douze fois impure*,—might well have compressed what they had to say into a pamphlet and brought it out as a brochure On the Care and Feeding of Women. Only the other day I came on a three-star passage by one of these artists (one does not see how he could have been a great writer, but he was) which for emetic efficiency and promptness can hardly be matched. Here is a paragraph from it:

> He who has preserved in his heart the flame of gallantry which burned in the last centuries surrounds women with a tenderness at once profound, gentle, sensitive and vigilant. He loves everything that belongs to them; everything that comes from them; everything that they are; everything they do. He loves their toilette, their knick-knacks, their adornments, their artifices, their naïvetes, their little perfidies, their lies, and their dainty ways. . . . He knows how, from the very first word, by a look, by a smile, to show that he adores them, to arouse their attention, to sharpen

> their wish to please and to display for his benefit all their powers of seduction. Between them and him there is established a quick sympathy, a fellowship of instincts, almost a relationship through similarity of character and nature. Then begins a combat of coquetry and gallantry, . . .

—but I closed the book at this point, lest haply I should pewk. The reader will probably be willing to take the rest of the passage on faith, as I am. One can see well enough what the besotted man is driving at in his darkened way, and can see that it is something very admirable; but spewing whole pages of neurasthenic slaver over it tends only to obscure and befoul it.

Then there is the school of the *psychologie de l'amour moderne*, the school which spreads itself on analysing and psychologising women as mysterious beings, unpredictable, unprincipled, predacious, infinitely subtle, and for the most part exceedingly nasty; such, for example, as the disgusting henhussies of Bourget's *Mensonges*. It gives one a turn of hopelessness to see Amiel edging himself into this gallery with a piece of simply inimitable nonsense:

> A woman is sometimes fugitive, irrational, indeterminable, illogical and contradictory. A great deal of forbearance ought to be shown her, and a good deal of prudence exercised with regard to her, for she may bring about innumerable evils without knowing it.

Amiel was a much-travelled philosopher, an excellent critic and man of letters, with all the culture of Europe in his head, yet he did not see that what he says here is equally applicable to either sex. He is adverting to qualities and behaviour which are characteristic of the psychically-anthropoid; and the vast overwhelming majority of *Homo sapiens*, women as well as men, are psychically-anthropoid. Psychically-human females do not exhibit such traits, nor yet do psychically-human males.

The third school, the lyrical or panegyrist, glorify woman as a kind of Institution. If they are French, they glorify her as a National Institution, like the Academy or the Comédie Française, which none but Frenchmen can properly appreciate and reverence. All of them do this; from Michelet up and down, all are guilty. *Crimine ab uno disce omnes*; the documentary evidence is complete in the pages of *La Femme* and *L'Amour*.

The curious thing is that the men of all three schools actually believed in the dreadful balderdash which they put forth about women. There is no doubt of it; no one could counterfeit such fatuous sincerity. This has the effect of giving a fantastic semblance of reality to such figures of womanhood as I have never seen and never expect to see, nor do I wish to see, whether on earth, in heaven, or in the waters under the earth.

IV

One of my valued friends is an Armenian merchant, dealing in objects of art. Armenians are known the world over as uncommonly shrewd merchants, and my friend is no exception; I can bear witness to this, for I have seen him in action. When I go in his shop he knows he has nothing in stock that I would take as a gift, let alone pay money for. I go in, seeking nothing, expecting nothing but an hour or so of his interesting and instructive companionship. Hence our conversation is free, disinterested, intimate, affectionate. I get a great deal out of it in respect of many recondite matters pertaining to the Oriental world of thought and action, and I think he also gets something. What we get, however, is not at all what we would get if I approached him in his capacity as merchant; and without pretending to answer for him, I may say that what I get is infinitely more valuable. This story may not seem apposite to a discussion of sex-relations, but it is, as I shall now show.

I think there can be "no manner of doubt, no probable, possible shadow of doubt" that men need women far more than women need men. I am not speaking of relative susceptibility to "the sexual urge." All that is as it may be, but it is entirely out of present consideration. Women may like men and want them, but on a forced put they can, and do, get on very handily without them. Men may not like women or want them, but without them they can hardly get on at all. I do not know why this should be so, though I can think of several contributory reasons, as any one can; but however the fact may be accounted for, there it seems to be.

Obviously this fact causes women, by and large, to appear before men in a double capacity. They appear in the capacity of friends and fellow-beings, casual associates; but they also appear in the capacity of merchants, exercising a sort of natural monopoly, and looking for trade. In their capacity as merchants they regard men primarily as potential customers. They have a merchant's eye out for the best customers available among those who present themselves, and they have the monopolist's instinct for regulating the terms of their market according to careful calculation of what the traffic will bear. The standard British novelists, such as Trollope, Thackeray, Jane Austen, consistently exhibit women in this capacity, and women's assumption of it is everywhere a matter of observed and acknowledged fact.

One may reluct a little at an exposition of this matter in such plain terms, perhaps, but when one understands the laws governing mankind's conduct one perceives at once that there can be no reasonable complaint of the fact, and therefore no particular point to glossing it over. Woman's basic needs and desires are the same as man's; they need and desire a steady and stable supply of food, clothing and shelter. In the effort to ensure this supply they tend always, precisely as men do, to follow the path of least resistance—Epstean's law. In the great majority of instances that path leads by way of bargaining with men through marriage. The Church of England's formula for solemnising marriage reflects the operation of Epstean's law by introducing the clause, "with all my worldly goods I thee endow." In instances where "social security" is effected by other means, such as an adequate inherited income, the path of least resistance does not usually run that way, save where a dominant motive of pure greed affords newspapers a chance to make a splurge over "the union of two great fortunes." Such instances are relatively infrequent. Nor would I dream of intimating that these needs and desires are the only ones that women have, for that would be simply silly; I say no more than that they are basic, primary, which most obviously they are. It is the part of wisdom in all circumstances, however, to keep steadily in mind the fact that Epstean's law bears just as powerfully on women as on men. Whatever a woman's needs and desires may be, from the least to the greatest, she tends always, as men do, to satisfy them with the least possible exertion; that is to say, by exploitation whenever exploitation is practicable. There are circumstances in which one is sometimes tempted to lose sight of this, but it is inadvisable to do so.

And now to my main point, indeed my only point, which is sincerely practical. If you approach women with the faintest suggestion of being a potential customer, you may expect to find the ensuing relation tinctured heavily with a spirit of mercantilism exactly analogous to that which my Armenian friend displays when some one comes in to look over his stock. The ways in which this spirit is displayed are of infinite variety and exceedingly attractive; my Armenian friend is one of the most accomplished coquettes I ever saw, when it suits him to turn the pressure on a potential customer. But these elaborate little arts all tending steadily in one direction, coynesses, backings and fillings, turns of finesse, are so well understood that there is no need to multiply words about them. Any one who does not understand them simply shows himself not only most unobservant, but also deplorably ignorant of literature, for even the literature of the modern Emancipation makes its roughneck heroines display them all.

On the other hand, if you approach a woman as I approach my Armenian, on the understanding that nothing is to be expected in the way of business, the ensuing relation will turn out to be infinitely rewarding. Unless all my experience and observation go for nothing, it will be devoted and enduring, intimate, candid, understanding, truly affectionate and disinterested. It will assay much richer in all these qualities than any comparable relationship between men, because it brings into reciprocal action qualities which are naturally complementary, thus correcting defects, smoothing down excesses, and carrying on a general course of strengthening and enlargement of both mind and spirit. To give but one illustration, I have learned ten times as much practical wisdom from women as from men, in virtue of all the superiority of women's realism and objectivity. It must be understood that in all I have been saying on this point I speak only of the psychically-human woman; of the psychically-anthropoid or mass-woman I can of course say no more than for her male congener.

The understanding I posit should be arrived at tacitly; I never told my Armenian friend in so many words that I was not interested in his merchandise, nor did he ever openly suggest an indisposition to selling me anything. But however arrived at, the understanding must be established in sincere good faith. No counterfeit, albeit ever so well made, will pass the test; and here may be seen the force of what I said a moment ago about the spirit of the *cavaliere servente* as being the best for men's cultivation. In Thélème and the Courts of Love it was thoroughly drilled into the lady's head that she had nothing in the world that her *cavaliere servente* was after. She could not sell him a pennyworth of anything. He was by her side day in and day out for no reason but that it suited him to be there. Under those conditions, whatever either of them got out of their association was not subject to "the higgling of the market." It came as a gift freely offered, not asked for or suggested. The whole philosophy of their relationship is summed up in the deep observation of Filena to Wilhelm, "If I love you, what business is that of yours?"

CHAPTER THIRTEEN

In the course of things, those which follow are always aptly fitted to those which have gone before; for this series is not like a mere enumeration of disjointed things, which has only a necessary sequence, but it is a rational connexion: and all existing things are arranged together harmoniously, so the things which come into existence exhibit no mere succession, but a certain wonderful relationship.

—MARCUS AURELIUS.

ALL I saw during the later 'twenties and the 'thirties pointed straight to the rather sombre conclusion that *Homo sapiens* has,—and, as I believe, can have,—no sense whatever of history's continuity. Even among the more experienced peoples of Europe I found few who understood that because the nineteenth century was what it was the twentieth century must be what it is, and that there is no way of cutting in between cause and effect to make it something different from what it must be. On the surface, the scene was one of incredible confusion, absurdity, futility. One would say that all the extravagances which lunacy could devise were running wild. But on looking beneath the surface one saw a spectacle of majestic and necessary order. Cause and effect, Emerson's implacable "chancellors of God," were working at their task without haste and without rest, in all precision and in all regularity.

These great agencies were building up a stupendous body of testimony to the august truth that there never was, never is, and never shall be, any disorder in nature; and so one surveyed their work with the scientific curiosity which attracted the elder Pliny to the eruption of Vesuvius. If ever there were a clear demonstration that anthropologists have drawn the line between *Pithecanthropus erectus* and *Homo sapiens* at the wrong level, the period 1920-1942 has furnished it. Throughout these years one saw—as one sees now and I suspect will always see—a baldly journalistic view of humanity's doings prevailing everywhere. Men and events were taken, as they now are, as phenomena virtually isolated, virtually improvised, with nothing behind them but their immediate exciting cause. Only the other day I heard some one saying what an appalling thing it is that the destiny of all Western society should be in the hands of two paranoiacs, a homicidal maniac, a mediæval *condottiere* and a mountaineer brigand. But such a view is utterly journalistic, utterly futile, for with Western society at this stage of the course it has pursued since 1850, what must its leaders inevitably be? History prescribed these men upon the world, prescribed their courses of action, and marshals them in those courses with an iron hand. History goes on to its end, carrying all incidental and temporary leadership in its sweep, and throwing it away when it has served its little shred of particular purpose. "I have seen so many kings," sighed old Rossini plaintively, as he declined an invitation to meet Napoleon III.

One who contemplates the spectacle of a society's impending dissolution has little energy to waste upon any emotions but those of awe and reverence for the natural forces which have brought about this vast *débâcle*. The ordinary feelings of concern, pity, sympathy, are transcended and effaced by the exaltation of sheer wonder and admiration. "I consoled myself for the approaching death," wrote the younger Pliny, "with the reflection: Behold, the world is passing away!" Wonder is evoked by the magnificence of the process; admiration is evoked by its unearthly beauty. The quick and sensitive eye of Marcus Aurelius perceived that "in the ripe olives the very circumstance of their being near to rottenness adds a peculiar beauty to the fruit." So at each phase in the disintegration of a society one remarks the peculiar and supremely affecting beauty of inevitableness, the beauty which shines out from the sequences of causation.

Everywhere one saw evidence that the pace of society in its "course of rebarbarisation" had been greatly quickened since the turn of the century. As one phase after another unfolded, it was interesting to see how suddenly the eminent characters associated with a previous phase fell into oblivion. In Europe I saw Woodrow Wilson as the great luminous figure of the second decade. At the opening of the third decade people almost had to think twice before they could remember who he was. When I came to America in 1929 he seemed to be as shadowy and remote a personage in the country's history as Zachary Taylor or Ten-cent Jim Buchanan. In the second decade William II was "the mad dog of Europe," the object of universal execration. Lloyd George won a post-war election by promising to hang him. In the third decade hardly any one troubled himself to wonder whether he and Lloyd George were still alive. So also it was with the representatives of a period's culture. The versifiers, romancers, painters, musicians of the 'twenties were eclipsed in the 'thirties; the men of religion, the *soi-disant* economists, the proponents of social theory, dropped into obscurity. The dead among them were promptly forgotten, and the survivors led a spectral unconsidered life, like that of the surviving politicians.

In my view the insensate irrational rapidity of these fluctuations clearly indicated that Western society had everywhere lost its stability and that its collapse was nearer than one might think. Mr. Ralph Adams Cram says most truly that a visitor from another world would see those years as a space "in which all sense of direction had been lost, all consistency of motive in action; all standards of value abolished or reversed. . . . With no lucid motive for doing anything in particular, self-appointed arbiters in almost every field of human activity from painting to politics were starting the first thing that came into their heads, tiring of it in a week, and lightly starting something else. . . . The futile philosophies, the curious religions, and the unearthly superstitions of the last days of Rome were matched and beaten by a fantastic farrago of auto-intoxication, while manners and morals lay under a dark eclipse."

This vivid picture is accurate; it is a picture which suggests a ruinous social disorder. Yet if Mr. Cram's visitor had the mind of a Pliny he would see that there was no disorder there. Pliny saw that a simple redistribution of energy was taking place in a perfectly orderly way, whatever might be the effect on Herculanum and Pompeii. The witless agitation of the people—Julia with her necklace, the man with his hoard of gold, the baker leaving his bread in the oven,—bore orderly witness to impending disaster due to the fact that the towns should not have been built where they were. So, as viewed by the light of reason, the behaviour of Western society in the last two decades is a simple matter of *prius dementat*, orderly, regular, and to be expected. It presages calamity close at hand, due to the fact that society's structure is built on a foundation of unsound principles.

II

Mr. Cram's visitor from another sphere would have enjoyed many a hearty laugh at the discussions of "civilised warfare" which I heard going on among statesmen and publicists of the period. The naïve seriousness with which this resounding absurdity was debated gave immense amusement to one who saw things as they were. I could never quite make up my mind whether or not the statesmen and publicists had their tongue in their cheek about this matter. They were so far out of habitual contact with any kind of reality, their lives were so drenched in make-believe, that very possibly they were in earnest and their weird verbosity was prompted by some kind of conviction which, however fatuous, was sincere. At all events, they took the matter with as much solemnity as if it had some substance of fact; and until their lucubrations grew tedious they were entertaining enough as prime examples of their kind.

For my own part, the war of 1914 convinced me that thereafter the conduct of warfare should revert to the primitive policy of extermination. This was the original intention of warfare; to take perhaps the most familiar example, it was the intention exhibited against the Palestinian tribes by the Israelites under Joshua, according to the Scriptural legend. This policy, however, was soon amended into a policy of sparing and enslaving eligible survivors, taking occasional women for use as instruments of pleasure, and occasional men for use as labour-motors. Nevertheless, where enslavement was for any reason impracticable or economically disadvantageous, the earlier policy has been resumed; as it was, for example, in the instance of the American Indians, by the Spaniards in the south and by ourselves in the north. Versailles clearly demonstrated that enslavement is no longer practicable as a policy of major warfare; and the profit-and-loss account of the nineteenth century's adventures in imperialism show as clearly that it is no longer practicable as a policy of minor warfare. It costs more than it comes to.[1]

In 1918, therefore, I saw every reason why in future the logic of war should be run out to its full length in a policy of systematic extermination. I could find no objection to this on moral grounds, since by no conjuration can warfare be thought of as either more or less than organised assassination and robbery. In its nature nothing else can be made of it, and in its history it is nothing but a progressive taking of advantage, with assassination and robbery as the end in view. Again, on economic grounds there can be no objection, for every economic consideration points straight the other way. Finally, objection on humanitarian grounds would seem the acme of inconsistency. If humanitarianism can reconcile itself to swallowing nine-tenths of the logic of warfare,—as apparently it has no

[1] On this conclusion cf. C. J. H. Hayes, *A Generation of Materialism*, ed. Harper, p. 238, and the discussion preceding.

trouble in doing,—one must put down its reluctance to swallow the remaining tenth as a rather nauseating affectation. After Versailles my impression was that in subsequent wars the policy of enslavement would go more or less gradually into desuetude and would be replaced by the primitive policy of extermination; and that impression still remains with me.

As time went on through the 'twenties and the 'thirties, one could see the sentiment and moral sense of mankind in continuous preparation for something of the kind. Burke's acute observation kept recurring to my memory, that if ever a great change is impending, "the minds of men will be fitted to it." I refer to the progressively lowered estimate put upon the value and quality of individual human life. To one who can remember where that estimate stood even so late as forty years ago, the difference is startling in its significance. Respect for life is at the vanishing-point, and respect for the dignity of death has disappeared. The preparation I speak of as indicated by this change was not, of course, deliberately designed. It is merely one casual induration among the many which are incidental to progress in our course of re-barbarisation.

One slight bit of testimony, so slight that I speak of it only because it has an amusing side, is the change one sees in the branch of popular literature known as the mystery-story. I am not concerned with the widespread vogue of this type of literature, but with its structure, with what one might call its architectural pattern. Stories of crime have always had a great vogue, and I see no valid reason why they should not have it. In so far as literature is at all to be taken as a pastime, this form of literature seems to me as innocuous as any. As for its being an incentive to crime, which I understand some say it is, I believe the few instances alleged are extremely doubtful.

But whereas formerly the mystery-story was built around any and every kind of crime, it is now invariably, as far as my observation goes, built around the one crime of murder. Murder seems as necessary to the architecture of the modern story as a roof is to the architecture of a modern house. I once asked a publisher who does a good deal with mystery-stories why this should be so. He said in some surprise that he had not the faintest idea; he had never thought of its being so until I spoke of it. Murder was so much the regular thing that he had taken it as a matter of course, not noticing its monopoly. Murder had a place with Dickens, but I do not remember that it was at all to the front with Wilkie Collins or Gaboriau. Nor do I recall that the mighty Sherlock had anything to do with murder, save in one instance, unless you count in a couple of attempts at murder which he foiled.

I can not hold my memory strictly accountable, so I speak of this matter under correction. There can be no question, however, about the later product. Therefore one might take it that the change from the practice of Doyle, Collins, Gaboriau, or even the fifty-per-cent record of Poe, to that of the writers of the 'thirties does reflect, however faintly, a corresponding change in the estimate popularly put upon the value and sanctity of human life. This interested me because by far the best creative work I found going on in the 'thirties was done by those mystery-writers who had a real story to tell and who showed themselves painstaking workmen in the telling of it. The only writer I could put with them in the rank of merit (and they will agree with me, I am sure, in putting her a little ahead of them) was Mrs. Thirkell, who carried on in the fine tradition of Jane Austen with exquisite insight, exquisite sympathy and captivating charm. One notable mystery-writer has shown in *Gaudy Night* that Lord Peter Wimsey and his lady-love could make themselves quite as competent and engaging in association with other mysterious illegalities as with murder. What a pity! one says, that they were not given another chance or two; for really, one does not read about their adventures for the rather hollow satisfaction of finding out "who done it" and why and how. One reads because the accounts of their adventures are excellent examples of the art of story-telling. The fact that his lordship never had another chance is pretty good evidence, to my mind, that the observation I have made is not altogether fanciful.

III

The "hurricane of farcicality" which the Spanish philosopher Ortega y Gasset speaks of as raging through Western society at this time played inordinate tricks with the structure of economic law. Many no doubt remember the "new economics" hatched in the consulship of Mr. Coolidge, whereby it was demonstrated beyond question that credit could be pyramided on credit indefinitely, and all hands could become rich with no one doing any work. Then when this seductive theory blew up with a loud report in 1929, we began to hear of the economics of scarcity, the economics of plenty, and then appeared the devil-and-all of "plans," notions about pump-priming, and disquisitions on the practicability of a nation's spending itself rich. America's economic aberrations during 1920-1942 have often been compared to those let loose in the later career of John Law, but I thought the comparison was lame, even as any matter-of-fact comparison was bound to be. These vagaries defied all criticism, surpassed all comment; they stood entirely outside the purview of serious consideration. I could find no match for them, not even in the prodigies witnessed by Gulliver in the academy of Lagado, or the marvels wrought at the court of Queen Whims, as described by Rabelais in the twenty-first and twenty-second chapters of the Fifth Book.

The oddest of these infatuations is perhaps worth a word or two because only now, at the time I am writing this, it seems to have reached its peak. Ever since 1918 people everywhere have been thinking in terms of money, not in terms of commodities; and this in spite of the most spectacular evidence that such thinking is sheer insanity. The only time I was ever a millionaire was when I spent a few weeks in Germany in 1923. I was the proud possessor of more money than one could shake a stick at, but I could buy hardly anything with it. I crossed from Amsterdam to Berlin with German money in my bill-fold amounting nearly to $1,250,000, pre-war value. Ten years earlier I could have bought out half a German town, lock, stock and barrel, with that much money, but when I left Amsterdam my best hope was that it might cover a decent dinner and a night's lodging. One might suppose that a glance at this state of things would show the whole world that money is worth only what it will buy, and if it will not buy anything it is not worth anything. In other words, one might suppose people would be set thinking, not at all about money, but about commodities.

But nothing of the kind happened. The general preoccupation with money led to several curious beliefs which are now so firmly rooted that one hardly sees how anything short of a collapse of our whole economic system can displace it. One such belief is that commodities—goods and services—can be paid for with money. This is not so. Money does not pay for anything, never has, never will. It is an economic axiom as old as the hills that goods and services can be paid for only with goods and services; but twenty years ago this axiom vanished from everyone's reckoning, and has never reappeared. No one has seemed in the least aware that everything which is paid for must be paid for out of production, for there is no other source of payment.

Another strange notion pervading whole peoples is that the State has money of its own; and nowhere is this absurdity more firmly fixed than in America. The State has no money. It produces nothing. Its existence is purely parasitic, maintained by taxation; that is to say, by forced levies on the production of others. "Government money," of which one hears so much nowadays, does not exist; there is no such thing. One is especially amused at seeing how largely a naïve ignorance of this fact underlies the pernicious measures of "social security" which have been foisted on the American people. In various schemes of pensioning, of insurance against sickness, accident, unemployment and what-not, one notices that the government is supposed to pay so-much into the fund, the employer so-much, and the workman so-much. Only the other day I read that some *paperassier* in the Administration at Washington,—or no, on second thought I believe it was a *paperassière*,—had forged out a great new comprehensive scheme on this principle, to be put in effect after the war. But the government pays nothing, for it has nothing to pay with. What such schemes actually come to is that the workman pays his own share outright; he pays the employer's share in the enhanced price of commodities; and he pays the government's share in taxation. He pays the whole bill; and when one counts in the unconscionably swollen costs of bureaucratic brokerage and *paperasserie*, one sees that what the workman-beneficiary gets out of the arrangement is about the most expensive form of insurance that could be devised consistently with keeping its promoters out of gaol.

The sum of my observations was that during the last twenty years money has been largely diverted from its function as a mere convenience, a medium of exchange, a sort of general claim-check on production, and has been slily knaved into an instrument of political power. It is now part of an illusionist's apparatus to do tricks with on the political stage—to aid the performer in the obscenities incident to the successful conduct of his loathsome profession. The inevitable consequences are easily foreseen; one need not speak of them; but the politician, like the stockbroker, can not afford to take the long-time point of view on anything. The jobholder, be he president or be he prince, dares not look beyond the moment. All the concern he dares have with the future is summed up in the saying, *Après moi le deluge.*

IV

At any time after 1936 it was evident that a European war would not be unwelcome to the Administration at Washington; largely as a means of diverting public attention from its flock of uncouth economic chickens on their way home to roost, but chiefly as a means of strengthening its malign grasp upon the country's political and economic machinery. In such circumstances, as Prévost-Paradol observed at the time of Louis-Napoléon's Italian adventures, it is usually absolute governments which look to this means of maintaining the security of their régime. My European friends had watched with fascinated amazement the goings-on in our economic Witches' Sabbath, and wondered whether in the circumstances the Administration would make a decisive move,—which we agreed it might easily and effectively make,—to forestall the outbreak of war. We had a good many conversations about this. My opinion was that the Administration would make no move. I reminded my friends of the formidable domestic difficulties which the British régime was facing in 1914, and how that while these difficulties made it certain that the régime would take the action it did, they also made it politically impracticable for it to declare its intentions until after the first gun had been fired.[2]

If in July 1914 Sir Edward Grey had served Prince Lichnowsky with a firm notice of the régime's intentions, it is a hundred to one that war would have been considerably deferred; but England would have been left split up by convulsions far worse than those of the eighteen-forties, and the Liberal régime would be tossed to the dogs. Mr. Asquith's Government evidently took the realistic view that British connivances had already made war a certainty; they had made British intervention also a certainty; and, this being so, things had best be arranged to let the war break at a time when it would be likely to do the most good and the least harm to British political interests. The results justified this judgement; politically, Britain came out of the war a very heavy winner, though in other respects, of course, she did not. After 1936, as I told my friends, our Administration seemed to me to be

[2] These difficulties were: the impending consolidation of labour into the One Big Union; the pressure for home rule for Scotland and Wales as well as for Ireland; and the pressure for land-value taxation. All these matters were due to come to a head simultaneously in the summer of 1914.

in much the same situation as Mr. Asquith's after 1911, and I expected it to act in the same way and for the same reasons; as in fact it did.

Nevertheless the outbreak of war in 1939 took me quite by surprise; I had no expectation of its breaking before another year. I was both a good prophet and a bad prophet, as it turned out. In 1935 I put myself in print that the break would come in the summer of 1939, as it did. A year or so afterwards, circumstances caused me to change my mind and put the time a year ahead, so in the spring of 1939 I was assuring all my American friends that they had still another long year to go before they need begin to worry; and they turned the laugh on me in royal style a few months later. I suppose the moral is as one of my friends said: Make your prophecy and then stick to it. One may as well do that, for forecasting a war within a year or two is mainly guesswork. An "incident" can always be arranged or manufactured or better yet, provoked, as we have often seen; and then the fat is in the fire. In recent years, as far as I can remember, every pretext for war has been carefully hand-tailored. The *Maine* was, the invasion of Belgium notoriously was, and so were von Bülow's "damned missionaries." As for the present war, the Principality of Monaco, the Grand Duchy of Luxemburg, would have taken up arms against the United States on receipt of such a note as the State Department sent the Japanese Government on the eve of Pearl Harbour.

Knowing its antecedents, one could regard the current war only as one did the last, as an incident in a long and regular sequence of cause and effect. It is so completely in order, so completely in the natural succession of things, that one can feel little concern with its fortuitous ups-and-downs or with its immediate outcome. A few months ago a member of the Administration asked me if I thought we were "gypped on this war," and I replied briefly that I did. I could not enter into any discussion of the matter, for my questioner would not have understood a word I said; or perhaps might not even have believed me if I had explained that anything like military victory or military defeat was farthest from my thought. I could not explain that a boatman moving around in the gulf of St.-Malo or in the Bay of Fundy is not at all interested in what the waves are doing, but is mightily interested in what the tide is doing, and still more interested in what it is going to do.

After the war of 1914, Western society lived at a much lower level of civilisation than before. This was what interested me. Military victory and military defeat made no difference whatever with this outcome; they meant merely that the waves were running this way or that way. The great bulk underlying and carrying the waves, the tidal mass, was silently moving out at its appointed speed. So likewise I might have told my questioner that we are "gypped on this war" because not victory, not defeat, not stalemate, can possibly affect the tidal motion of a whole society towards a far lower level of civilisation.

Therefore this war, like the last, has held no interest for me. I have had no curiosity about its progress, have read nothing of it, and all I have heard has been casual. I did not go in with any of the non-interventionist movements, partly because I knew their efforts were futile, but mainly because I was not sure they were well-advised. I knew, with Bishop Butler, that things and actions are what they are, and the consequences of them will be what they will be; and therefore the attempt to cut in on those consequences is not to be gone into lightly. Indeed, my respect for "the chancellors of God" is so profound that if at any time I could have defeated the Administration's intentions by turning over my hand, I greatly doubt that I would have done it. I certainly would not have done it in 1914, and I am quite sure I would not have done it in 1939.

One must wonder how many of the multitude now reading *War and Peace* read the sections devoted to historical and philosophical analysis; and of those who do read them, how many read them carefully enough to understand them; or are capable of understanding them, however carefully they may read them.

V

Wherever I went in Europe I was struck by the persistence of the old original idea that America, and especially the United States, has no reason for existence except as a milch cow for Europe. People there were apparently born with this idea, as they might have been in the days of Columbus and Balboa. I observed it not only in the higher walks of society, but also in the lower. I observed also that Americans do not quite understand this persuasion, which is why I speak of it here. As far as I could see, there was no meanness about it, no spirit of grafting or sponging, or of bilking a rich and easy-going neighbour. It seemed rather to be the simple, natural expression of a sort of proprietary instinct. The general harmony and fitness of things required that America's resources should at all times be at the disposal of Europe for Europe's benefit. Especially it was imperative that when Europe got in any kind of scrape, America's plain duty was to take the brunt of it, and to stand by when the scrape was settled, and clean up the débris at American expense.

I was prepared to find this view prevailing in England, but not so well prepared to find it on the Continent, though undoubtedly I should have been. The two views, however, differed slightly. Ever since Elizabeth's spacious days, the general run of Englishry seem bred to the idea that all peoples, nations and languages should be privileged to keep seeing to it that Britannia is supported in the style to which she has been accustomed; and naturally the United States is expected to come down handsomely whenever the hat is passed. The Continental European's view is more prosaic; he has no notion of doing America any favour by tapping her resources, but merely pockets the proceeds in a matter-of-fact way, and thinks no more about it. The French Government, for example, entered up the American war-loans as a "political debt"; in other words, they were all in the day's doings, and nothing to worry about.

It was this matter of the war-debts that suggested a misapprehension on America's part. Most Americans were of Mr. Coolidge's mind, that "they hired the money, didn't they?" and when they saw that the money was not coming back, they felt that they had been let in, and were pretty warm about it, which was natural. Just as naturally the Europeans, who did not share Mr. Coolidge's view of the situation, were irked at being regarded as dead-beats and swindlers; and the result was a great deal of useless recrimination and bad blood. The Europeans simply did not get Mr. Coolidge's drift, and Americans did not quite understand that a traditional line of thought which had persisted unbroken for four hundred years was something to be reckoned with.

I could not help seeing also that America had unwittingly done a great deal to keep this line of thought going. For a century and a half America has consistently displayed towards Europe, and especially towards England, a great sense of inferiority. Its attitude, both official and social, has been one of ill-bred servility alternating with one of ill-bred truculence. When I thought of Hay, Reid and Page in my own time it seemed to me that Mr. Dooley's remark about our ambassador "going to Buckingham Palace as fast as his hands and knees would carry him" was neither unkind nor uncalled-for. When one looks at the unending effervescence of American snobbery displayed in social matters,—such as court-presentations abroad, and at home the insensate pawing and adulation bestowed upon "distinguished foreigners,"—one can hardly wonder that Americans should be assessed at the valuation they put upon themselves.

Then again, over long periods America has been taking great masses of unacceptable population off Europe's shoulders; partly to satisfy industrialists in search of cheap low-grade labour, and partly from motives of a highly questionable humanitarianism. These immigrants caused great streams of money to flow out of America to the folks at home; and up to 1914, many came only with the intention of going back for the rest of their lives as soon as they had got together enough money for the purpose. The consequent political evils, due to our system of universal suffrage, have been most calamitous; but, aside from that, it is clear that this reckless policy of immigration must have done a great deal to strengthen the conviction that America's only mission in life is that of being a good steady producer for Europe.

VI

The redistributions of population in Europe, brought about by the war of 1914, showed some interesting phenomena. They made it seem probable that if the process went on much longer, Europe would be inhabited by a population of hybrids, mongrels, like the population of the United States. In many obvious ways, this would be by no means a bad thing in the long-run; but for the time being, the ignorance and predacity of politicians were bound to make it troublesome. Among the many knotty morsels in the messes of hash which these prehensile gentry dished up under the name of succession-states, the problem of minorities was perhaps the most refractory. This problem at best is always difficult, and under the idiotic prescriptions laid down at Versailles, nothing could be done about it.

Surveying the plight of minorities in Europe, I was reminded of the appalling consequences of political intervention upon the problem of the Negro minority in America. The effect of emancipation-by-fiat was never better put than by Mr. Dooley; it "turned th' naygur out iv th' pantry an' into th' cellar." It discharged upon the country a huge avalanche of industrial specialists—mostly single-crop agriculturists—with nothing to do, and no provision made for their getting anything to do. This was bad enough, but political intervention had yet to show that it could do its worst. The Fourteenth and Fifteenth Amendments were a device deliberately contrived by Ben Wade, Ben Butler, Thad Stevens and their co-beauties to perpetuate the dominance of a Republican party representing the economic interests of the industrial North. Politically, this device did all that could be expected; it was successful to the last degree; but it made the problem of the American Negro (in my opinion) permanently insoluble by any means consistent with reason, decency or humaneness.

With the very grave problem presented by another American minority, the Jew, political considerations have until very lately had little to do, except in the matter of regulating immigration. The seriousness of this problem is being recognised, but its terms are confused in the public mind. Apparently very few know what its actual terms are; and as long as this confusion and ignorance persist, the way is open to all sorts of misapprehension, suspicion, unreasoned hatred, and every undesirable complication. It must be said that the peculiar temper and disposition of the American Jew—I refer of course to the preponderating element among them, the inferior order—enhances this confusion most unfortunately. He resents vehemently any discussion of his people's status as an American minority, and he is alone among minorities in the pursuance of this wholly irrational policy. This morbid sensitiveness is not without reason, certainly, and its reason is plain. Nevertheless, as the wiser and more intelligent Jews are well aware, it adds greatly to the problem's confusion, and thereby reacts most unfavourably upon the Jew himself.

Some time ago, noticing that the problem had become more pressing and that its actual terms were not at all understood by the majority, I had the idea of writing a small book which should show exactly what, in my judgement, the terms of the problem are. This had never been done categorically, as far as I knew, and I thought it should be. My book would keep scrupulously away from the Jewish side of the fence; it would be addressed to none but my own people, the American majority, peoples of Western European stock. As a matter of good taste and courtesy it would of course do this; but since responsibility for the exercise of reason, justice, tolerance and good temper rests always heaviest on a majority in these circumstances, I felt that it was with the majority that the book should concern itself. I had the book about two-thirds ready when the war unexpectedly came on, public attention was diverted, and the pressure of the problem lightened; so I laid the book aside, to be picked up again and published at a more favourable time.

I have no idea how the problem of these two American minorities will finally be settled. I regret to say my conviction is that they will be dealt with in the traditional manner, with immediate results which one does not care to contemplate; that is to say, they will not be settled at all. I know, however, that the problem of no minority anywhere can be settled unless and until two preliminaries are established. First, that the principle of equality before the law be maintained without subterfuge and with the utmost vigour. Second, that this principle be definitively understood as carrying no social implications of any kind whatever. "I will buy with you, sell with you, talk with you, walk with you, and so following," said Shylock; "but I will not eat with you, drink with you, nor pray with you."

These two preliminaries demand a much clearer conception of natural as well as legal rights than I think can ever prevail in America. The French have this conception well established. If I choose to associate with Negroes, and they choose to have me do so, whatever the terms of the association may be, I am within my rights and so are they. If I insist on other Negroes forming like associations, I exceed my rights; if Negroes insist on others of my race forming them, they exceed their rights. The doctrine of equality does not carry any competence in the premises to justify either the Negroes or myself. The most agreeable and improving social relations which I have enjoyed of late in America have been with a coterie of Jews living in Pennsylvania. If they had found me unacceptable and had excluded me, the doctrine of equality would have suffered no infringement; nor would it if a Negro hotel-keeper or Jewish restaurateur had turned me away; nor if the white proprietor of a theatre had refused to let it for a performance by Negro or Jewish actors and actresses. The principle of equality carries no implications of this kind, and the attempt to foist them on that principle is an error of the first magnitude.

Sometimes I felt vaguely dissatisfied at finding so little in the state of Europe and its peoples to excite my sympathy. It seemed as if perhaps the sources of sympathy within my nature might be drying up; yet I knew in reason that this was not so. Everything was so completely in the sequences of cause and effect that one could not become sentimental any more than one could sentimentalise the suicidal policy of the lemming. Mankind had been striving after forms of organisation, both political and social, too large for their capacities; believing that because they could organise a small unit like the family, the village, even the township, with fair-to-middling success, they could likewise successfully carry on with a state, a province, a nation. Just so the lemmings on their migrations, finding themselves able to cross small bodies of water, think, when they come to the ocean, that it is just another body of water like the others they have crossed; and so they swim until they drown. Season after season, they make these attempts, unable to learn that the thing is impracticable. Likewise, age after age, mankind have made the attempt to construct a stable and satisfactory nationalist civil system, unable to learn that nothing like that can, in the nature of things, be done.

For the trials and tribulations of America during the last twenty years, like the great Mommsen, I could feel neither sympathy nor interest. I often thought of a story which I heard from a friend years ago, and heard again from him only the other day. His mother was expostulating with Mommsen for some extremely severe strictures which that eminent man was making upon the United States. She offered the usual plea-in-avoidance to the effect that he ought to have more sympathy with us in our shortcomings, because we were such a young nation. Mommsen replied austerely, "Madame, your nation has had open before it the whole history of Europe from the beginning; and without exception you have consistently copied every mistake that Europe has ever made. I have no sympathy whatever for you, and no interest in you."

CHAPTER FOURTEEN

Nothing in education is so astonishing as the amount of ignorance it accumulates in the form of inert facts.

—HENRY ADAMS.

In spite of my French turn for scepticism and for "burning my nightcap every morning," which Louis XI recommended as sound diplomatic practice, sheer curiosity has now and then let me into some rather pointless adventures. They were of the sort which I knew well enough would come to nothing, but I thought the experiment would in itself, probably, be interesting enough to make it worth while. My editorial experience was a case of that kind; I have shown my reasons for undertaking editorial work for which I had not the slightest professional qualification, and I have also shown what came of it. I think it was towards the end of the 'twenties, though I do not remember just when, that I was asked to do some teaching. One of my friends who was busy in that line, a man for whom I have great respect and affection, was very strong for my taking up with the proposal, and so I did. The idea was that I should settle down to it as a full-time occupation, but I demurred at that. My roots were firmly fixed in Europe, and I had no notion of pulling them up. It was agreed finally that I should come over for two months each winter, and give two courses. I did this for two years, and then having had enough of it to satisfy my curiosity, I gave it up.

Ever since I left college I had felt recurrent spasms of

interest in the American system of education. The revolution which took place towards the turn of the century made an impression on me, enough so that I was rather keen to see what would come of it, and therefore whenever I was in this country I looked over its development in a general way. In course of time I came to some pretty definite conclusions about this development, and about its social effects. I even went as far as writing two or three fugitive essays for Harper's and the Atlantic on certain phases of the subject. But all this was from the outside. I had no experience, no practical acquaintance with the educational machinery which the revolutionary forces had designed and built. So when the chance for an inside view came along I decided that it would probably be worth taking.

The students who sat under me were presumably, I believe, something of a picked lot; something, that is, rather above than below the level of intelligence set by "the average student," whatever that may signify. They may have been all of that; I am not in a position to commit myself on this point. What struck me with peculiar force was that only one out of the whole batch was taking work with me because he wanted to learn something about my subject. Most of them were taking it as a filler. They sat where they did because they had to sit somewhere in order to meet some requirement in an intricate system of "credits," and the most convenient place for them to sit happened to be in my lecture-room. Some were there for purposes connected with their prospective ways of getting a living. The majority, however, for all I could make out, were there because they were, at the moment, nowhere else; they put me in mind of the cheerful old drinking-song which we used to sing to the tune of *Auld Lang Syne*:

We're here because
We're here because
We're here because
We're here.

In spite of persistent effort, neither they nor I could produce any more plausible reason why they were there, or for that matter, why they should be anywhere. The point is that with one exception, these persons did not regard the subject as one to be pursued disinterestedly for its own sake. They were not even moved to it by an impulse of intellectual curiosity; they simply cared nothing about it.

This state of things was not exceptional, or at all peculiar to the institution which I served. Any one who understood the philosophy of economism and who knew how well our educational system had been formed to fit its requirements, would expect to find just those conditions prevailing in any American college or university. He would expect to find the student body divisible into two groups, the first made up of those who were there in a sort of social quarantine. They had come to get a further respite from going to work, or to make advantageous social contacts, or because it was in fashion for everybody to go to college, or for some equally irrelevant reason or combination of reasons. The second and larger group would be made up of those who were in pursuit of such studies as bore directly on their preparation for getting a living. Outside these groups one might expect to find now and then a person of some pretensions to intelligence, some conception of education as a formative process; one who had intellectual interests unconnected with getting a living, and who had perhaps also a vague suspicion that the philosophy of economism falls a trifle short of covering the whole content and purpose of our existence on this earth.

II

I was greatly interested in seeing that our system of free popular instruction was producing results, both negative and positive, which were quite different from those which its original designers expected it to produce. As Herbert Spencer has shown, no man or body of men has ever been wise enough to foresee and take account of all the factors affecting blanket-measures designed for the improvement of incorporated humanity. Some contingency unnoticed, unlooked-for, perhaps even unforeknown, has always come in to give the measure a turn entirely foreign to its original intention; almost always a turn for the worse, sometimes for the better, but invariably different. It is this which predestines to ultimate failure every collectivist scheme of "economic planning," "social security" and the like, even if it were ever so honestly conceived and incorruptibly administered; which as long as Epstean's law remains in force, no such scheme can be.

Our system was founded in all good faith that universal elementary education would make a citizenry more intelligent; whereas most obviously it has done nothing of the kind. The general level of intelligence in our citizenry stands exactly where it stood when the system was established. The promoters of our system, Mr. Jefferson among them, did not know, and could not know, because the fact had not been determined, that the average age at which the development of intelligence is arrested lies somewhere between twelve and thirteen years. It is with intelligence as it is with eyesight. No oculist can give one any more eyesight than one has; he can only regulate what one has. So education can regulate what intelligence one has, but it can not give one any more. It was this unforeseen provision in nature's economy which wrecked the expectations put upon our system. As for raising the general level of intelligence, the sluicing-out of any amount of education on our citizenry would simply be pouring water on a duck's back.

Aside from this negative result, I saw that our system had achieved a positive result. If it had done nothing to raise the general level of intelligence, it had succeeded in making our citizenry much more easily gullible. It tended powerfully to focus the credulousness of *Homo sapiens* upon the printed word, and to confirm him in the crude authoritarian or fetishistic spirit which one sees most highly developed, perhaps, in the habitual reader of newspapers. By being inured to taking as true whatever he read in his schoolbooks and whatever his teachers told him, he is bred to a habit of unthinking acquiescence, rather than to an exercise of such intelligence as he may have. In later life he puts this habit at the unreasoning service of his prejudices. Having not the slightest sense of what constitutes a competent authority, he tends to take as authoritative whatever best falls in with his own disorderly imaginings.

Thus a system of State-controlled compulsory popular instruction is a great aid in making *Homo sapiens* an easy mark for whatever deleterious nonsense may be presented to him under the appearance of authority. One does not have to go farther than the account which the *Pickwick Papers* give of the great election at Eatanswill to see how this is so. The spread of literacy enabled Mr. Pott of the Gazette and Mr. Slurk of the Independent to approach the credulousness of a greater number of people than they could otherwise reach, and to debauch their credulousness much more effectively. It enabled Mr. Pott to play upon the meanest prejudices of the Blues, and Mr. Slurk to inflame the worst passions of the Buffs; and thus to keep alive the feud of ignorant partisanship, like the feud of the Greens and Blues in Rome and Byzantium so long ago, or the feud of Whigs and Tories, Democrats and Republicans, Black Shirts and Red Shirts, in more recent years. Mr. Pott and Mr. Slurk knew as well as the editor of today's newspaper knows, that what best holds people together in pursuance of a common purpose is a spirit of concentrated hate and fear. They knew that their constituents, Blue and Buff alike, were a mere mob, intellectually as irresponsible as the wild dogs of Algiers, and that an appeal to intelligence would be vain, nay, embarrassing. "Mere reason and good sense," said Lord Chesterfield, "is never to be talked to a mob. Their passions, their sentiments, their senses and their seeming interests are alone to be applied to. Understanding, they have collectively none." I am reminded here of an acute French critic's remark made almost a century ago, that this observation of Lord Chesterfield constitutes one of the most serious arguments against representative government. In my opinion it is by far the most serious argument; indeed, I believe a century of experience has shown that it is the only argument needed. One may confidently rest one's case on it.

I observed that the course of our educational revolution had followed the regular pattern common to all revolutions; but knowing the inflexible laws which prescribe that pattern, I was not disappointed or taken aback. "The sense of the inevitable" which Mr. van Loon speaks of had warned me that the inevitable upshot of other revolutions would be the inevitable upshot of this one. As soon as the system was on its way to become a going concern with the taxing-power of the State behind it, the path of least resistance lay open to a rapidly-increasing flow of persons whose interest in education was secondary. These were careerists of sorts, impelled by the fundamental law of conduct, that man tends always to satisfy his needs and desires with the least possible exertion. Then the general estimate, the currency-value, of education,—the generally-accepted idea of what education is and ought to be, —was set by the worst form in circulation, a form which had virtually nothing to do with education, but only with training; and those forms which had more to do with education were forced out. Then finally, after the system had passed a certain point of development in size, power and prestige, the percentage of net profit (putting the matter in commercial terms) began to show a steady decline.

Furthermore, the curiously composite public character of the system, as I observed it in the late 'twenties, interested me as having likewise come out inevitably according to pattern; the pattern set in earlier times by the Church, and now by the State. As a State-controlled enterprise maintained by taxation, virtually a part of the civil service (like organised Christianity in England and in certain European countries) the system had become an association *de propaganda fide* for the extreme of a hidebound nationalism and of a superstitious servile reverence for a sacrosanct State. In another view one saw it functioning as a sort of sanhedrim, a levelling agency, prescribing uniform modes of thought, belief, conduct, social deportment, diet, recreation, hygiene; and as an inquisitional body for the enforcement of these prescriptions, for nosing out heresies and irregularities and suppressing them. In still another view one saw it functioning as a trade-unionist body, intent on maintaining and augmenting a set of vested interests; and one noticed that in this capacity it occasionally took shape as an extremely well-disciplined and powerful political pressure-group.

During my brief and unserviceable career as an instructor of youth I had a good many hearty laughs whenever I thought of the quiet fun one might have with Mr. Jefferson if he could return to the Republic and see what his pet project of universal popular instruction had come to. I had studied his character rather carefully, and could not make out that the great and good old man had been blessed with an over-keen sense of humour. Apparently he had enough to go on with, but not much more, and what he had was of a dry type. I think, however, he would have risked a wry smile at the spectacle of our colleges annually turning out whole battalions of bachelors in the liberal arts who could no more read their diplomas than they could decipher the Minoan linear script. He might also find something to amuse him in the appearance of eminent shysters, jobholders, politicians, and other unscholarly and unsavoury characters, on parade in gowns and hoods of the honorary doctorate. Yet it would probably occur to him that academic misdemeanours of evil example were not unknown even in his own day. Only some half-dozen years after Mr. Jefferson's death, Harvard College admitted to its doctorate a man whom John Quincy Adams very properly described as a barbarian, incapable of putting a grammatical sentence together, and barely able to spell his own name—Andrew Jackson.

One can not be sure that Mr. Jefferson would look with the

eye of humour upon certain other results of the system's working. I suppose that in the whole country today one would have to go a good long way to find a boy or girl of twenty who does not automatically take for granted that the citizen exists for the State, not the State for the citizen; that the individual has no rights which the State is bound to respect; that all rights are State-created; that the State is morally irresponsible; that personal government is quite consistent with democracy, provided, of course, it be exercised in the right country and by the right kind of person; that collectivism changes character according to the acceptability of the peoples who practice it. Such is the power of conditioning inherent in a State-controlled system of compulsory popular instruction.

When it came to matters like these, Mr. Jefferson was an extremely serious and outspoken person. I doubt that he would be in the least amused by the turn which his pet project has given them since his time; and not only in his own country, but in all countries where his project has taken root. On the contrary, I believe he would regard the entire exhibit with unstinted disgust and contempt.

III

Back in the days when I was doing editorial work, immediately after the war, I had heard so much exasperating talk about education that I became heartily sick of the word. War, like whisky, engenders seasons of repentance, and that was one of them. The post-war dislocations, disturbances and distresses got no end of well-meaning people stirred up over the idea that nothing of the kind should ever be allowed to happen again. They wrote, printed, lectured, organised clubs, associations, forums, brought forth reconstruction-plans, peace-plans, and the devil-and-all of other plans and projects designed to educate war off the face of the earth. I was astonished at their number; one would hardly believe there could be so many. Everything I remember of them now is that they were all very strong for education, highly articulate, highly ineffectual, and did not last long.

My occupation obliged me, for my sins, to keep more or less track of these doings, but I went no further than that with any of them; and with most of them, if the truth must be told, I rather scamped my job. None of them contemplated anything really fundamental. One might agree that if people can be educated to a common will in pursuance of a common purpose to abolish war, the purpose will no doubt be accomplished; but the main question surely is whether, if one "regards mankind as being what they are," the thing can be done at all; and the second question, if the first be answered in the affirmative, is how to set about it. I saw no evidence that the main question had ever even entered the heads of these enthusiasts, or that the second had been entertained in any but a superficial, hand-over-head fashion which could produce nothing practicable or even sensible. Some of the more adventurous spirits, apparently under the effects of Mr. Wilson's inspiration, went so far as to propose educating all mankind into setting up a World State which should supersede the separatist nationalist State; on the principle, so it seemed, that if a spoonful of prussic acid will kill you, a bottleful is just what you need to do you a great deal of good. I did not join forces with any of the groups engaged in these endeavours. I was as much against war as they were, and as much in favour of education as any one could be; and I also had the highest respect for their earnestness and devotion. But I knew, as they apparently did not, that if you go in for education you must first make sure of having something educable to educate; and second, you must have some one with a clear and competent idea of what he is about, to do the educating. I saw no prospect that either condition would be met. With the average of intelligence standing immovable at the thirteen-year-old level, I knew that the first one could not possibly be met; and as for the second, even in the case of the educable, it would be a Sisyphean job to offset the processes of intensive conditioning which the State continually applies to its citizens, beginning from the first day of their conscription into its system of compulsory instruction, and ending on the last day of their lives.

Another numerous body of opinion had a grievance against war, but it was rather particular than general. They did not make so much of moral and humanitarian issues as the others did, though probably in principle they disapproved of war quite as heartily. Their particular contention, however, was that never again should the United States pull anybody's chestnuts out of the fire but its own. The outcome of the war bore hard on those who had swallowed the jobholders' glib mendacity about the enterprise being a war to end all wars and to make the world safe for democracy. When it finally became clear that the war was no such noble undertaking as all that, but was merely a disreputable scuffle for loot, exactly like the wars which for untold ages had preceded it, those who had accepted it in good faith as a crusade for righteousness felt that they had been outrageously let in, and made no bones of saying what they thought about it.

I was not one of this number, for I had already cut my eyeteeth on the Spanish War. My observations of foreign affairs since the days of McKinley and John Hay convinced me that what British jobholders were wanting in 1914 was exactly what British jobholders had wanted in 1898. It was clear to me in 1898, as I have already said somewhere in these pages, that the British Foreign Office had constantly before its eyes the vision of a world at peace, dominated and operated by British imperialism, with the United States kept in hand to act as a bouncer and pay heavily for the privilege, whenever malcontents became obstreperous. I could make nothing else of Mr. Hay's conduct; of the British Colonial Secretary's "blowing the gaff"; and of our military and diplomatic doings in the Pacific. The Spanish War had turned out to be a tradesmen's war; there was no doubt of it. So when the war of 1914 came on, I bent a jaundiced eye upon its officially-advertised aims and motives, for I knew too much of what had been going on in European politics since 1910 to believe a word of them. When the secret treaties came to light after the Bolshevist revolution, and the reports of Belgian diplomatists in Berlin, Paris and London were published, the whole rationale of the war was shown to be just what one would know it must be. When the peace-terms were seen to correspond with the terms of the secret treaties and not with those of the infatuated Mr. Wilson's Fourteen Points, it could surprise no one. When the League of Nations proved to be only a blind for jobholders intent on maintaining the *status quo*, what else could one expect?

I felt somewhat sorry for the gudgeons who had been hooked by the lies of jobholders and their tagtails of the press, pulpit and platform, as one must always feel sorry for the victims of any set of common swindlers; but I did not see how anything could be done about it. I thought the hardest trial they had to bear must be the memory of all the appalling drivel they had poured forth in their spasms of pseudo-patriotic ardour. During the war I often witnessed the sorry spectacle of old acquaintances, normally quite cool-headed persons, emitting great volumes of lurid nonsense about "the mad dog of Europe" and his murderous designs on the world in general; and how if Britain and France should fall, the whole structure of Western civilisation (for so they naïvely called it) would collapse in ruin. What must they have thought of themselves when daylight finally broke in on them!

I never disputed or discussed these views,—what was there to discuss?—but I often recalled them afterwards when projects of "education for peace" were being broached. I could imagine how far any of these projects, or all of them put together, would be likely to get with an average popular mentality capable at any time, on twenty-four hours' notice, of being sent clean daft by any egregious canard that officialdom saw fit to disseminate. Writing from Rome in 1536 to the bishop of Maillezais, the great realist Rabelais grimly cites Claudian's line, *Mobile mutatur semper cum principe vulgus*. So it did in 1914, virtually overnight; and conditions being what they were, I saw no way of ever educating it to do otherwise thereafter.

But after all, as I reflected on the wild whirling words of my acquaintances, I asked myself is not all this just democracy? As I understand the term, it is of the very essence of democracy that the individual citizen shall be invested with the inalienable and sovereign right to make an ass of himself; and furthermore, that he shall be invested with the sovereign right of publicity to tell all the world that he is doing so. I do not know whether these rights are implicit in the Magna Carta, but if a sufficient political interest were at stake no doubt the Supreme Court could discover that they somehow are. I do know, however, that they are expressly stipulated in the American Bill of Rights; they are declared beyond peradventure in the First Amendment to the Constitution of the United States. Well then, if any citizen or body of citizens chooses to exercise these sovereign rights, on any pretext or on none, is it competent for another member of the democracy to demur or interfere? I think not; but however this may be, why in the name of common sense should an intelligent person have the least wish to interfere?

So when in their course of killing off the Kaiser and his myrmidons by word of mouth, my vehement acquaintances now and then paused to catch their breath, I would say, "Yes, yes, exactly—just so—I quite understand you," and let it go at that.

Dans le pays des bossus
Il faut l'être
Ou le paraître.

IV

I have always been profoundly grateful for my luck in having been enabled in my early youth to understand that education is one thing and training quite another, and thus to avoid the vicious errors resulting from confusion of the two terms. It can not be too often reiterated that education is a process contemplating intelligence and wisdom, and employing formative knowledge for its purposes; while training is a process contemplating sagacity and cleverness, and employing instrumental knowledge for its purposes. Education, properly applied to suitable material, produces something in the way of an Emerson; while training, properly applied to suitable material, produces something in the way of an Edison. Suitable material for education is extremely scarce; suitable material for training abounds everywhere. The young men I saw during my brief term of service as a teacher (not those in particular who sat under me, but generally) were manifestly ineducable beyond the thirteen-year static level of intelligence; but they were fully endowed with cleverness and sagacity, and were capable of being excellently well trained in any number of ways.

When one considers man's place in nature, one gets a firm grasp on this distinction. In our loose and inaccurate speech, we say commonly that man rose to dominance over the rest of the animal world in virtue of his superior intelligence. I can find no evidence that this is so. It seems clear, on the contrary, that he rose to this position of dominance in virtue of his immeasurably superior cleverness and sagacity. He had the sharp-set Edisonian sagacity to notice all manner of things that were about him, to observe their relations and reactions, what they did and how they worked, and he had the Edisonian cleverness in rearranging, modifying and adapting them for the satisfaction of his needs and desires. But intelligence, properly so called, would seem to have been as sporadic, as unevenly distributed, as it is now, and its average level undoubtedly neither lower nor higher.

When I was an undergraduate student I read the elaborate work called *Anti-Lucretius*, by the accomplished French cardinal-statesman or statesman-cardinal, Melchior de Polignac, written to refute the neo-Epicurean doctrines which had been promulgated at that time by Gassendi and others. I was much impressed by a long passage in the sixth book, in which the cardinal shows how primitive man got his start in the world by observing the practices of other animals and improving on them. Philosophically, the *Anti-Lucretius* can hardly be said to have hit the mark, perhaps, but it is an excellent specimen of seventeenth-century hexameter, well worth my quoting a few lines from the passage I have mentioned. They give a thought-provoking view of various tricks which our sagacious and clever ancestors picked up in this way, such as dam-building, deer-stalking, netting birds and fish, mining, and even the lighter arts of dancing, acting and petty larceny:

> Hinc aliquas vitiis, aliquas virtutibus olim
> Insignes dixere feras; hominique fuisse
> Primitus exemplo, atque opera ad complura magistras:
> Ut canis occultum silvis deprendere Damam
> Nare sagax, et odora sequi vestigia praedae,
> Veneri docuit. . . .
> Forte etiam insidias Vulpes, artemque latendi,
> Perque canaliculos fodiendae subtus arenae
> Monstravit, fecitque viam ad querenda metalla;
> Unde homines docti coeperunt viscera terrae
> Rimari. . . .
> Et quid non Elephas, quid mimo Simia gestu
> Non praestat; vafra et Felis; saltator et Ursus? . . .
> Paxillos in aquam primus defigere Castor
> Instituit, laribusque inimicum avertere flumen,
> Et ligna intrito atque intritum jungere lignis; . . .
> Callida quinetiam dum tendit Aranea laxos
> In foribus casses, internectitque sagenam,
> Retibus et pisces et aves captare dolosis
> Admonuit.

So the passage goes on through many more instances of the same kind. But as far as my reading goes, the clearest and most interesting brief précis of what pure sagacity and pure cleverness have done for mankind is found in the sixth chapter of Mr. Charles F. Lummis's remarkable work called *Flowers of Our Lost Romance*. This excellent book was published in 1929, so I suppose it has been long out of print, but if one can find a copy of it anywhere it will be worth all the trouble one has had to look for it.

It was this great endowment of cleverness and sagacity which enabled the frail, feeble and unintelligent *Homo sapiens* in the first instance to survive, and then to gain dominance over his more physically-powerful competitors in the struggle for existence. Furthermore it was this, and this only, which has enabled him to build up the prodigious apparatus of civilisation which with unconscious humour he persists in regarding as evidential of civilisation itself. I can not make out where intelligence played any part in the process; still less, wisdom. The satirist's view of man's creation is certainly not without the appearance of reason. One can see an uproarious cosmic jest (and I think by no means a bitter one; on the contrary, I should regard it as harmless, even on the whole, benevolent) in the idea of creating a being with enough sagacity and cleverness to harness all the forces of nature in constructing the most elaborate mechanism of civilisation, and then not giving him intelligence enough to civilise himself, or even to understand what civilisation means.

Here then, in the inordinate lack of balance between these two sets of forces,—sagacity and cleverness on the one hand, intelligence and wisdom on the other,—I perceived a valid reason why the social agglomerations of mankind are so unstable. They can be stabilised only by the continuous exercise of a very considerable and generally-diffused intelligence and wisdom; and these are simply not to be had, they do not exist, have never existed, and at present one sees no prospect that they ever will. *Homo sapiens* has already gone so astonishingly far in the progress which Goethe predicted, without any corresponding advance in intelligence and wisdom, as to make it easily conceivable that in the long-run he may perish through his own inventions. Goethe himself, with a poet's insight, had an uneasy suspicion of something like this. In the next sentence after his prediction he says, "I foresee the time when God will have no further pleasure in man, but will break up everything for a new creation." There is a pleasing touch of irony in the thought that the forces which have enabled *Homo sapiens* to survive and dominate, and to indulge in all manner of inflated conceits about himself, his merits, and his importance,—that these forces may very easily be the ones to bring about his annihilation. The broken sentence found graven on the tomb of one of the Scipios, words which for sombrous majesty have no equal in any literature, might well serve as an epitaph upon the race. *Qui apicem gessisti . . . mors perfecit tua ut essent omnia brevia, honos fama virtusque, gloria atque ingenium.*

V

Circumstances being as they are, one has no trouble about seeing that a State-controlled system of popular instruction is bound to lean heavily to the side of training, since the trainable masses stand immeasurably in excess of the educable few. But by looking a little beyond this, one can perceive another reason, equally valid, why the system should tend to be stepmotherly with the educable few; that reason being that the coercive collectivist State is distinctly uninterested in the cultivation of intelligence and wisdom. This is understandable, and there can be no complaint of it, for the State has no uses to which persons of intelligence and wisdom can be put. It is notorious that the State's affairs can be successfully carried on only by persons of sagacity and cleverness, heavily tempered with improbity. We all accept this fact as matter-of-course and agreeable to the nature of things, which it unquestionably is; the proof of it is found in the invariable character of those who are most conspicuous in administering those affairs. Sometimes when an autocratic ruler wishes to make an impression of enlightenment, he will put men of intelligence and wisdom in some conspicuous sinecure as window-dressing, or confer some kind of ostentatious patronage on them, as Catherine II did with d'Alembert and others of the Encyclopædists; but in all these instances the motive is political. Speaking of Napoleon's patronage of men such as Fontanes, Joubert, Chateaubriand, Count Lüxburg put it very well that "he considers these people as drugs of the imperial pharmocopœia, ingredients to be mixed up in the chemical mass of an emperor's government."

But throughout history the man of intelligence and wisdom has been merely so much useless lumber in view of the State's purposes. Voltaire's gay epigram on *le superflu, chose très-necessaire* has distinctly not been applicable to him. Often indeed, like the Swifts, Arnolds, Butlers, Gilberts, Shaws, he has been something of an embarrassment. In England at the time of the Tangier incident, I could not keep back a smile,—rather sardonic, I am afraid,—at the thought that if the British State had ten thousand of the world's wisest and most intelligent men at its disposal, it could not find a single thing for them to do which would not be most dreadfully embarrassing. When I was next in England, four years later, intelligence and wisdom would not have exempted a Socrates, Jesus, Confucius, if of military age, from conscript service as a private in the front line, side by side with the half-witted; what other use would the State have had for his proficiencies? It all seemed natural and reasonable enough, and I could not get stirred up about it, as so many were. What was the best that the State could find to do with an actual Socrates and an actual Jesus when it had them? Merely to poison the one and crucify the other, for no reason but that they were too intolerably embarrassing to be allowed to live any longer.

On the other hand, the State can use as much highly-developed sagacity and cleverness as its institutions can turn out. There is room to spare for these everywhere throughout its bureaucracy and in the wide field of its practical politics. The State could do nothing with a thousand Emersons, but it would count itself lucky if it could build its personnel on the foundation of a thousand persons who had all of Edison's highly-trained sagacity and cleverness, and none of his integrity. There is no need to press this point, however; every one understands it. Why, then, should a State-controlled system of instruction do more than go through the motions of dealing with an educable minority? I see no reason why it should. It is perfectly logical that it should not; the disparagement of intelligence and wisdom is all in the general "course of rebarbarisation" on which Spencer saw so clearly that Western society had set forth nearly a century ago. It is inevitable, and therefore the part of wisdom is not to resent it or deplore it or think overmuch about it.

At one time I had the notion that our system might do a little better than it was doing by the educable minority. I thought that with all its innumerable training-schools for the ineducable, it might establish two or three modest institutions which should be strictly educational, devoted to cultivating intelligence in those who gave proof of having it, and holding out the attainment of wisdom as an end preëminently desirable for its own sake. The idea seemed unpretentious enough, and putting it into effect as an experiment would cost relatively little. I went on the assumption that although persons of intelligence and wisdom were no asset to the State, they might be something of an asset to society, and were therefore worth a moderate amount of attention. I had not actually given the matter much thought, however, and as soon as I turned it over in my mind I perceived that it was nothing to be taken seriously; for obviously, whether or not such persons are an asset to society depends altogether on the kind of society you have, on what philosophy governs it, on what it is trying to make of itself, what it is driving at. As soon, then, as I found myself back on the solid ground of reason and logic, I saw that our system was all in the right, and that my notion of the educable minority being a potential social asset was quite wrong.

If the whole content and purpose of mankind's existence can be summed up in terms of the production, acquisition and distribution of wealth, it is impossible to see where intelligence and wisdom come in for a footing. A society completely committed to the philosophy of economism has no more use for them than the State has; naturally so, since in such a society the State is the organised expression of economism.[1] Hence such a society has nothing to gain by the presence of wise and intelligent persons; they are not a social asset. The best it can find to do with them is to make them hewers of wood and drawers of water for the sagacious and clever majority. The young person of intelligence who sets out to "get wisdom, get understanding," as the Jewish Scriptures exhort him to do (and it is interesting to look up these exhortations and see how many and how forcible they are) does so in full knowledge that society will continually be reminding him in various well-understood ways, mostly rather harsh, that he is wasting his time and should be doing something useful.

All this again is so completely in the course of nature, so orderly and logical, that I saw no reason why one should feel any bitterness about it or complain of it, though I knew that many did feel great bitterness. I remember having been much impressed many years ago by the dedication of a novel by Jules Vallès, the revolutionist of 1870 and member of the Commune. I think the title was *Le Bachelier*, though I am not sure; I was so little taken with the book itself that I have forgotten. The dedication ran:

> À tous ceux qui, nourris de grec et
> de latin, sont morts de faim.

But I asked myself why, when all comes to all, should they not die of starvation? I saw no reason. They were useless to the State, useless to economism, and they mustered far too few votes to interest a political collectivist humanitarianism, so how could either the State or society be reasonably expected to keep them alive? "And to think," cried Voltaire, in a burst of wrath, "that an army-contractor makes $4000 in a day!" I could

[1] For an illustration of this point I may again refer to Mr. Marquand's novel *passim*; and I might take this occasion to remark that *H. M. Pulham, Esquire* is in my judgement the nearest thing to adult fiction that has come from an American pen in many years.

not share his indignation. That army-contractor was a man of sagacity and cleverness who was performing an indispensable service to the State's iniquitous undertakings; and if he could turn a trick to net himself $4000 by way of a day's pickings, his service was no doubt worth it from the State's point of view. During the war of 1914 I saw fortunes made in this way by sagacious men who one might think were considerably overpaid, but a moment's reflection would show that the question depended on the point of view from which one estimated the value of their services. From the point of view of civilised man, that is to say the psychically-human being, those services were of no value; but from that of the anthropoid mass-man they were of great value. Hence I could find nothing out of the way in the State's liberality, and so far from sharing Voltaire's indignation against it in a like case, I thought it was very just. As I saw the matter in 1914, the psychically-anthropoid masses of democracy were accepting the State's designs and even whole-heartedly glorifying them; and moreover, *ex hypothesi* it is never the State's business to promote civilisation. So to expect the State to take Voltaire's point of view on the sagacious war-profiteer seemed to me most illogical; and for a critical observer to take that point of view seemed not only illogical, but also,—which is no doubt a more serious irregularity,—undemocratic.

VI

When I was surveying educational matters at closer range than ordinarily, what impressed me most was the dissatisfaction of professional educationists with the results produced by our system. Complaints on this score, coming as they did from many of the most distinguished men in the service, seemed almost innumerable, and they were expressed with a forcefulness betokening disappointment and grievance. One conference of educationists, I remember, wound up in fairly general agreement, according to the press-reports, that our system is a failure. The president of a huge straggling university said despondently that our undergraduate colleges had been trying for forty years to find an effective substitute for the discarded classical curriculum, and had not yet succeeded. Reports made under the auspices of various foundations amounted actually to indictments. On a distinguished public occasion one educationist said that the type of education offered by our million-dollar high schools is about one-twentieth as valuable as the type offered by the little red schoolhouse of a past generation. I am told that these lamentations continued unabated long after I had ceased to keep any track of them. In fact, only two or three years ago I happened on a searching deliverance from the president of one of our largest colleges for women, and found it quite in the old familiar vein. I quote a few lines from it because in a general way they set forth the main ground of all the complaints I had been reading in the 'twenties:

> Any one who has opportunity to meet and study in large numbers the alumni of the American colleges is likely to have attacks of depression. In spite of the vast investment of money and energy in these institutions it is only too clear that in a great many cases education has failed to "take," or the infection has been so slight that few traces are to be perceived after five or ten years of the wear and tear of American life.

I thought that this complaint which as I said is typical, would stand a little sifting. While I had felt every sympathy with the system's critics and was in complete agreement with them about the validity of the facts which they brought forward, I could not agree that the system was in quite such a bad way as they thought it was. They impressed me as being either victims of confusion about what exactly the system was supposed to drive at, or else victims of a rather serious failure in realism, a failure to see things in their true nature and appraise them for what they are. In forming estimates of this kind, one must above all be realistic; one must remain as little as possible unaffected by prejudice, convention or sentiment, no matter how generally laudable these may be. On all these grounds I was as far on the side of the complainants as it was possible for a child of the old educational régime to go; I was with them as far as the combined forces of prejudice, convention and sentiment could carry me. Nevertheless, in a clear view of the requirements which the State puts upon the system, and the requirements which the ruling social doctrine of economism puts upon it, and the inexorable prescriptions which nature puts upon it, I could not see but that it was doing an extremely good job.

In the first place, how can education "take" when those who are exposed to it have had nature's gift of complete immunity conferred on them at the age of twelve or thereabouts? Any such expectation is manifestly and preposterously exorbitant. Training will "take" to some extent in almost any instance where it does not encounter absolute imbecility, but education will not. If education contemplates intelligence and wisdom—and what else can it contemplate?—one who for years had been president of a notable college for women must surely have perceived that the vast majority of his students were ineducable. He could do great things for them in the way of sagacity and cleverness; he could make them excellent routineer biologists, botanists, geologists, chemists, perhaps even passable cooks and housekeepers if his institution carried the requisite equipment; he could make them good grammarians, philologists, even historians, all of a psittacene type; but educate them he could not.

In the second place, why should education be expected to "take" in a society where the qualities of intelligence and wisdom are of necessity classified not even as by-products of its corporate life, but as waste-products? These qualities notoriously play no part in the production, acquisition and distribution of wealth, and therefore a social philosophy which regards this process as accounting for the whole content and purpose of mankind's existence must write them off as so much slag.

So in all this I found no reason why a clear-minded person should be "likely to have attacks of depression." I certainly experienced none. "Things and actions are what they are," said

Bishop Butler, "and the consequences of them will be what they will be." There the State was, fixed, immovable, standing as the great instrument of economic exploitation; there also was the philosophy of economism; there also was a system of compulsory popular instruction, answering to the requirements of both. In its great work of training and conditioning the ineducable masses, I thought our system was doing, on the whole, a first-rate job, and I said so publicly. As for the educable minority, they were merely casualties of the time and circumstances into which they were born, and that was that. The whole course of things seemed to me perfectly logical, orderly, with each step making the next one inevitable in the long sequence of cause and effect, "the chancellors of God," as Emerson so well and truly calls them. There seemed no incentive to depression or fault-finding anywhere in the sequence; the aspect of nature's great Inevitable is too august, too admirable, to admit of either.

For a brief time I had a notion that in the interest of simple straightforwardness and honesty all systems such as ours might do very well to give up their nugatory fiddling with degenerate fag-ends of what used to be known as the "humanities," and throw them on the dust-heap for good and all. I did not set much store by this notion, however, for one could see plainly that they must come to that in the natural course of things; indeed, in the 'twenties one could see that they must come to it very soon. Coercive collectivism was on its way throughout the Western world, and logically the first thing for the coercive collectivist State to do, as soon as it had got itself well established, would be to shut down firmly on all instruction which did not bear intensively on conditioning its children and young people to an unquestioning *ex animo* acceptance of the State's will; and this would of course do away with even the sleaziest sort of education. It may be imagined with what interest I remarked how promptly the Fascist government of Italy fulfilled my expectations by doing just that, and since then how regularly the other great coercive collectivist governments in both hemispheres have followed the Fascist example.

It has been profoundly interesting to me to observe how closely the nationalist State's technique of conditioning its citizens into an attitude of docile servility follows that of the mediæval Church. Up to the sixteenth century the Church was the great instrument of exploitation, as the State is now. The individual was born into the Church, and the Church's superintendence regulated every step of his daily existence as long as he lived. Its coercions, interferences and exactions were limited only by calculation of what the traffic would bear. In pursuance of its purposes it devised an elaborate system of conditioning; and in the sixteenth century, when the nationalist State took over its purposes and hamstrung its competition, it also took over its technique of cultivating obedience and docility in its subjects. On this point I can do no better than to quote from one of Mr. Carlton J. H. Hayes's admirable essays on nationalism:

> Nowadays the individual is born into the State, and the secular registration of birth is the national rite of baptism. With tender solicitude the State follows the individual through life, teaching him in patriotic schools the national catechism, and commemorating his vital crises by formal registration not only of his birth, but likewise of his marriage, of the birth of his children, and of his death. And the death of national potentates and heroes is celebrated by patriotic pomp and circumstance that make the obsequies of a mediæval bishop seem drab. . . . Nationalism's chief symbol of faith and central object of morality is the flag, and curious liturgical forms have been devised for 'saluting' the flag, for 'dipping' the flag, and for 'hoisting' the flag. . . . Nationalism has its parades, processions and pilgrimages. It has, moreover, its distinctive holy days, and just as the Christian Church adapted certain pagan festivals to its own use, so the National State has naturally borrowed from Christianity. . . . Every national State has a 'theology,' a more or less systematised body of official doctrines which have been deduced from the precepts of the 'Fathers' and from admonitions of the national scriptures, and which reflect

the 'genius of the people' and constitute a guide to national behavior.

It has taken a good three hundred years for the superstitions cultivated by the Church's system of conditioning to show signs of wearing off, and they are not yet by any means worn off. From this one may infer that the kindred superstitions cultivated by the nationalist State's system have a fairish lease of life, and that their manifestations will remain pretty much what they are. For a man of his ability and experience, the late Senator Borah seemed to me singularly naïve in his saying that "the marvel of all history is the patience with which men and women submit to burdens unnecessarily laid upon them by their governments." To me the marvel is that any one can marvel at it.

Thus logic and the course of events in the 'twenties combined their forces to convince me that the well-disposed persons whom I saw hopefully relying on education to bring about world-peace, to achieve some semblance of a civilised society, or to fulfil some other grandiose collective purpose, were leaning on a broken staff. Their hopes were based on an egregious misconception of man's place in nature, of his intellectual and psychical accessibility, of the laws which mainly determine his conduct; and finally, they were based on an enormously erroneous conception of the State's character and function. Such being the case, it appeared to me impossible that these hopes could come to anything but speedy and overwhelming disaster, as they now seem to have done.

CHAPTER FIFTEEN

Omnia exibant in mysterium.

—THOMAS OF AQUIN.

Illi sunt veri fideles Tui qui totam vitam suam ad emendationem disponunt.

—IMITATIO CHRISTI.

IN MY schooldays in Illinois, sometimes when we had a free evening three or four of us would be asked out to some house in town where we would find a group of companionable pretty girls waiting for us. We had what might now seem a curiously chivalrous sentiment towards these girls, regarding them as something to be deferred to, pampered and protected. Perhaps our fine old friend Major Pendennis would have called it one of the "damned romantic notions boys get from being brought up by women," but there it was. On one of these pleasant social evenings we tried our hand at table-turning. The great wave of interest in spiritist manifestations which swept over Europe and America in the eighteen-forties had pretty well subsided, but one still found backwaters of it here and there. We had never heard of table-turning, but the girls had got wind of it somehow and were eager for a trial. By spreading our finger-tips on a table-top and using some formula—I have forgotten what it was,—to concentrate our attention, we soon had the table rocking at a great rate, and even moved it all around the room.

Inspired by this success, we tried another experiment. Seating a girl in a heavy arm-chair, four of us stood around her, two on a side. Each of us put the tips of his forefingers together, his arms extended full length. Then three times in unison we raised our arms high and lowered them, inhaling deeply and exhaling as we did so. When our arms came down for the third time, we put the joined tips of our forefingers under the edge of the chair-seat and lifted the load of chair and girl four feet in the air as if it were a *Windbeutel.* There was no hocus-pocus about it; the chair was good sound Victorian walnut, and the girl was a hulking wench who must have run to a hundred and thirty, net; and the odd thing was that in lifting all that mass, none of us felt more than a feather's weight on his finger-tips. We repeated this once or twice, with the same result. Then we tried lifting without going through the preliminary motions, and failed. We tried again as before, but breaking the rhythm, making the preliminary motions out of unison, and this also was a failure.

We had not the faintest idea of how these odd phenomena "made themselves," as the French say, but they tapped no vein of superstition in any of us, nor did they move us to take stock in any theory of a spiritist agency at work. The thing was too trivial for that, even in the minds of schoolboys. Table-tipping and hoisting a corn-fed strapping hussy four feet or more in the air would seem an incongruous business for a disembodied spirit to be entertaining himself with, unless he were a jocular fellow like Rabelais's Cincinnatulo, who liked to mystify people; which I suppose is conceivable. We did not speculate about it, but took it merely as a trick of some kind which we did not understand, and thought no more about it.

Once shortly after this incident I tried spirit-writing out of pure curiosity; I had just then heard of it for the first time. I got several "messages" of such a commonplace character that I could not associate them with the personages from whom they purported to emanate. One which laid claim to come from a deceased aunt, warned me against tobacco and liquor, this being about the last thing which that particular aunt would have in mind to do. I put all this down as sheer nonsense of no evidential value whatever, as far as any external influence was concerned.

One Sunday morning, not long after I had left college, I was in the gallery of the church of the Holy Trinity, Brooklyn. The choir had just begun the *Venite* and I was all absorbed in the magnificent music when suddenly I was struck with horrible illness and faintness. Something impelled me to turn around, and there I saw sitting in an indolent attitude, his eyes fixed on me with a dull, sinister phosphorescence, a man who might have passed for a twin brother of King Edward VII. The sight of him affected me with the utmost horror and loathing; I never experienced such a sensation even in encountering a water-moccasin. I somehow managed to stagger out of the building, and in a few minutes I recovered completely.

Some months later, in the same place and at the same point in the service, the same thing happened again, precisely as before. I had meanwhile been attending the church quite regularly, always in the same pew, and all memory of the incident had passed out of my mind.

About two years afterwards I was walking up Court Street late one night in a driving rain with my old roommate at college whose home was in South Brooklyn. The street was quite deserted; no one had passed us. All at once I was taken with a hideous illness and faintness, and put my hand on my roommate's shoulder to steady myself. He asked what the matter was, and I said, "I don't know, but I feel as if I had been shot hard by something." At that moment some one passed us, half-hidden by an umbrella; he turned his head as he went by. It was the same man.

At a friend's house one evening in the 'twenties I met a Russian operatic tenor, a fine artist. I had already heard him distinguish himself as Hermann in a marvellous performance of *Pique-Dame*, such as one could never forget. This evening after dinner my friends persuaded him, much against his wish, to show off a curious trick. Standing before him, you presented the back of your hand; he put the tips of his forefingers together and pointed them at it, about three inches distant. In a minute or so you would feel a strong jet of ice-cold air coming out of his forefingers against your hand as out of a blowpipe. He did this "with great toil and vexation," like Thaumast in his colloquy with Panurge; he said the effort so exhausted him that if he did the trick oftener than twice at a stretch he was completely done in, which reminded me of Vassily's collapse, in Tourgueniev's *Strange Story*. He did not know how the thing was done, and I wondered how he discovered that he had this peculiar gift. I never heard of another instance of it; though that is saying little, for it may be in every professional magician's repertoire, for all I would know. There was certainly no unconscious collusion about it, for the subject was not told what to expect.

These three or four extremely trivial experiences in the realm of what is called the hyperphysical or extraphysical are all I ever had. I think I may not have the psychical sensitiveness which invites them; I doubt that spiritists would find me a good medium. I knew nothing, really, about spiritism proper until 1911 when I was in London, and the late William T. Stead talked with me for two hours about his adventures in that sphere. He showed me spirit-photographs, writings, evidences of levitation, and some of the stories connected with these were most remarkable. What interested me chiefly was his saying that he had got thought-transference down to such a fine point that he had practically given up the use of his telephone. Only that morning, he said, he had fixed his mind on getting back an umbrella which some one had borrowed, and the man promptly turned up with it just before I came in. I was reminded of my grandmother's strange experience at the time of her father's death in England. There seems to be something in this matter of thought-projection. Goethe left record of some striking instances of it, as did Mark Twain, and as no doubt many others have done. The notable instance of the French officer, Captain de Géroux, and his impressionable sister, an instance amounting to clairvoyance, is well authenticated. The idea that disembodied spirits play any part in thought-projection, however, seems to me gratuitous.

II

By all the evidence of sense-perception there appeared to be "something in" the Russian tenor's odd performance, as there was in our table-turning and chair-lifting, and as there is in the phenomena of telepathy, clairvoyance, thought-transference, the *Poltergeist*, and so on. When one has said that, apparently one has said all there is for one to say. But even so, it is also apparently as much as one can say about many of the commonest phenomena observable in our everyday existence. I have often wondered why Protestant theologians make so much of the Scriptural miracles and mysteries when one sees daily so many miracles which are far more impressive and no end more purposeful. The fact that ice floats instead of sinking, which I understand to be a most exceptional phenomenon in nature's economy, seems to me much more impressive than the miracle of Elisha's ax-head, or of Jesus and Peter walking on the waters of Galilee. It also seems much more to the point, when one reflects on what this planet would be like if ice did not float, and what would happen to all forms of life if it should cease to float.

Maintaining the order of nature appears to me quite as respectable a miracle as an isolated, momentary and relatively very insignificant interruption of that order would be. Gravitation, always varying directly as the mass and inversely as the square of the distance, holds the stars in their courses to the farthest reaches of the universe; and here, on a third-rate planet moving in a tenth-rate solar system, it also enabled me this morning to find my shoes exactly where I left them when I took them off last night. I should say that by way of a miracle, either of those performances would be quite as respectable as the other, and quite as respectable as any to be found mentioned in Holy Writ. Mr. Long, the translator of Marcus

Aurelius, says most truly that "we can not conceive how the order of the universe is maintained. We can not even conceive how our own life from day to day is continued, nor how we perform the simplest movements of the body, nor how we grow and think and act, though we know many of the conditions which are necessary for all these functions." As I see it, there is small choice among miracles in this world, for no one has the faintest idea of how, still less why, the order of nature came to be arranged as it is; no one knows how or why the stars came to follow their courses or my shoes came to stay put overnight. "Natural law" accounts for nothing, for natural law means not a thing in the world but the registration of mankind's experience. Not long ago I read of a fine exhibition of intellectual integrity by a physicist lecturing on magnetic attraction. He told his students that he could describe the phenomena, put them in order, state the problem they present and perhaps carry it a step or two backward, but as for the final "reason of the thing," the best he could say was that the magnet pulls on the steel because God wants it to.

Some of the Roman Catholic theologians are more to my mind. "All things keep continually running out into mystery," said St. Thomas of Aquin, seven hundred years ago. In matters where the mystery is more or less sensational or apparently irregular, like our chair-lifting or Mr. Stead's thought-transference, and where any hypothesis about it is as hard to disprove as it is to prove, my Platonist interest in "the reason of the thing" runs out, and my agnostic French strain keeps me content to have no hypothesis whatever. Like Mr. Jefferson, I have always been content to "repose my head on that pillow of ignorance which a benevolent Creator has made so soft for us, knowing how much we should be forced to use it."

The unknown author of the *Imitation* was moved to offer a prayer of such wisdom that I have always kept it by me for use as an emergency-brake when my Platonist spirit of inquiry showed signs of getting out of hand. "Grant, O Lord, that the kind of knowledge I get may be the kind that is worth having."[1] I have already mentioned somewhere far back in these pages that one of the deepest impressions made on me in my childhood was made by my perceiving that ignorance exists, that people know actually very little about anything, nor are they equipped for knowing much more than they do. My friend Henry Stanley Haskins, in his remarkable little work, *Meditations In Wall Street*, puts it drily that "the eyes, ears, nose, taste and touch are the only parts of our equipment that we can't rely on for complete and accurate information." As I grew older I learned that the uses of ignorance, when kept within its proper scope, are great and salutary, and nowhere more so than in matters pertaining to the realm of the spirit. If our knowledge of the causes operating in that realm were complete and certified, I do not believe we should be any better, any wiser in managing our mundane life, or, in spite of the buoyant sentence of Lucretius, any happier. I am sure I should not be; and therefore for me at least, such knowledge is not of the kind that is worth having.

III

If I were asked to name the most striking spectacle observable in my time, I should say it was the long round-trip voyage which science made away from metaphysics and back again to the most egregious mess of metaphysics that ingenuity could devise. When I was a lad, science had tossed metaphysics into the junkpile. The scientific Left, headed by Moleschott and Büchner, had gone in for Strafford's policy of "thorough" against the idealist philosophers, especially Hegel. Straight materialist monism was the thing; the universe was to be interpreted strictly in terms of matter and force. Boscovich's hypothesis had even resolved matter itself into "centres of force," whatever those might be. Consciousness was a function of the brain; "the brain secretes thought as the liver secretes bile." The moderate and sensible Huxley, Romanes and others,

[1] Da mihi, Domine, scire quod sciendum.

thought it was not quite so simple as all that, and dissented vigorously. But metaphysics were at a ruinous discount all round, and in particular the metaphysics of Christian theology were condemned in terms so severe as to make the *exitiabilis superstitio* of Tacitus seem mild and judicial.

Science went on with its investigations of matter and force, consciousness, space and time, like the donkey after the carrot, but the carrot apparently as far away as ever. When one was through with atoms, molecules, ions, electrons, protons, and so on, where was one, what had one actually got? Now I see that one great mathematician goes a bit ahead of Boscovich by resolving matter, not into centres of force, but into "groups of occurrences," and thinks that matter as an actuality, a thing-in-itself, may not exist at all. Another savant thinks that matter is a characteristic of space, while still another suggests that space is a characteristic of matter. Another sage has decided that space has a definite diametrical limit, beyond which there is no space, no matter, not only no anything, but literally no nothing.

I am far from setting myself up as a judge of these deliverances, but in all diffidence I maintain that in their totality they amount to as fine an exhibit of metaphysics as anything the Schoolmen can show. In the course of their efforts to express the inexpressible, define the indefinable, and imagine the unimaginable, these master minds have made the metaphysical grand tour and are back once more in the old familiar port of the Middle Ages, safe and sound. When I heard of a disagreement about the shape of space, one pundit holding that space is cylindrical and another that it is globular, I went back for refreshment to the eleven great theses of Pantagruel, which Rabelais says were "debated after the manner of the Sorbonne, in the Schools of the Decree near St. Denis de la Chartre, at Paris." I especially wished I might hear our two great men of science debate Pantagruel's third thesis, which seems so particularly in their line: "Whether the atoms, turning about at the sound of the Hermagorical harmony, would make a compaction or a dissolution of the quintessence by subtraction of the Pythagorean numbers." In point of intelligibility I do not see a pin to choose between the metaphysics of the Athenasian Creed and the fresh-laid metaphysics set forth in current scientific doctrines concerning matter, space and time. As between the two, I turn from both and seek safety on the old and well-tried ground of agnosticism.

IV

By the time I was thirty I had read quite a bit of theological literature by fits and starts, for no reason in particular but that the subject-matter was interesting and the literature superbly good. I had no religious doubts or misgivings to resolve. Somehow I had completely missed out on the eruption of *Sturm und Drang* which is supposed, I do not know how correctly, to accompany adolescence, and which is said to give rise oftentimes to religious self-searchings. That period of my life was marked by no more spiritual stress than any other; that is to say, by none. I think, though it is mere conjecture, that this exemption may have been due to the heavy pressure of other matters. I had so much baseball to play just then, so much responsibility about dogs, so much fishing, sailing, swimming, skating, iceboating, horseback-riding, and other general-utility jobs of like nature to attend to, that when these duties were over for the day I was too bone-tired to worry about my spiritual status, or indeed to worry about anything. Perhaps also the lack of emphasis laid on the minutiæ of religious beliefs and observances during my childhood may have had most to do with it. However it may have come about, I do not recall in all my life any religious experience that was disturbing, any harrowing doubts, any stretch of bumptious juvenile atheism, or anything of the kind. And so it was, I suppose, that I approached the magnificent literature of religion with as few prepossessions, as unbiased a mind, as any one could have.

I did hardly anything with comparative religion, except as

other reading had brought me into casual contact with the religions of Greece and Rome, and now that in later years I have scratched the surface of that study I wish I had done more. The part of Christian literature which I found most acceptable was the work of writers who had applied an enlightened common sense, combined with an enlightened fervour, to "the divine impossibilities of religion," and who drove most directly at practice. On the other hand, I found the part of it which was devoted to metaphysical and institutional system-building or system-propping largely unacceptable, as savouring less of religion than of science or, as I thought, pseudo-science. Arnold's *Literature and Dogma* gave me a thoroughly satisfactory account of Christianity's nature and function. His conception of religion as "morality touched by emotion" satisfied me. The object of religion, as I saw it, is conduct; and whatever mode or form one's religious persuasions may take, if it bears fruit in sound conduct it is *ad hoc* sound religion.

My philosophical counsellor Edward Epstean lately put this to me in a rather striking figure. He accepts the Pauline doctrine of the dichotomous man, the doctrine of the "two selves," about which I may presently have more to say, and he likens man's progress through life, with respect to conduct, to the progress of a rope-walker. Being dichotomous, man is always being put off balance by the promptings of the "lower and apparent self," and religion functions as a balancing-pole to bring him into equilibrium again and hold him steady under control of "the higher and real self." It makes no difference, my friend said in his forceful way, "whether that pole is made of Christian oak or Jewish steel or Confucian teak or Mohammedan bamboo, as long as the man finds it best adapted to doing what he wants done, and really makes it work."

Goethe said truly enough that man never knows how anthropomorphic he is. But man *can* know, if he has the very small amount of reflective power requisite to enable him to find out, and is willing to use it. The advantage of doing this is that if a person knows how anthropomorphic he is, and if he keeps the consciousness of it constantly in mind, he can then go on being as anthropomorphic as he likes, and no harm done. Some such idea may have been in the back of Joubert's mind when he said that "it is not hard to know God, provided one does not trouble oneself to define Him." Any nomenclature will do, any set of hypothetical attributes, if one is constantly aware that all these are a mere matter of words *thrown out*, as Arnold so happily puts it, at a reality immeasurably beyond one's power of expression.[2] One may speak of Deus, Zeus, God, Jehovah; of the *Ens infinitum infinité*, with Spinoza; of the Not-ourselves, making for righteousness, with Arnold; of the Unknown and Unknowable First Cause, with Spencer; of the Best one knows or can know, with Luther; but one may use these or any other terms with safety only if one knows to a certainty how anthropomorphic one is in one's use of them.

For my own part, aware that I am in any case shut up to anthropomorphism, I see nothing against making a complete job of it. Today I habitually think and speak of God as "a magnified and non-natural man," as did the two bishops against whom Arnold discharged his broadsides of deadly raillery. The attributes I assign Him are all human, and among the foremost of them I place a highly refined and lively sense of humour. I sometimes imagine Him as immensely tickled by the capers of his pretentious little creatures here below, and I have now and then suspected Him of arranging matters to make those capers show to the best advantage. We oldsters all remember Mr. Garfield's "heatless Mondays" in the last war, and how regularly on Sunday nights the mercury would drop headlong to an appalling death. After this had been repeated three or four times, one ghastly Monday morning Allen McCurdy met me

[2] One reason why the religious literature of the Jews is so inestimably precious is that it is thoroughly permeated by a sense of this. The Oriental mind does not take kindly to the subtleties of metaphysics. In the Old Testament the Jew lets his anthropomorphism range with the utmost-freedom, but one is all the time conscious that behind it is the hard, clear, cold-pressed, realistic common sense which is always instantly ready to say with Job, "Lo, these are *parts* of His ways; but how little a portion is heard of Him."

on the street and said, "Who's coming out ahead on this, d'ye think, God or Garfield?" The same amusing thought was in my own mind. I remember too, one day when Charles Beard and I were in one of what he used to call humorously our Meditations on the New Testament, he said, "I believe if you approach God in a perfectly frank, self-respecting manner, as one gentleman to another, He will meet you half-way and do the decent thing by you. But I have noticed nine times out of ten, if you go cringing and snivelling up to Him on your hands and knees and try to butter Him up, work Him for something, or make a deal with Him, He won't even listen; and the tenth time He will wait till you get real close up, and then kick the seat right out of your pants." This is an anthropomorphic view, surely; but in the premises, what view can be less so?

Aware that the mode of my own religious persuasions was most imperfect and must always be so, I felt great tolerance towards other modes, even those which were based on what seemed to me sheer superstition. As Flaubert says that politics are for the *canaille,* so with equal truth Joubert says that superstition is the only basis of religion which the lower order of mind is capable of accepting. In so far, then, as superstition alone is effectual in working on that order of mind to bring forth sound conduct, I regard it as respectable and not to be meddled with.

I read considerably in the English religious philosophers of the seventeenth century, especially the group called the Cambridge Platonists, which included Cudworth, John Smith, Whichcote, Glanvill, Culverwel. I imagine that they are quite forgotten now, though I do not know where at this present time one could get a more intelligent practical guidance towards the essential nature of Christianity and towards a more satisfying respect and love for it, than these men offer. To my mind, their great merit lies in keeping a firm grasp on actuality, in their insistence on the evidential value of mankind's actual experience, and in their emphasis on conduct. Even in skirting the edges of metaphysics, they never let themselves be swept off their feet. When Smith amplifies Luther's definition by saying,

"Where we find wisdom, justice, loveliness, goodness, love and glory in their highest elevations and most unbounded dimensions, that is He; and where we find any true participations of these, there is a true communication of God; and a defection from these is the essence of sin and the foundation of hell,"—when Smith says this, one feels that he has gone as far with a prescriptive system of dogmatic theology as it is safe to go; and he goes no farther. Taylor also, with his mind on metaphysical credenda, gives warning that "too many scholars have lived upon air and empty nothings, and being very wise about things that are not and work not." *And work not*—there he comes back, as these men are always coming back, to the basic ground of practice, of conduct; and how great is the reason why they should, for as Whichcote says, "men have an itch rather to make religion than to practice it." Conduct is the final thing, and dogmatic constructions which fail to give proof of themselves in bringing forth conduct are worse than useless.

▼

The history of organised Christianity is the most depressing study I ever undertook, and also one of the most interesting. I came away from it with the firm conviction that the prodigious evils which spot this record can all be traced to the attempt to organise and institutionalise something which is in its nature incapable of being successfully either organised or institutionalised. I can find no respectable evidence that Jesus ever contemplated either; the sort of thing commonly alleged as evidence would not be substantial enough to send a pickpocket to gaol. By all that is known of Jesus, He appears to have been as sound and simon-pure an individualist as Lao-Tsze. His teaching seems to have been purely individualistic in its intent. One would say He had no idea whatever of its being formulated into an institutional charter, or a doctrinal hurdle to be got over by those desirous of being called by His Name. If there is any reputable evidence to the contrary, I can only say with Pangloss, "It may be; but if so it has escaped me."

Organised Christianity has had the same fate which has beset all of mankind's attempts at organising itself around some great and good social purpose. The same influences have conspired to vitiate it that have vitiated all other-like attempts, and have done this in the same familiar way. Not much is known about Christianity's organisation in the first three centuries, but apparently what there was of it was relatively loose and informal. In any case, with due allowance made for intolerances, disagreements, bizarre aberrations, rabid fanaticisms,—and of all these there was no doubt plenty,—the main interest of its rank and file would seem to have been religious. Indeed, it is hard to see where any other kind of interest could have come in, for Christianity had no prestige, no wealth; it was a proscribed, persecuted, hole-and-corner affair, regarded by the State as seditious and by Roman society as contemptible, much as the American State and American society regarded Mormonism not so many years ago. Early in the fourth century, however, Constantine I, like the good politician which he was, foresaw the future of Christianity and established it as the official religion of the Lower Empire. His object was political, not religious; he was out to establish a régime of political absolutism, and he saw that an official religion could be made an extremely useful instrument not only for helping him on in that purpose, but also for keeping people docile under absolutism when it was achieved. So he gave the organisation considerable wealth, a great deal of prestige, and put it on its way to be what Mr. Middleton Murry calls "a good wife to the State." Ever since then the Christian organisation has pretty diligently fulfilled that function wherever it has been established by the State or subsidised by tax-exemption.

Constantine's act gave Christianity a social cachet, making it eminently respectable and fashionable. Then Epstean's law, which before that had not seen much chance to show what it could do, at once herded into the organisation a swarm of persons whose interest was not religious, but secular. Many of these were turned towards it by a careerist motive, but all by one-or-another motive of secular profiteering. For them it was the way of satisfying their needs and desires with the least possible exertion. In the fourth chapter of the Fifth Book, Rabelais gives a racy but substantial account of the operation of Epstean's law at the time of the Protestant Reformation; in fact, as an exposition of Epstean's law the whole episode of the Ringing Island is worth a careful reading.

Then on the heels of Epstean's law came Gresham's law, fixing the currency-value of religion by the worst type in circulation; that is to say, allowing no more face-value to "morality touched by emotion" than it allowed to a punctilious *pro forma* acceptance of ecclesiastical dogma and ritual, thus tending to drive the former out. Then finally came the law of diminishing returns, which saw to it that the greater the organisation grew in size, wealth and prestige after passing a certain point, the more the net spiritual product accruing from its operation tended to diminish.

VI

Not long ago a woman I have long known but had not seen for some years, said to me, "I have a surprise for you. I have become a Christian." This declaration gave me a slight chill. If it meant one thing, it was such an enormous pretension that I could hardly imagine a person of any delicacy who knew its implications would dare to advance it. If it meant another, one would hardly know how seriously to take it; not but what my friend was serious enough, but simply that a better-informed person might find that the statement pointed at something mostly meaningless or even largely stultifying. The question whether one is or is not religious is hard enough to answer; and the question whether one is or is not a Christian is in my opinion impossible to answer categorically; the answer might mean anything or nothing.

I do not find any evidence that Jesus laid down any basic doctrine beyond that of a universal loving God and a universal brotherhood of man. There is no report of His having discussed the nature of God or laying stress on any other of God's attributes, or that He ever said anything about them. He also exhibited a way of life to be pursued purely for its own sake, with no hope of any reward but the joy of pursuing it; a way of entire self-renunciation, giving up one's habits, ambitions, desires and personal advantages. The doing of this would establish what He called the Kingdom of Heaven, a term which, as far as any one knows, He never saw fit to explain or define. His teaching appears to have been purely individualistic. In a word, it came to this: that if every *one* would reform *one* (that is to say, oneself) and keep *one* steadfastly following the way of life which He recommended, the Kingdom of Heaven would be coextensive with human society. The teaching of Jesus, simple as it was, was brand-new to those who listened to it. Conduct, "morality touched by emotion," put forth as the whole sum of religion, was something they had never heard of.

Simple as the teaching of Jesus may have been, it was also very difficult. Following the way of life which He prescribed is an extremely arduous business, and my opinion is that those who can do it are, and have always been, relatively few; even those able to understand the terms of its prescriptions would seem to be few. If the record be authentic, Jesus appears to have been clearly aware that this would be so. Yet there is abundant evidence that Jesus was not merely offering an impracticable counsel of perfection, for the thing has been done and is being done; mainly, as is natural, in an inconspicuous way by inconspicuous persons, yet also by some like St. Francis and others among the great names one meets in the history of Christian mysticism, whom circumstances rendered more or less conspicuous.

Assuming that a person took these matters as stated, and that he faithfully followed out their prescriptions, I think that in the first century and probably in the second, he would have passed muster as a Christian. Later on, when Gresham's law, which had used St. Paul as its chief instrument, completed its work of intellectualising Christianity into an entirely different public character,—a character which it has maintained ever since,—the case was somewhat different. I greatly doubt that our hypothetical person could have got himself accepted as a Christian at any time in the latter part of the third century, certainly not in the fourth; and certainly not now, unless by some sort of low and unscrupulous collusion-in-perjury which would make hay of the official articles of the Christian Faith.

At the beginning of the fourth century organised Christianity showed a pattern set, not by Jesus, but by Gresham's law; a pattern essentially Jewish, but sophisticated by some Mithraic accretions. It had reverted to the Jewish conceptions of a particularised and bargaining God, and of a redeeming Messiah. This Christian Messiah, however, was Jesus, who was God's only Son, and with a third being, called the Holy Spirit, was an integral part of the Godhead. It had reverted to the old metaphysical ideas concerning blood-sacrifice, blood-atonement, refining them somewhat in the transference; it also reverted to an elaborate system of ritual ceremonies and a professional priesthood, and it took over the Mithraic Sunday.

One would be hard put to it to find that Jesus ever had in mind any forecast of anything like all this; there is certainly no suggestion of such a forecast anywhere in the Gospels. Nevertheless organised Christianity is still set in this pattern, and hence the question whether or not one is a Christian is not in most cases, I believe, susceptible of a categorical answer. For myself, I would not pretend to give any kind of answer. My impression is that in the course of a couple of centuries Gresham's law supplanted a stark and simple doctrine of practice by a stark and highly complex doctrine of belief; and how far the two can be reconciled I should say depends on the individual's powers of self-persuasion. I can do nothing whatever with reconciling them.

Concerning the legends of miracle and mystery which have grown up around the historic figure of Jesus, I notice with interest that my attitude of mind is exactly what it was when as a three-year-old child I encountered the New England

Primer's doctrine of original sin. For example, I would not affirm or deny that Jesus was born of a virgin mother; I would merely raise the previous question, How can any one possibly know anything about it?[3] Or, if I had been at the council of Nicæa in the year 325, and Arius had told me that Jesus was not an integral part of the Godhead, I would have asked him how he knew that; and if Athenasius had told me that He was, I would have asked him the same question. I have seen too many miracles and mysteries in the course of my life ever to take "the high *priori* road" of affirmation or denial with respect to any.

What impresses me about such matters, however, is not so much the paucity of evidence available concerning them, as that, for all I can see, they are essentially immaterial, adventitious. All the credenda to which Gresham's law has committed organised Christianity seem to me not nearly so difficult in their improbability as in their pointlessness. I do not see that they have any bearing upon practice. If it were proven beyond doubt that Epicurus was born of Athene's brain and came into the world like Gargantua, by way of his mother's ear, I do not see how the fact could affect either the soundness of his philosophy or its applicability. So likewise if all the mass of organised post-Pauline Christianity's metaphysics were proven true or false tomorrow, I do not see that one's view of the historic Jesus and His teaching would be in the least affected.

For some years I have been observing that organised Christianity is in a poor way; it has come into some disrepute, but far more into general disregard. It has lost the power of making itself feared, and has gained no power of making itself loved; its ancient prestige has dwindled to the point where Epstean's law can no longer do any business with it. Its officials are uneasily aware of this, and some of them are looking about

[3] Parthenogenesis occurs in several groups of the animal world and is probably much more common than has been supposed; hence one might agree that it would be perfectly competent for nature, if so minded, to produce an instance of it, or indeed any number of instances, among mankind. That such an instance has or has not in fact occurred, however, is purely a matter of evidence.

for a new apologetic which shall enable "the Church," as they call it, to recover its lost ground. I doubt their success, and I think with reason. The more forthright of the Church's officials distribute the responsibility for this disintegration between an irreligious materialistic society and a spineless secularised Church. I suspect that there is far more to it than that. I suspect the trouble is that people at large, even good people, religious people, even those who by Mr. Cram's classification are to be reckoned as human, have simply stopped thinking of religion in institutional terms; they have become *ad hoc* individualists.

If this be so, I can not deplore it; neither can I argue any calamitous consequences from it, but quite the contrary. I can conceive of a post-Pauline Church going to destruction, carrying with it the whole cargo of metaphysics which Gresham's law has loaded on it, yet leaving the historic Jesus standing before society in a clearer light than ever. I have every respect for Sir Thomas Gresham's memory, but I take leave to think that the religious apologetic produced by the mighty power of his law,—an apologetic based on metaphysics, miracle and magic (there is no word for it but that one),—is no longer serviceable.

The only apologetic for Jesus's teaching that I find in any way reasonable is the one which Jesus Himself propounded—experience. His way of life is not to be followed because He recommended it, or because He was virgin-born, or was a part of the Godhead, or could work miracles, or for any other reason than that experience will prove that it is a good way, none better, if one have but the understanding and tenacity of purpose to cleave to it; neither of which I have, and I believe very few have. Here once more is where the hard gritty common sense of the Jew comes out, in his instinctive recourse to the apologetic of experience: "*O taste and see* how gracious the Lord is." It was also the signal merit of the Cambridge Platonists that they recognised experience as the sum-total of Jesus's own apologetic. Smith, in his discourse on the *Method of Attaining to Divine Knowledge*, urges it in more impassioned language than any of the others, with the possible exception of Culverwel. "Ἔστι καὶ ψυχῆς αἴσθησίς τις," Smith says, in a noble passage. "The soul itself hath its sense, as well as the body; and therefore David, when he would teach us how to know what the divine goodness is, calls not for speculation but sensation. *Taste and see* how good the Lord is." Continuing, Smith remarks the progressively increasing power of spiritual insight accruing from the discipline of experience—

> We shall then converse with God τῷ νῷ, whereas before we conversed with Him only τῇ διανοίᾳ, with our discursive faculty, as the Platonists were wont to distinguish. Before, we laid hold on Him only λόγῳ ἀποδεικτικῷ, with a struggling, agonistical and contentious reason, hotly combating with difficulties and sharp contests of divers opinions, and labouring in itself in its deductions of one thing from another. We shall then fasten our minds on Him λόγῳ ἀποφαντικῷ, with such a serene understanding, γαλήνῃ νοερᾷ, such an intellectual calmness and serenity as will present us with a blissful, steady and invariable sight of Him.

As with the other inscrutable phenomena which I have mentioned, I think there is "something in" the phenomenon of a progressively clarified spiritual insight at which these words are thrown out. It appears by all evidence as something specific, and the sense of it perhaps as to some degree communicable. Beyond this I can say nothing, and I doubt that anything can be said.

VII

I was much interested in some further conversation with Edward Epstean on the subject of religion, tending to show that organised Christianity has made somewhat a mess of its conception of sin and of what to do about it. The point of our talk took me back to Mr. Beard's remark which I have quoted, about the stultifying ineptitude of orthodoxy's cringing approach to God as in the prayers we all repeat and the hymns we all sing. Mr. Epstean's view was based on his Pauline assumption of the dichotomous man, the man of "the two selves," one divine and the other bestial, and he thought that progress on the way of life recommended by Jesus is better made by an energetic strengthening of the former than by direct efforts to repress and weaken the latter. Whether or not the basic assumption be sound, I believe that the method is eminently sound, and that in laying stress on the opposite method organised Christianity has brought a great deal of avoidable, enervating and rather cruel distress upon those of its adherents who took its pretensions seriously.

"When God created man," Mr. Epstean said, "He was not out to create a race of competitors, nor could He have done that without upsetting the whole run of His universe; at least, we can't see how He could, and we do see that He very evidently didn't. He created man part divine, part bestial, and the two elements have been at war within the individual ever since. When the bestial side gets the better of it for the moment, as it will every now and then, and you go wrong, don't bother over repenting and nagging yourself about it. Let it go,—forget it,—to hell with it!—and put your energy harder than ever on building up the divine side. Don't try to repress the bestial side. Repression is negative, enervating. Put all your work on the positive job, and you can afford to let the bestial side take its chances."

I am not so clear in my mind as I once was about the dichotomous man; Mr. Cram has made some serious difficulties for me on that score. But this does not affect the validity of Mr. Epstean's view, considered as a matter of method. As such, I think it may be regarded as the one in all respects most consistent with the general discipline contemplated by Jesus's teaching.

CHAPTER SIXTEEN

Quod amplius nos delectat, secundum id operemur necesse est. ·

—ST. AUGUSTINE.

The primary and sole foundation of virtue, or of the proper conduct of life, is to seek our own profit.

—BARUCH SPINOZA.

FROM what I have now written I think one may easily see how it came about that by the time I was in my early thirties I found myself settled in convictions which I suppose might be summed up as a philosophy of intelligent selfishness, intelligent egoism, intelligent hedonism. It may be seen also how subsequent observation and reflection confirmed me in this philosophy. With a squeeze here and a pull there, any of those terms, selfishness, egoism, hedonism, might be made to fit in a hand-me-down fashion; but I do not like them, because they connote something academic, elaborate, something which needs a great deal of explaining. My findings are too simple and commonplace for anything like that. If it were obligatory to put a label on them, I should say, with Goethe's well-known remark in mind, that they amount merely to a philosophy of informed common sense. To know oneself as well as one can; to avoid self-deception and foster no illusions; to learn what one can about the plain natural truth of things, and make one's valuations accordingly; to waste no time in speculating upon vain subtleties, upon "things which are not and work not";—this perhaps is hardly the aim of an academic philosophy, but it is what a practical philosophy keeps steadily in view. Because the *Meditations* of Marcus Aurelius so consistently does keep just this in view, it still remains, and for those who can take it will probably always remain, the best of handbooks to the art of living.

The fundamental validity of egoism and hedonism seems to me indisputable, as it did not only to the Cyrenaics and to Epicurus, but to Christian moralists like Butler and Wilson among Protestants, to Spinoza among Jews, and to the mighty Augustine of Hippo among Catholics. But putting all such authority aside, I hold it to be a matter of invariable experience that no one can do anything *for* anybody. Somebody may profit by something you do, you may know that he profits and be glad of it, but you do not do it *for* him. You do it, as Augustine says you *must* do it, are bound to do it (*necesse est* is the strong term he uses), because you get more satisfaction, happiness, delight, out of doing it than you would get out of not doing it; and this is egoistic hedonism.

By consequence I hold that no one ever did, or can do, anything *for* "society." When the great general movement towards collectivism set in, about the middle of the last century, "society," rather than the individual, became the criterion of hedonists like Bentham, Hume, J. S. Mill. The greatest happiness of society was first to be considered, because in that the individual would find a condition conducive to his greatest happiness. Comte invented the term *altruism* as an antonym for egoism, and it found its way at once into everyone's mouth, although it is utterly devoid of meaning, since it points to nothing that ever existed in mankind. This hybrid or rather this degenerate form of hedonism served powerfully to invest collectivism's principles with a specious moral sanction, and collectivists naturally made the most of it. It bred a numerous race of energumens, professional doers-of-good; and surrounding these were clusters of amateur votaries whose concern with improving society was almost professional in its intensity. When in the later 'nineties I first observed this fetichistic exaggeration of society's claims against the individual I regarded it as transparent nonsense, as I still do. I also regarded the activities of its promoters as so ill-conceived and ill-advised as to be in the main pernicious, as the mere passage of time has now shown that they were.

In those days I noticed with amusement that some philosophers of "the social consciousness" had carried their speculations up into the higher realm of scholastic metaphysics. I could make nothing of Sir Leslie Stephen's notion of a "social organism" but that society exists as an objective entity apart from the individuals who make it up. I had long known that the Church lays claim to that sort of unsubstantial existence, but I was never metaphysician enough to get a very clear idea of how this could be so. I should say that if a Church or "the Church" no longer had any members it would no longer have any existence; and I should say the same of society. Albertus Magnus and his great pupil Thomas would sniff at Sir Leslie Stephen's "social organism" and the curious product, apparently ectoplasmic, which he calls a "social tissue," and they would at once catch the fine old familiar fusty aroma of universals existing objectively.

For my part, although for the sake of convenience I use the term *society* freely enough, I am not sure but that a fairly plausible argument could be made out for the thesis that there is no such thing as society. I say this, however, with no intention of coming forward as a modern William of Ockham, to fight the nominalist-realist battle all over again. I merely observe that I have never been able to see "society" otherwise than as a concourse of very various individuals about which, as a whole, not many general statements can be safely made. The individual seems to be the fundamental thing; all the character society has is what the prevailing character of the individuals in its environment gives it. If they mostly work in factories, you have an industrial society; if they are mostly civilised, you have a civilised society; if they mostly drink too much, you have a drunken society; and so on. A tendency to disallow and disregard the individual's claims against society, and progressively to magnify and multiply society's claims against the individual, seems to me fatuous in its lack of logic. I have regularly had occasion to notice that grandiose schemes for improving society-at-large always end in failure, and I have not wondered at it because it is simply not in the nature of things that society can be improved in that way.

I have known many persons, some quite intimately, who thought it was their duty to take "the social point of view" on mankind's many doings and misdoings, and to support various proposals, mainly political, for the mass-improvement of society. One of them is a friend of long standing who has done distinguished service of this kind throughout a lifetime, and is directly responsible for the promulgation of more calamitous and coercive "social legislation" than one could shake a stick at. In a conversation with me not many months ago, this friend said mournfully, "My experience has cured me of one thing. I am cured of believing that society can ever be improved through political action. After this, I shall 'cultivate my garden.' "

Il faut cultiver notre jardin. With these words Voltaire ends his treatise called *Candide*, which in its few pages assays more solid worth, more informed common sense, than the entire bulk of nineteenth-century hedonist literature can show. To my mind, those few concluding words sum up the whole social responsibility of man. The only thing that the psychically-human being can do to improve society is to present society with *one improved unit.* In a word, ages of experience testify that the only way society can be improved is by the individualist method which Jesus apparently regarded as the only one whereby the Kingdom of Heaven can be established as a going concern; that is, the method of each *one* doing his very best to improve *one*.

In practice, however, this method is extremely difficult; there can be no question about that, for experience will prove it so. It is also clear that very few among mankind have either the force of intellect to manage this method intelligently, or the force of character to apply it constantly. Hence if one "regards mankind as being what they are," the chances seem to be that the deceptively easier way will continue to prevail among them throughout an indefinitely long future. It is easy to prescribe improvement for others; it is easy to organise something, to institutionalise this-or-that, to pass laws, multiply bureaucratic agencies, form pressure-groups, start revolutions, change forms of government, tinker at political theory. The fact that these expedients have been tried unsuccessfully in every conceivable combination for six thousand years has not noticeably impaired a credulous unintelligent willingness to keep on trying them again and again. This being so, it seems highly probable that the hope for any significant improvement of society must be postponed, if not forever, at any rate to a future so far distant that consideration of it at the present time would be sheer idleness.

Admittedly, mankind have never shown themselves capable of devising a sound and stable collective life for themselves, or one that exhibited any actual advance of civilisation beyond the point reached by other attempts which have preceded it. As evidence of this, the collective life established in Crete has always seemed to me the most completely conclusive in history. Its conditions were unique; no such combination of favorable circumstances is known to have existed anywhere. The salient circumstance was that continuously for one thousand years, from 2500 to 1500 B.C., the Cretans lived not only free from attack by outsiders, but also free from fear of it. They traded all around the eastern Mediterranean, and there is every indication that those thousand years were a period of unexampled peace and prosperity. They built up an elaborate apparatus of civilisation perfectly suited to all their needs and fancies, singularly modern in matters of convenience and comfort, such as drainage, household water-supply, plumbing, bathtubs. The arts flourished vigorously. One would say that if ever a people had the chance to demonstrate that society is indefinitely improvable, the Cretans had it. Everything was in their favour; climate, resources, wealth, commerce and, above all, peace and immunity from interference. Moreover, a thousand years of this is a good long time, quite long enough to show some detectable results. Apparently, however, the improvement of Minoan society went static at a point not much ahead, if any, of the point where ours stopped. As with us, so evidently with the Cretans, cleverness and sagacity did wonders in developing the mechanics of civilisation, but the intelligence and wisdom requisite for developing civilisation itself were simply not there.

I can make nothing of it but that in the attempt to stabilise anything more highly differentiated than the primitive patriarchal form of society, mankind are attempting something which is quite beyond their powers. Not too often has the mass-man made any conspicuous success even with the patriarchal form. Really, when one thinks of it, what a preposterous thing it is to put the management of a nation, a province, even a village, in the hands of a man who can not so much as manage a family! Friar John of the Funnels uttered golden speech when he asked how he could be expected to govern an abbey, seeing that he was not able to govern himself. *Absurdum quippe est ut alios regat qui seipsum regere nescit* was a good legal maxim in the Middle Ages, and it remains forever as a maxim of sterling common sense.

So seeing, with Goethe, no present prospect that mankind will become happier, wiser or better than they now are, or than they were in their highly-privileged circumstances on the island of Crete five thousand years ago, I see as little prospect that their collective life will show the marks of a civilised society any more clearly than did the Minoan collective life of 2000 B.C. To the calm and profound thought of Marcus Aurelius this reflection seems to have been always present. The things to come, he says, will certainly be of like form with the things of the past, "and it is not possible that they should deviate from the order of the things which take place now. Accordingly, to have contemplated mankind's life for forty years is the same as to have contemplated it for ten thousand years; for what more wilt thou see?" Henry Adams ends his autobiography with a moving remembrance of two lifelong friends. Perhaps, he says, the three may be allowed to return to earth for a holiday and look things over, say in 1938, their centenary year; "and perhaps then, for the first time since man began his education among the carnivores, they would find a world that sensitive and timid natures could regard without a shudder." No such world awaited them in 1938, as we can testify.

II

In former days when I believed in the doctrine of the Enlightenment, that evolution is strictly progressive and that *Homo sapiens* and his society are indefinitely improvable, my "contemplation of mankind's life for forty years" was on the whole a rather puzzling business, but by no means discouraging. True, the stretch of history from Sumer and Akkad down to 1850 did present a pertinacious sameness. But then had come the great period of *Naturforschung*, the progress of discovery and invention, which would surely speed up the evolutionary process. It made such swift, spectacular and salutary changes on the surface of life that beyond doubt it must effect some corresponding changes, slight as they might be, in life's essential quality, in the essential quality of *Homo sapiens* himself. No such changes, however, became discernible, nor the symptoms of any. Still, I thought, the span of six thousand years is but a moment in the evolutionary course; one must be patient and content. But while I was sustaining myself with thoughts of what mankind and their society would be like at the end of sixteen thousand years of progressive evolution, the observations of de Vries and others made it clear that the Darwinian formula must undergo a far more drastic amendment than Weismann had suggested; that evolution is by no means necessarily and invariably progressive; that it may on occasion be catastrophic, and its course quite unpredictable. Then archæology produced unassailable evidence of an order of civilisation prevailing thousands of years ago in Crete, Egypt and Mesopotamia, which was in no respect inferior to our own, and in some respects almost certainly higher; and thus the whole foundation of the overwhelming determinist optimism which pervaded the Western world at the turn of the century was blown to pieces.

I have already spoken of the uneasy premonition that this huge structure of optimism was about to collapse, and of the tone of resentful disappointment, discouragement, despondency, which appears in the literature of the period. Many gifted minds felt that the Enlightenment was a mere mirage, and its grandiose promises were only so much sweetened wind. Some, like Henry Adams, surveyed the life of mankind with gentle and amiable resignation; some, like Tourgueniev, with a profound and noble grief; some, like de Maupassant, with bitter dejection; some, like Flaubert, with almost frantic disgust. I could not share this despondency, though I was as puzzled as any one. Sometimes during the war of 1914 I suspected that I might be too insensitive, too much a creature of the moment, to get myself into the frame of mind of these great men, though actually I knew well enough that this was not so. There seemed, as a matter of common sense, something clearly wrong with the basic assumptions of the Enlightenment, but I did not know what it was, and the fact itself, if it were a fact, did not seem to call for such acute distress. Later on, Mr. Cram's brilliant thesis showed me plainly what was wrong, and all my puzzlement evaporated. In a passage of eloquent prose de Maupassant, whose conclusion runs curiously close to Mr. Cram's, turns his back on Condorcet and Rousseau with this sentence:

> Ah, yes, we shall ever continue to be borne down by the old and odious customs, the criminal prejudices, the ferocious ideas, of our barbarous forefathers, for we are but animals and we shall remain animals, led only by the instincts that nothing will ever change.

If this be so, I thought, mankind are unquestionably living up to the measure of their psychical capacities, they are doing the best they can. Why, then, should their collective life provoke disappointment, distress, despondency, on the part of those who contemplate it "as from a height," as Plato says it should be contemplated? I saw no reason why it should do so.

Every day I divert myself with watching, outside my window, a concourse of chickadees, woodpeckers, tree-sparrows, nuthatches and other small birds, feeding on grain, seeds and suet which the household puts out for them. They had lost no time in discovering that they could satisfy their needs and desires with less exertion by exploiting the household than by scratching up a living for themselves; hence they are always promptly on hand. Presently two jays appear, imperialist freebooters whom I have named respectively Joseph Chamberlain and Cecil Rhodes. They consider the situation, then fly off and report to a lurking band of jay-profiteers who descend in a body, disperse the original exploiters, and "take over."

This scene would disappoint no one, distress no one, because that is the way birds are, and everybody knows it, and knows also that nothing can be done about it. They are living up to the measure of their psychical capacities; they are doing quite the best they can. There is an interest and even a certain kind of beauty, in the faithfulness with which they fulfil the majestic and terrible law of exploitation, Epstean's law, and there is beauty also in the little nefarious tricks and stratagems incident to its fulfilment. One is led to reflect deeply on the enormous scope, the innumerable ramifications and implications of this law which operates as inflexibly in the lowest range of animate nature as in the highest; and there is great profit in these reflections.

So one feels no distress or despondency at the sight of like behaviour on the part of psychical anthropoids, as when imperialist jobholders resorted to war for political purposes in 1898 and 1914, or as when in 1900 British exploiters evicted and took over from Dutch exploiters who, in their turn, had evicted and taken over from Kafirs; or again as when in 1918 British exploiters took over from German exploiters in Africa.

During the war of 1914 I regarded the movements of both sides with singular indifference, sometimes scarcely knowing which was which. My little dialogue with Brand Whitlock in Brussels, which I have mentioned somewhere back in these pages shows that my reaction to the situation, although at that time almost purely instinctive, was sound. That is the way people are. The war was detestable enough, but the anthropoid jobholders who engineered it and the masses whom they coerced and exploited were doing the best that the limitations of their nature admitted of their doing, and one could expect no more than that. There was even a certain grave beauty, such as one observes in a battle of snakes or sharks, in the machinations which they contrived in order to fulfil the law of their being. One regarded these creatures with abhorrence, yes; sometimes with boredom and annoyance, yes; but with despondency and disappointment, no.

III

Like the general run of American children, I grew up under the impression that mankind have an innate and deep-seated love of liberty. This was never taught me as an article of faith, but in one way and another, mostly from pseudo-patriotic books and songs, children picked up a vague notion that "the priceless boon of liberty" is really a very fine thing, that mankind love it and are jealous of it to the point of raising Cain if it be denied them; also that America makes a great speciality of liberty and is truly the land of the free. I first became uncertain about these tenets through reading ancient accounts of the great libertarian wars of history, and discovering that there were other and more substantial causes behind those wars and that actually the innate love of liberty did not have much to do with them. This caused me to carry on my observations upon matters nearer at hand, and my doubts were confirmed. If mankind really have an unquenchable love for freedom, I thought it strange that I saw so little evidence of it; and as a matter of fact, from that day to this I have seen none worth noticing. One is bound to wonder why it is, since people usually set some value on what they love, that among those who are presumed to be so fond of freedom the possession of it is so little appreciated. Taking the great cardinal example lying nearest at hand, the American people once had their liberties; they had them all; but apparently they could not rest o'nights until they had turned them over to a prehensile crew of professional politicians.

So my belief in these tenets gradually slipped away from me. I can not say just when I lost it, for the course of its disappearance was not marked by any events. It vanished more than thirty years ago, however, for I have consciously kept an eye on the matter for that length of time. What interested me especially is that during this period I have discovered scarcely a corporal's guard of persons who had any conception whatever of liberty as a *principle*, let alone caring for any specific vindications of it as such. On the other hand, I have met many who were very eloquent about liberty as affecting some matter of special interest to them, but who were authoritarian as the College of Cardinals on other matters. Prohibition brought out myriads of such; so did the various agitations about censorship, free speech, minority-rights of Negroes, Jews, Indians; and among all whom I questioned I did not find a baker's dozen who were capable of perceiving any inconsistency in their attitude.

According to my observations, mankind are among the most easily tamable and domesticable of all creatures in the animal world. They are readily reducible to submission, so readily conditionable (to coin a word) as to exhibit an almost incredibly enduring patience under restraint and oppression of the most flagrant character. So far are they from displaying any overweening love of freedom that they show a singular contentment with a condition of servitorship, often showing a curious canine pride in it, and again often simply unaware that they are existing in that condition. Byron, one of the world's greatest natural forces in poetry, had virtually no reflective power, but in the last lines of his poem on Bonnivard, who "regained his freedom with a sigh," he displays a flash of insight almost worthy of Sophocles, into mankind's easy susceptibility to conditioning.[1]

I do not know the origin of this idea that mankind loves liberty above all things, but the American revolution of 1776 and the French revolution of 1789 apparently did most to give it currency. Since then it has done yeoman's service to an unbroken succession of knaves intent on exploiting the name and appearance of freedom before mankind, while depriving them of the reality. Such is the immense irony of history. The goddess of liberty, as she lay in the arms of de Noailles and Lafayette, was a beautiful and alluring figure; but after she had been passed on to the arms of Mirabeau, then handed on to the embraces of Danton, Robespierre, Saint-Just, Marat, Barras, Carrier, and finally Bonaparte, she was left in an extremely raddled and shopworn condition. "Good old revolution!" said one of my friends in a meditative mood, during the stormy times of 1936 in Paris. "*Liberté, Égalité, Défense d'uriner*. They still keep the fine old motto posted up, I see, but it doesn't seem to mean much more now than it did when Robespierre was running things."

I might have witnessed some of the revolutions which occurred in my time, but having a pretty clear notion of what they would come to, I paid little attention to them. Like Ibsen and Henry George, I have little respect for political revolutions, for I never knew of one which in the long-run did not cost more than it came to. Beheading a Louis XVI to make way for a Napoleon seems an unbusinesslike venture, to say the least of it. Passing from the tyranny of Charles I to the tyranny of Cromwell is like taking a turn in a revolving door; the exertion merely puts you back where you started. If every jobholder in Washington were driven into the Potomac tonight, their places would be taken tomorrow by others precisely like them. Nor have I any more respect for what the Duke of Wellington

[1] It should be unnecessary to say that this susceptibility exists only in respect of faculties which they possess. It is the error of those who are dazzled by illusive schemes for the mass-improvement of society to imagine that it exists in respect of faculties which they do not possess.

called "a revolution by due course of law" than I have for one of the terrorist type. In this country, for example, unseating predatory and scampish Republicans to give place for predatory and scampish Democrats, and *vice versa*, has long proved itself not worth the trouble of holding an election. I have also been extremely cautious about taking revolutionary "ideologies" at anything like their face value. I have found that the façade of ideology counts for little; it is the too, too solid flesh of the human material behind it that really counts. A very able Frenchman of the eighteen-thirties, one who wanted nothing and who steadfastly refused to enter public life, said, "Political opinion in France is based on the fact that the louis d'or is worth seven times as much as the three-franc écu." To the best of my observation, this is the only kind of "ideology" to which political opinion, revolutionary or otherwise, has been answerable in any country. Furthermore, my sense of this has made me always look very closely at the instigators, promoters and fautors of revolutionary activity. In this I have taken pattern by an Englishman who witnessed the French revolution of 1848, and left this record:

> From that day forth I have never dipped into any history of modern France, professing to deal with the political causes and effects of the various upheavals during the nineteenth century in France. They may be worth reading; I do not say that they are not. I have preferred to look at the men who instigated those disorders, and have come to the conclusion that had each of them been born with five or ten thousand a year, their names would have been absolutely wanting in connexion with them. This does not mean that the disorders would not have taken place, but they would have always been led by men in want of five or ten thousand a year. On the other hand, if the d'Orléans family had been less wealthy than they are, there would have been no firmly-settled Third Republic; if Louis-Napoléon had been less poor, there would in all probability have been no Second Empire; if the latter had lasted another year, we should have found Gambetta among the ministers of Napoleon III, just like Emile Ollivier.

So much, then, for the binding force of "ideologies." The one phenomenon which interested me in this connexion has been a general revival of the practice which the Roman State employed when it was on its last legs, of quieting discontent by a palliative system of bribery and subsidy in the form of doles, pensions, "relief" and the like. As Mr. G. B. Shaw said scornfully, "You can buy off any revolution for thirty bob." For obvious reasons these measures mark a long step forward in a society's "course of rebarbarisation," and are in fact rather desperate; their end is so plainly visible from their beginning. Dumas turned a neat phrase when he said that Necker, who had been called back to the Treasury after the fall of the Bastille, was "trying to organise prosperity by generalising poverty." That is what such measures plainly amount to, and it is all they amount to.

IV

It would seem to be in the order of nature that the history of mankind's efforts to stabilise a collective life should be the same hereafter as it has been in the past, a history of repetitions following a singularly exact pattern. Out of a period of anarchy and dissolution mankind have come together in the production of something which for lack of a better word may be called a culture, frail and tottering at the outset, but becoming gradually stronger, and describing an upward curve in power and importance. As it rises, the forces of Epstean's law, Gresham's law and the law of diminishing returns act upon it with progressively increasing energy, and when it has reached a certain height the combined play of these forces drives it down again into another period of anarchy and dissolution. There has been a curious periodicity observable in this performance; the rise and fall of these cultures has been a matter, roughly, of five hundred years each.

Hence history is on the side of those observers who see Western culture as standing today where Roman culture stood at the end of the fourth century; standing, that is, at the verge of extinction. Seven years ago I ventured a prediction with special reference to the impending fate of American culture, but *a minori ad majus* my findings, as it now appears, were equally applicable to the whole body of Western culture:

> What we and our more nearly immediate descendants shall see is a steady progress in collectivism running off into a military despotism of a severe type. Closer centralisation; a steadily-growing bureaucracy; State power and faith in State power increasing, social power and faith in social power diminishing; the State absorbing a continually larger proportion of the national income; production languishing; the State in consequence taking over one "essential industry" after another, managing them with ever-increasing corruption, inefficiency and prodigality, and finally resorting to a system of forced labour. Then at some point in this progress a collision of State interests, at least as general and as violent as that which occurred in 1914, will result in an industrial and financial dislocation too severe for the asthenic social structure to bear; and from this the State will be left to "the rusty death of machinery" and the casual anonymous forces of dissolution will be supreme.

Seven years ago this forecast was regarded as utterly fanciful and preposterous. I doubt that the most inveterate optimist can so regard it now.

With regard to the régime of collectivism which under one-and-another trade-name has fastened itself firmly upon Western society, I can view it only as a logical and necessary step in a general "course of rebarbarisation." Spencer speaks of society's evolutionary progress from the militant type, which is purely collectivist, to the industrial type, which is marked by less and less of State interference with the individual. The collectivism of today is plainly a reversion from the industrial or semi-industrial to the militant type, and is therefore quite what one would expect to see coming forth at this stage of a society's rebarbarisation.

Considering mankind's indifference to freedom, their easy gullibility and their facile response to conditioning, one might very plausibly argue that collectivism is the political mode best suited to their disposition and their capacities. Under its régime the citizen, like the soldier, is relieved of the burden of initiative and is divested of all responsibility, save for doing as he is told. He takes what is allotted to him, obeys orders, and beyond that he has no care. Perhaps, then, this is as much as the vast psychically-anthropoid majority are up to, and a status of permanent irresponsibility under collectivism would be most congenial and satisfactory to them.

Given a just and generous administration of collectivism this might very well be so; but even on that extremely large and dubious presumption the matter is academic, because of all political modes a just and generous collectivism is in its nature the most impermanent. Each new activity or function that the State assumes means an enlargement of officialdom, an augmentation of bureaucracy. In other words, it opens one more path of least resistance to incompetent, unscrupulous and inferior persons whom Epstean's law has always at hand, intent only on satisfying their needs and desires with the least possible exertion. Obviously the collectivist State, with its assumption of universal control and regulation, opens more of these paths than any other political mode; there is virtually no end of them. Hence, however just and generous an administration of collectivism may be at the outset, and however fair its prospects may then be, it is immediately set upon and honeycombed by hordes of the most venal and untrustworthy persons that Epstean's law can rake together; and in virtually no time every one of the régime's innumerable bureaux and departments is rotted to the core. In 1821, with truly remarkable foresight, Mr. Jefferson wrote in a letter to Macon that "our Government is now taking so steady a course as to show by what road it will pass to destruction, to wit: by consolidation first [i.e., centralisation] and then corruption, its necessary consequence."

The idea of a self-limiting or temporary collectivism impresses me as too absurd to be seriously discussed. As long as Newton's law remains in force, no one can fall out of a forty-storey window and stop at the twentieth storey. So, as long as Epstean's law remains in force there can be no such thing as a ten-per-cent collectivist State for any length of time. One might just as sensibly speak of a ten-per-cent mammalian pregnancy.

It seems quite pointless to speculate upon what may succeed the present period of disintegration and dissolution, for whatever it may be, those who are now living will not see it, nor yet will their grandchildren. So much seems fairly certain, since the duration of these periods has hitherto run roughly to something like two hundred years; and therefore if we set the beginning of our period at 1870, we might say that only about one-third of its term has expired. Many observers, relying on history, expect it to be followed by another renaissance, another rise and fall, fulfilling the regular five-hundred-year cycle, and running out into another term of dissolution. This seems reasonable, but the matter is too far off to make any conjecture about its details worth while. I think it is much more profitable to spend one's energy on the effort to get a measure of the period in which we actually are living, and be content to let the future bring forth what it may.

Henry Adams, relying on the validity of Carnot's principle, appears to have thought that the rise and dissolution of societies would go on indefinitely, pretty much on the pattern which they have hitherto followed, until the equilibrium of physical forces should be established at absolute zero, in the silence and inanition of universal death. The later findings of physicists, however, suggest that Carnot's law needs a radical overhauling, and that the conclusions which Adams drew from it are open to doubt. But aside from this, one can not safely predict even so much as that the periodic ups and downs of mankind's socio-political agglomerations will continue indefinitely, because one never knows what nature is going to do. To the best of our knowledge nature abruptly shut down on production of the great saurians, and replaced them as abruptly with mammals. By analogy it would be perfectly competent for nature, if and when she were so disposed, to shut down abruptly on production of the neolithic psychically-anthropoid variety of *Homo sapiens*, which now exists in an overwhelming majority, and replace it with the psychically-human variety, which now exists only sporadically. This seems highly improbable as matters stand at present; but so, presumably, did the fate of the saurians. All one can say is that such a feat is not impossible with nature; it could happen; and if it did happen, the one sure thing is that the subsequent history of mankind and mankind's institutions would be entirely different from what it had been in the past.

V

If there were any credit due me for the conduct of an extraordinarily happy and satisfying life, I should feel diffident about speaking of it; but there is none. The foregoing pages will show, I believe, that all I have done towards the achievement of a happy life has been to follow my nose. I can say with Marcus Aurelius in that best of all autobiographies, the first book of the *Meditations*, that "to the gods I am indebted for having good grandfathers, good parents, good teachers, good associates, good kinsmen and friends, nearly everything good." With him I can also say that whatever unhappiness I have had was "through my own fault, and through not observing the admonitions of the gods and, I may almost say, their direct instructions." I learned early with Thoreau that a man is rich in proportion to the number of things he can afford to let alone; and in view of this I have always considered myself extremely well-to-do. All I ever asked of life was the freedom to think and say exactly what I pleased, when I pleased, and as I pleased. I have always had that freedom, with an immense amount of uncovenanted lagniappe thrown in; and having had it, I always felt I could well afford to let all else alone. It is true that one can never get something for nothing; it is true that in a society like ours one who takes the course which I have taken must reconcile himself to the status of a superfluous man; but the price seems to me by no means exorbitant and I have paid it gladly, without a shadow of doubt that I was getting all the best of the bargain.

One evening when Amos Pinchot and I were at dinner in the Players' Club, we heard the news of a very dear friend and fellow-member's death. We talked of him a long time, feeling that the club would never be quite the same to us without him, nor would life itself be quite the same. "Yes, we shall miss him," Amos said, finally, "but just think of the crowd that is going to be down at the railway-station when our train pulls in!" I thought this whimsical turn of phrase was an unusually charming expression of the great hope that has beset mankind for uncounted generations. Socrates, standing before his judges, told them with simple eloquence of the fine time he was going to have when he could talk things over with Minos, Rhadamanthus, Triptolemus and the heroes of Troy; and how happy he would be to go on looking into the order of nature and searching for the plain natural truth of things, in company with the great philosophers who had preceded him. He made it clear that he thought very little of the life he was leaving by comparison with the life that awaited him; and so when Crito asked him how he wished to be buried, he said, "Bury me any way you like, if you can catch me." Then, laughing, he turned to Simmias and the others, and said it seemed he could never quite get it through Crito's head that the dead body which remained would not be Socrates at all, and that the real Socrates would still be keeping on at his old line of trade, the same as ever, but under circumstances vastly more favourable.

The same dream and desire, the same hope and expectation, appear throughout the history of mankind. Cicero, the Macaulay of Roman letters, always a great rhetorician, but also, like Macaulay, probably as honest a rhetorician as he knew how to be, voices this expectation in the noble periods which he puts in the mouth of the elder Cato: "Oh, what a glorious day it will be when I can set forth to that association and companionship of godlike minds, and take leave of this crowded filthy rout and rabble!" Probably not many of us but have at one time or another indulged some such fancy. My own mind has dwelt on eschatological matters as little and as casually as any one's, perhaps, but sometimes I have thought what a wonderful treat it would be, for instance, to pass the time of day with Rabelais and his incomparable Scots translator Sir Thomas Urquhart, as they stroll arm-in-arm through the Elysian fields to forgather with Lucian, Aristophanes, Erasmus, Cervantes and such other kindred spirits as might be happening along. Or again, to move in that galaxy of great Frenchmen who ushered the nineteenth century out into the *dies tenebrarum atque caliginis* which is the twentieth century. Or again, to refresh myself with the keen, well-bred, sceptical and humorous wisdom of the race of gentlefolk from whom, however unworthily, I had my earthly being. Or again, to fraternise once more with other rare souls whose acquaintance graced my passage through this life; most of them in rather humble station, superfluous persons, entire strangers to the tenets of economism, content that the sublime and exquisite quality of their lives should pass unnoticed and unpraised of men.

It is always one's privilege to entertain dreams and desires of this order, no doubt, but when they transform themselves into anything like definite hope and expectation one must ask oneself how far they can be justified. To this there is but one answer: Not at all. The persistence or extinction of consciousness, the survival or extinction of personality, is purely a matter of evidence, and there is no available evidence tending either one way or the other. "What is there in the realms below?" cries Callimachus at the tomb of Charidas,—and the mournful answer comes, "Great darkness!"[2] The mystery of consciousness has never been penetrated. Huxley and Romanes long ago observed that the transition from the physics of the brain to the facts of consciousness is unthinkable. Consciousness which, as Huxley said, is neither matter nor force nor any conceivable modification of either, is perceived by us to exist only in association with that which has the properties of matter and force.

[2] Palatine Anthology, vii, 524.

Whether or not it must always so exist, we do not know. If one says it can and does exist independently or in some other mode of association, we can only ask what evidence he has that this is so; and if one says it can not, we must ask the same question. I know of no valid ground for any *a priori* conclusion; the matter is entirely one of evidence, and since (fortunately for us, I think) there is not a shred of evidence available, one's only refuge is on the safe ground of agnosticism. If evidence were ever discovered that Socrates was right,—that it is in the order of nature for those like himself who are eminent in the practice of the psychically-human life to overlive physical death,—the discovery would not surprise me. I might even go so far as to say that such a provision of nature would seem to me most agreeable to what little I know or can know of her august economy. But evidence either for or against any such provision of nature is wholly lacking, and therefore no one of intellectual integrity can say more than this that I have said.

Probably a good many, as age advances, have tried to settle with themselves whether or not they would choose to live their lives over again if they had the offer of it. The two old ex-Presidents, Thomas Jefferson and John Adams, raised this question in the correspondence which they carried on after their public career had closed; one of the few truly great correspondences in literary history, and one which the deadly force of Gresham's law has now made virtually inaccessible. Mr. Jefferson had no doubts. "You ask," he wrote his old friend, "if I would agree to live my seventy, or rather seventy-three, years over again? To which I say, yea." His experience of life had been so pleasurable, interesting and in all ways desirable, as to make it well worth repeating. John Adams did not see it quite that way. At eighty he was hale and alert, making his short legs carry him three or four miles a day, his mind and memory were good as ever, and he was willing to acknowledge that he had never known a day which had not brought him more pleasure than pain. He was not tired of life by any means, but as for going over it all again, he thought once was enough.

Enough is precisely the right word. One might agree that life has far more joy than sorrow, as my life has had,—immeasurably more,—and yet might feel, as Adams did, that even of the best of things one can have enough. I remember as a child congratulating an old relative on her seventy-third birthday, and wishing her many happy returns. She said, "Oh, don't wish me anything like that; I have lived long enough." Perhaps one's decision is shaped largely by temperament; perhaps some incline to the *ne quid nimis* more readily than others. When I was five or six years old my father's oldest brother who was visiting us, a rich man for those days, offered me a silver quarter. I thanked him with due formality, and he said gruffly, "Polite fellow, anyway,—I'll have to give you another one for that." I thanked him as before, and he gave me another and still a fourth, at which I drew back, and said, "No, thank you, I've had enough." My uncle made no comment on this, but some time afterwards when I noticed that he seemed to be considering me attentively, he said to my mother, "Can't make the chap out. Only person I ever saw that knew when he had enough money." The turn of my temperament may have been stiffened later on when I was pumped full of Aristotle's far-famed formula of virtue and the philosophical excellence of the μηδὲν ἄγαν, but apparently the original turn of temperament was there, for to the best of my recollection I was never taught to be moderate in my desires,-and can only suppose that some instinct, helped out by the absence of any serious temptations to be otherwise, put me in the way of it.

So while one must be unspeakably thankful for all the joys of existence, there comes a time when one feels that one has had enough. However happily one has "warmed both hands before the fire of life," however much may remain that is greatly worth seeing and hearing, one gradually slips into a state of grateful certainty that one has seen and heard enough. For a while there survives a pleasurable interest, as Flaubert says, in "watching life grow up over one's head, like the grass,"—in seeing how certain habits of mind, modes of thought, sets of principles, by which one's own life has been rigorously guided, have now become for others a mere matter of history, unregarded and for the most part unknown. But this interest is slight and fitful, and does not last; and one finds oneself, like the two old ex-Presidents, surveying the scene of contemporary activity with profound detachment.

Nevertheless normally, as in the case of these superb old men, this is far from degenerating into a culpable *taedium vitae*. I remember once lately discussing with a friend the instance of some one we knew who had become bored with existence and had taken his own way out of it. I said I could not object to suicide on the ethical or religious grounds ordinarily alleged, and I saw nothing but uncommonly far-fetched absurdity in Rousseau's plea that suicide is a robbery committed against society. My invincible objection to suicide is, if I may put it so, that it seems to me so distinctly one of the things that a person just does not do. An instance of the kind we were discussing always sets up a certain sharp disappointment, a sense of failure, of inability, as our slang goes, to take it on the chin;—in all, it gives rise to a regretful sense that the victim was not quite the man we thought he was. In my view, the only justification for suicide is consideration for others. If for any reason one becomes a permanent burden on others, greater than they can well bear, or should be called upon to bear, I would applaud his following the example of the learned Euphrates, whom Pliny speaks of so highly, and taking himself out of their way.

With regard to the dread of death, one has one's worry for nothing when death comes in the course of nature, for the dread evaporates in face of the event. Indeed, in any case one has one's worry for nothing, as every person who studiously contemplates the order of nature is well aware. Marcus Aurelius reminds himself that "he who fears death either fears the loss of sensation or a different kind of sensation. But if thou shalt have no sensation, neither wilt thou feel any harm; and if thou shalt acquire another kind of sensation, thou wilt be a different kind of living being, and thou wilt not cease to live." This is all one can know, doubtless, but it is also all one needs to know.

"*OUR ENEMY, THE STATE*, hit me between the eyes when I read it as book review editor for the New York Times. During the past 60 years history has surely proven his thesis correct."

John Chamberlain
Syndicated columnist, historian, author, former editor at Life, Fortune, Barron's, and the New York Times.

ISBN 0-87319-023-8
112 pages, Trade Paper, $9.95

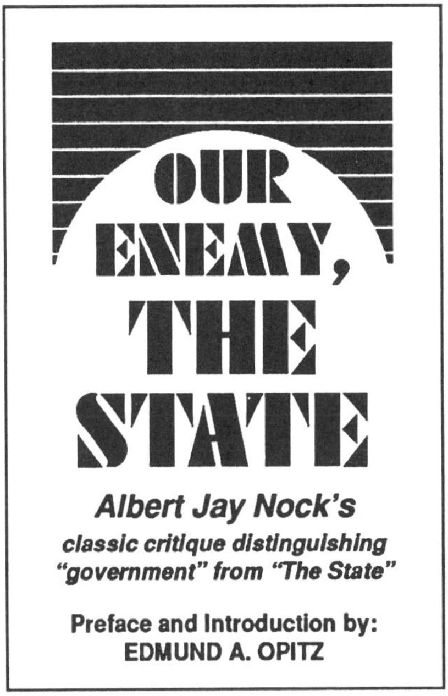

"Albert Jay Nock's, *MR. JEFFERSON*, is a superb biographical essay, beautifully written and penetrating in analysis; Mr. Nock understands Jefferson so well that one despairs of going at all beyond him."

Richard Hofstadter
Columbia University

ISBN 0-87319-024-6
224 pages, Trade Paper, $12.95

Had we changed the names and dates, the reader would assume, *THE LAW* was written in 1994 - not to the people of France in 1850.

ISBN 0-87319-039-4
128 pages, Mass Mkt. Paper, $6.95

THE LAW

Frederic Bastiat's

Classic Treatise of Legislative "Legal Plunder"

Introduction by:
EDMUND A. OPITZ

Gems of Nock's thought, selected from 14 of Nock's books by Robert Thornton and arranged by subject matter.

ISBN 0-873189-040-8
105 pages, Trade Paper, $7.95